Praise for *The Place I Live The People I Know*

"It is like going to a party and meeting lots of nice, interesting people who tell you all about themselves."
—**Jane Krivine**, Director, Freddie Krivine Tennis Foundation

"The stories are so interesting and show the makeup of Israel in a direct way that few other books do."
—**Sally Kaufmann, MD**, Jungian Analyst, San Francisco

Also by Lori Bard Mendel

HELLO! WORLD, Mara Books, 1970

Interview with Martin Grotjahn, A CELEBRATION OF LAUGHTER,

Werner M. Mendel, Mara Books, 1970

The
PLACE
I LIVE
The
PEOPLE
I KNOW

*Profiles from the
Eastern Mediterranean*

LORI MENDEL

ARCHWAY
PUBLISHING

Archway Publishing books may be ordered through booksellers or by contacting:

Archway Publishing
1663 Liberty Drive
Bloomington, IN 47403
www.archwaypublishing.com
1-(888)-242-5904

ISBN: 978-1-4808-1440-0 (sc)
ISBN: 978-1-4808-1441-7 (e)

Library of Congress Control Number: 2015900091

Printed in the United States of America.

Archway Publishing rev. date: 01/30/2015

To the people I know, who have expanded
my ideas about friendship

Preface

In Tel Aviv for the weekend after visiting Egypt in 1985, I was standing on the corner of Ben Yehuda and Frishman Streets—the faces, the music, the smell of frying falafel, the energy. *This is for me! I can do this! I could just come and be here!* No house to sell, no husband, no children, a not-so-significant job—I was free.

I returned to Los Angeles, resigned my fundraising job at Daniel Freeman Hospital, and came back to Israel with the name of an Israeli family given to me by a member of the board of directors. It was the beginning of a life of intense human contact. I learned that you can sit in the front seat of the taxi. You can talk to anyone, and anyone can talk to you, and they do. The sales people in stores are familiarly rude. I can tell any child to tie his shoelaces and any child can ask me for bus money. My students called me by my first name and told me about their personal lives. There are no lines between age/gender/social class and no line separates personal and business.

I made friends, found a job that evaporated, ran out of money, and concluded that there were six things I would have to do to survive here. I returned to Los Angeles, spent a year debating and a year preparing and landed in Tel Aviv in 1989, with my suitcase and my bicycle.

On a beautiful spring morning in 2012, walking around Kibbutz Ashdod Ya'acov, near the Kinneret, looking through the banana trees and date trees, I could see across the valley to Jordan. My friend Sara would have a reception for her son's wedding later that afternoon. I had come by bus the previous afternoon, Friday, joined Sara's family for dinner, and slept overnight. *How wonderful it is that I have so many good friends I could visit, each one with a story. This is a treasure! I must find a way to tell those stories!*

Over the past year, I traveled from Eilat in the south to Kibbutz Ne'ot Mordecai in the north near the Syrian border, visiting with my friends to hear their stories. I would like to share their stories with you, the reader. Some escaped the Holocaust in Europe, some are *sabras*—born here—some are new immigrants. Some played a part in building the state, a few are from the Arab sector, but all are ordinary people who have lived their lives in this extraordinary country and make up part of the story of life in Israel. For those who were willing, we met for about an hour, I asked questions and took notes and recorded. I sent each person the write-up for approval.

Here are the questions I asked:

Where and when were you born?
What is your situation today?
What is your burning issue?
How is it that you are in Israel?
Where did you grow up?
Where are your parents from?
Who helped shape your life?
What did you think your life would be like when you were fifteen?
What setbacks have you faced?
What would you do differently?
What are some good things you have done in your life?
What is it like for you to live in Israel now?
What else would you like to include?

You will meet Eva, Ziva, Leah, and Maya, who are the children of Holocaust survivors. You will meet Erika, who experienced it herself;

Connie, who lived through the war in England; Chava, who lived in Germany but could no longer do so and became Israeli; Abe, who came from Berlin almost too late; and Ephraim, who was grateful for having time to study while hidden in the attic during the war in Holland.

You will miss the story of Eli, whose experiences were so complicated he wasn't able to contribute. He recounts,

> I will not tell of the events when my mother, with her last remaining valuables, her wedding ring, etc., managed to buy Aryan papers for us. There were some difficulties because I had the papers of a nine-year-old girl, and my cousin, who was then one and a half, had the papers of a three-year-old girl. Eventually, my mother got a job housekeeping two houses, which were hotels before the war, where the Gestapo, with their families, made their homes under the occupancy.
>
> Even though I was very conscious of my status as a Jew in flight, I was still able to enjoy myself. One day, I was up in a tree about three meters, when I saw a German woman helping my little cousin open his fly so that he could pee. Understanding the danger of that happening, I dived from the tree on top of the woman and my cousin, explaining he was too shy to let anyone help him.

You will meet Vlad, and Lina, and Florence, and Robbie, and Stella, and Liora, who came as young people to Israel from Russia, Georgia, Algeria, England, Uzbekistan, and Argentina. Some of the participants, like Sara, Tali, Moni, Bat-ami, Heeli, and Nati, were born in Israel. Some came to Israel for their own reasons from France, the United States, and Zimbabwe, like Ashkar, Zev, Gershon, Yosef, and Vivienne. Some were born here in Palestine, in what would become Israel, like Munther, Hussam, Bishara, Hader, and Maha, a lovely and lively woman who was so conflicted about the situation it took her a long time to decide to participate. Most everyone recounted their most precious event as the birth of their children.

What connects us? Why do we feel at home here? What do we share? The feeling of home — the whole country is home. In the old days, you could knock on any door and ask to take a shower. I don't know if this is still true. Hitchhiking used to be a useful way of getting around, especially for soldiers, women as well as men. But because of "the situation" this is no longer a good idea. Once, I lost my wallet while biking home from the tennis courts. The taxi driver who found it returned it to me and invited me for dinner with his family. A friend visiting from Paris was concerned he would be among strangers if he went alone to a resort near the Kinneret. I told him there are no strangers here and you always meet someone you know when you go out. You can't live a double life. The Ministry of Foreign Affairs is called, in Hebrew, *Misrad HaHutz*, The Office of Out. If you go abroad, you go *hutz l'aretz*, out of the Land. And when Israelis go abroad, most go with friends.

The concept of anonymity does not exist here. Many of our current social mores, our behavior, and our assumptions were developed by the immigrants who wanted to realize the egalitarian ideals of the Russian Revolution in the 1920s, to live a life of Labor Zionism. This was exemplified on the *kibbutzim*, which has shaped life here, even if everybody did not live on a kibbutz. How much of that remains in our current society?

As the United States is an experiment in democracy, so Israel is also a work in progress. There is fierce love for the country and great despair over problems like the occupation and the divide of the religious and secular, which are not yet resolved. I hope you will discover what holds us together, what makes this home for all of us in our diversity.

Participants

In order of appearance

Gershon Baskin, PhD
Brooklyn, 1956

GERSHON IS INVOLVED IN MANY PEACE-SEEKING ORGANIZATIONS. HE WAS A KEY FIGURE in the release of Gilad Shalit. I met him when I participated in an organization he started, the Israel Palestinian Center for Research and Information (IPCRI). He writes a column about the situation for the Jerusalem Post. "— they need to be perceived as being more balanced. There are three people like me who write for them to try to give balance to the right-wing crazies." He has boundless energy and optimism and shares it generously.

Here is a segment from a recent column in the Jerusalem Post.

I receive many invitations to attend conferences around the world on subjects connected to the Middle East and the Israeli-Arab conflict. My travels have brought me into contact with people all over the world. The common thread among them is that they care about the Middle East, are knowledgeable about the Israeli-Arab conflict and support peace.

My travel plans took me to Rabat via Paris. I had a six-hour layover in Paris, not really enough time to see anything, but enough time to meet some people.

I posted on my Facebook page that I would have several hours in Paris and would be happy to meet someone for lunch. Well, within a couple of hours I had several invitations to choose from. Reaching out and connecting is too easy not to take advantage of the wide world of cultural experience one click away.

They had all "Googled" me to learn more about me and my positions. It was a great afternoon. My "role" in these situations is often to answer a lot of really good questions and to keep hope alive with my optimistic nature and my deep belief that our conflict is resolvable. I told them that I believe that most Israelis and Palestinians really do want peace. We need to convince our leaders to take the step forward with sincerity (and with the assistance of experts) and peace is within reach.

How is it that you are so optimistic?
A genetic defect! I can't do anything about it. It just happens. From my mother! I'm always hopeful. This goes back to my Jewish sense. We, as a people, have survived for thousands of years. When our survival was threatened, we found ways to overcome. I think our survival is threatened now by our own deeds. We are in the process now of committing national suicide. I hope our sense of survival, the urge of Jewish survival — will make us do the right thing. I am not some space cadet. I am very grounded. I am one of a handful of people here in the country who knows the history of the negotiations and have the accumulated knowledge and experience. This is not a conflict that is intractable. This conflict is resolvable. We know how to solve this. We have learned the

lessons of past mistakes, but we don't have to make the same mistakes; we can make new ones. History doesn't have to repeat itself. We have the wisdom and the common sense and the brain power to overcome this. The peace process doesn't have to lead to failure. It can actually succeed! Peace is my burning issue. Ending the Israeli-Palestinian conflict and making peace.

When I was eight, I told my parents I wanted my *bar mitzvah* in Israel. I have no idea where that came from but it's not important. When I came at thirteen, I visited my cousins and I had an overwhelming feeling — looking out from their terrace in Givatayim towards Tel Aviv: it felt like home.

I decided at sixteen that Israel was my home, where I wanted to live. I got involved with Young Judaea, a Zionist youth movement, when I was fourteen. I was president of the Long Island region of Young Judaea in my last year in high school and then spent a year in Israel on the Young Judaea Year-Course program in 1974-1975. When I made *aliya* (emigrated to Israel) in 1978, I joined a program called Interns for Peace and in that framework I lived in Kfar Qar'a for two years – a Palestinian village inside of Israel. That was the beginning of my life in Israel. It was an amazing experience. I gained so much more than I gave.

At that time, young people were involved in drugs so my parents thought that what I was involved in - politics and talking philosophy - was a clean and healthy activity! They encouraged it, looking around them.

I grew up in Long Island, New York. I did my first year of university at Tulane University in New Orleans. I wanted to get out of the Northeast to an environment I didn't know, to see if I could manage where I didn't know anyone. It sounded good: jazz and food. I had a wonderful year. I would have stayed, but I got involved with a group from Young Judaea – we were on "Year Course" together and we chose to be in New York to live together, work in the movement and we made aliya together. Some of them are still here in different parts of the country.

Both my parents were born in America, in Brooklyn. My maternal grandparents in Galicia; my father's grandparents were from Belarus, what they used to call White Russia.

My mother had more influence on me than anyone else. She was killed in a car accident five years ago. She had too many things left in her life to do. She was an amazing person. I was also inspired by her sister, who was more political than my mother. She had my mother's intelligence but a keener social awareness. This shaped me and inspired me.

I had a best friend when I was young who had extraordinary intelligence. I felt the closest thing to jealousy I ever experienced of his ability to get an A and never study! I worked hard to be like him, to increase my reading level — I was reading every day and asking my mother, "What does this word mean?" My friend grew up to be a total nothing — a crime against intelligence. He has done nothing with his life. We met two years ago in NYC and are still connected on Facebook.

When I was ten or twelve, I had the key to the Democratic Party headquarters! I was already engaged in politics and thought I would be a US senator. I was campaigning in the Civil Rights Movement and against the war in Vietnam.

I've been working for peace for thirty years and we're not there yet. The Second Intifada was a huge setback — watching the destruction — the violence, rage, people getting killed. More enemies of peace being born on both sides — we were so close — everything went to hell. It could all have been avoided. It could have all ended. The obstinacy and arrogance of Arafat and Barak. I remember Peres pleading with Barak: five days of no one getting killed. On the fourth night of the Second Intifada I was in Ramallah in the security headquarters with two members of Knesset. We had Prime Minister Barak on one phone and Arafat on the other. We were pleading with them to end the fighting that night. We were so close, but they were both stubborn men and we failed.

What would I do differently — hmmm. On a micro level, maybe this or that issue, this or that relationship, but on the macro, very few things. I had an opportunity to do the executive Master's program at the Kennedy School at Harvard. But I thought it would be too hard on my family and didn't. I don't know how I could have done it. I would like to have been at Harvard for a year.

The best and most outstanding and rewarding thing in my life, other than children and family, is having been a central part of bringing Gilad Shalit home. I think about that every single day. There was a good chance that kid might still have been in captivity. And maybe wouldn't have survived.

I am married with three children and live in Jerusalem. I am the Chairman of the Board for IPCRI. As of a year ago, I am no longer the executive director. I am also on the board of five other peace organizations. I am writing and lecturing for my livelihood, and for the past year I have been working for the company Gigawatt Global, a Dutch Company developing solar energy in Palestine and Egypt.

My eighteen-year-old is finishing high school, involved in Arabic Studies. My middle one, twenty, is involved in reshaping the *Nahal* (an army unit that used to be involved in settling the land) to make it more about social needs for urban youth. He is politically exactly like me. My daughter, twenty-six, is after an MA in Sustainable International Development and is now working as an associate producer for a film that she did research on for the producer. It's a film about Jews and Arabs in the Ottoman period. She is much more radical, more to the left than me. She is not a Zionist.

My life is a collection of experiences motivated and inspired by the enormous variety of people I know all over the world. My motto is "Never accept NO for an answer!" I really believe in the possibilities of human experience. All the wonderful people you can meet! I'm at a point in my life where possessions are not important. It is experiences and travel. I see beautiful things but I don't have to have them on my shelf.

Israel is home. I travel a lot and every time I feel good about coming home. I am always happy to come home. I have a deep emotional attachment to being here even with all our troubles and with all of our challenges. I am *engaged* in this country — everything in my life is about being here.

I am working on a book now about my experiences working for peace.

Maya (Simcha) Mendel Morag
Czech Republic, then it was Czechoslovakia, 1947

WHEN I FIRST CAME TO ISRAEL, I DID THE COURSE DESIGNED FOR TEACHERS WITH CRE-
dentials and experience. We were given access to the best the Education
Ministry had to offer. I was assigned to Maya as my master teacher. It was
fun to be in her sixth-grade class, as she was a creative, involved, patient, and
loving teacher. As it turned out, after visiting some high schools and seeing
the lippy kids and the miserable conditions, I decided I would never do that to
myself and started teaching privately in the business sector. My friendship with
Maya continues to this day. I have seen her grow her talented daughter and live
through crises with her now-husband. When the Russians first came and they
tried to survive by playing music on the streets, she said that if we each gave a
shekel, they would be OK. She initiated a wonderful birthday celebration for me
in the desert. She is spontaneous, sees the world through rose-colored glasses,
but has her feet on the ground, and enjoys living the moment.

I changed my name when I was twenty-seven. I will always thank
myself for going from Simcha, which was an old-fashioned name, to
Maya.

I have enjoyed teaching so many Israeli kids. (Every time I am
with Maya in Tel Aviv, some former student comes over to hug her.)
I'm happy with the way I was creative as a teacher and engaged with

my students. And I think I did a good job of taking care of my mother in her old days.

I am a surprisingly happy pensioner. I'm still tutoring and volunteering in the tourist information office of Tel Aviv, and I recently married the man who had been my significant other for more than twenty years. I have been living in Tel Aviv overlooking the Yarkon River, and I am mother to one daughter who is an excellent student at Tel Aviv University. Mickey, my husband today and the father of my child, is eighteen years younger than I am. And that has been proven successful!

I am making the best of my sweet freedom and my sweet free time.

My parents made aliya and brought me here when I was eighteen months, in 1949. They decided to leave Czechoslovakia and come to Israel out of their conviction that this was the place for Jews. During the war, they were in the Novaky labor camp in Czechoslovakia. They survived, mainly because my father was the driver for the head of the camp and was highly appreciated and loved by him.

Both are from Czechoslovakia — and all four grandparents. I speak Slovakian. They lived in the small town Topolcany which was practically closed on Yom Kippur, but not one Jew lives there today. Most of my family perished in the Holocaust. My grandmother was one of eight. None of her siblings survived, nor did most of my parents' cousins.

On my father's side, although he tried to protect them, his brothers, sister and mother were shot in the forest while escaping when the camp was liberated at the end of the war.

When we first came, we lived on Kibbutz Ha'ogen, where my parents' friends had already settled. When I was five we moved to Hadera, a nice little town then. We youngsters all knew each other and felt very much at home. I did elementary and high school there and later I taught in that same elementary school. When I was eighteen, I left Hadera to go to teachers' college in Jerusalem. I was there during the Six-Day War, when we captured the Old City. I left Hadera again to go to Australia for three years, where I taught in a Jewish school. And then I really left

Hadera for Tel Aviv when I was thirty-one. Being the same age as Israel and going through all the wars and stages that this country has gone through has definitely shaped my life.

I thought I would get married at an early age. I had no idea of where I would be, but I knew I would be a teacher from a very early age. I am not a planner! I'm a floater!

I went to Australia when I was twenty-two because my sister was living there and she decided for me (a floater, remember?!). I went to a teachers' college before serving in the army because my mother said I should. In the army I was supposed to be a teacher. But in those euphoric days following the victory of the Six-Day War the last thing I wanted was to serve as a teacher. More than anything else, I wanted to serve in Sinai. In the end I didn't serve in Sinai, but since I didn't give up trying, I ended up serving in the Intelligence in the tanks and also had the chance to be in Sinai for a while.

I keep thinking about what my parents went through and it makes me sad. I appreciate this country now more than before, in spite of all the discomforts, the hardship, and the pain that comes with it. Now and always it's been a great comforting experience, in spite of the constant state of war, being in a country where I am in the majority — it is only now that I fully understand the importance of having a Jewish state.

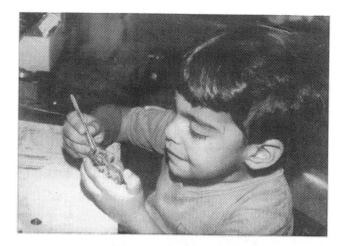

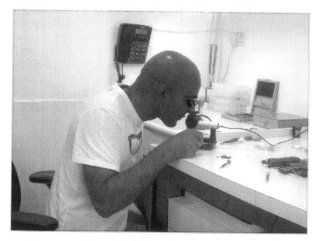

Oz Mesilati
Israel, 1976

I NEEDED A NEW WATCH BAND. AS I WALKED DOWN IBN GVIROL STREET I PASSED A VERY light and spacious watch-repair shop. The charming young man told me he was the watchmaker. In fact, he told me he was the third generation watchmaker in his family. I was intrigued by the story with all its complications.

I started to work when I was just almost seventeen. I opened this shop four years ago. The main shop is in Rishon where my brother works, where I worked until I left when I was thirty because I wanted to know if this is my work or something that my parents had imposed on me.

My brother and I are different. A watch for me is like a heart. It's not like when you repair a piece of jewelry because when you fix a watch it starts to beat like a heart. This is my passion.

In my family there are five children. My two brothers and I are watchmakers. My father had two wives but the whole family is together and we don't make a difference among us.

Starting about fifteen years ago people here in Israel began to know about expensive watches that cost $3,000-$4,000. I haven't been affected by the digital watch. In Israel there are not many watchmakers. I order my parts from Italy as I have good connections. I go once a year. I have a big family there — all in the watchmaker business. My uncle fixed a clock in Rome — he was the only one who could do it — but this is old fashioned and things change.

This store is perfect for me. I came back from traveling for a year in Australia; I didn't work for three years. I volunteered, I was a carpenter, tennis coach, and worked with horses. When I came back, I worked in my brother's shop just to explore. He had gone to Eilat and he asked me to fix a watch. I sat down and I started to cry. I knew that it was my work. This work saved my life. It's my passion. I used to be angry at my father, but now I know he gave me everything. I am grateful to be alive and to do my work and I appreciate him. I always say to him, "Thank you that you gave me this work."

Two hours ago, a friend came by and I started talking about my work. You can fix a watch a million times and every time it can be something different. This is harder than going to the doctor — the movement of the watch will not tell you. You have to find the problem — you discover along the way — even if I do this a hundred times. The Swiss do the best. There is a German brand that is also very good. But they don't compete — it's the Swiss. My favorite is Rolex. It's simple and good. It isn't show off. For sixty years it has been the same. The way the movement is built is very clever, very intelligent, and not easy to copy.

I have a sister who has been sick for ten months. She is going to die. What keeps me living is my work. I started with my uncle when I was fourteen. I left school when I was thirteen. I didn't like school. I told my mother I don't think something good will happen if I stay in school. It's boring. Until I was six I was here in Israel. Then one year in Italy, then back to Israel. When I was twelve my father left for Italy and one year later I went.

My mother was from Israel. My father met her here. My grandfather and grandmother left Tripoli and went to Rome. My father's family sent him here when he was nine in 1949. His mother was Jewish. But his father was Catholic. He was the only one they could send because

_Checkout Receipt

_ Henderson Library
_ 27 Nov 2018 03:34

****
_ The place I live the people I know : p
_CALL #: 956.940922 PLA 2015
_ 33097079909393   Due Date 18 Dec 201

_TOTAL: 1
****
Manage Your Account Online or By Phone
Renewals * Notices * Online Payments
Call TeleMessaging at 204-986-4657 or
1-866-826-4454 (Canada/US toll free)
Go online winnipeg.ca/library
****
_ verdue Fines:
ult Items 40 cents/day per item
dren's items 20 cents/day per item
ess, Bk Club kits $2.10/day per item

he was circumcised. But no one ever came to look for him; he had been sent in advance here, and he was shuffled from institution to institution. My father grew up here until he was twenty-eight without knowing about his family. He went to Italy to track down his family. After spending two weeks searching for his family but not finding them, and deciding to go back to Israel, my father was on a train with his pack of Israeli Noblesse cigarettes sticking out of his pocket. And his uncle, the one who was there when they sent him to Israel, happened to be on the same train. The uncle had visited Israel so he knew Noblesse cigarettes. And that is how my father found his family.

Years later, my father moved to Italy, leaving my mother behind, and learned watchmaking by observing his brothers. My father brought his wife to Italy to meet the family. When they said something funny at the table and everyone was laughing, my father kissed my mother on the lips. My Sicilian grandfather thought this was disrespectful. He said in Italian, "This is not right!" My father said, "This is my wife and I can kiss her any time!" My grandfather was a bad man; my grandmother was waiting for him to die.

My dad had me working on watches when I was fourteen. Later, it was my uncle who showed me another way. He taught me to appreciate, more than the work itself. He is in Italy. He is my good friend. I talk to him every day.

You can never be bored as a watchmaker. My uncle is sixty-three and he has the same passion. He is still young! Last year we sailed an 18-foot sailboat from Italy to Greece. We talked about work because it is never finished. I run to work every morning!

At thirteen I was really mature. I told my mother that I want to go to Italy to learn to be a watchmaker. It wasn't difficult to leave. If I stayed here my future would not be what I want. When I played soccer in Rome my friends laughed about my work.

I am just grateful for everything. I am grateful for the bad and the good — I was crying about why my father and mother are not together, but now I am different and am happy that I am different.

I imagined this store a LONG time ago — five years ago when I was traveling in Australia and driving all around. I knew it would be like this. I didn't know where — it could have been Rishon, but I thought about Tel Aviv. I have a girlfriend for a year. She was working in the bakery next door. She's Russian. In the beginning it was not serious because she was not my type. But after three months, when we had a situation I didn't like I said, "It's over." She said that everything she had asked for in her life was someone like me and she was not going to lose me. And now we are OK. We have a long journey — I think that she is the one, which I never said before.

I keep doing what I love — my work. My friends want to win millions — I don't work long hours so that I don't burn out. Don't take my passion from me — I don't want to be rich. If someone comes with a special watch I want to fix it. I want to meet the challenge. More the challenge than the money. But of course the money counts — you might spend twenty hours on this watch. My work has saved me from my troubles with my family. I want to be alive so that I can be a watchmaker. I'm crazy about my work!

I traveled around a lot — I've been to a lot of places. I thought about moving from Israel — but no. It's my home! You can't change. I tried to live in Australia but decided it's impossible. I am not so patriotic. There is good and bad here, but it's home.

Sara Beery

Tiberius, 1947

I MET SARA WHEN SHE WAS THE WIFE OF DANI, WHO ORGANIZED BIKE TRIPS. SHE WAS always jolly and hospitable when our group of riders came to their Kibbutz Ashdot Yaakov. I always felt welcome and at home when I spent some holidays at the kibbutz. She has shared insights of what life used to be like on the kibbutz. The children were brought up to think of others, and it took a long time to learn to think about oneself. Now that many kibbutzim are privatized that concept probably no longer exists. I have watched Sara's sons grow up.

A recent visit was the inspiration for this collection of interviews.

I grew up in the kibbutz. All my life has been here, except for one year in Tel Aviv and the two years in Thailand. In Tel Aviv I worked as a housekeeper. And of course the two years in the army. In the kibbutz, after people finished the army they would work in the kitchen, the garden. I felt that I must try something else. So I went to Tel Aviv to try. In the family I worked for, the husband was a doctor, so I lived near Ichilov hospital. And his wife was American. I had a good time because I came from the kibbutz education. The wife gave her two children sterilized education only at home. It was a big contrast to my life that had been free and no shoes!

Of course I live here. I was born here! When I was twenty-five I went to Thailand and lived there for two years because Dani had a job there. I asked, could I really live in Thailand? To live in a place I must know the language, the jokes and what is behind the meaning, and the songs. I feel really comfortable here. In Thailand, at the end we had to decide: live in New Zealand or Thailand or Israel? My family, friends, language; everything is here. I feel comfortable and don't have to work hard to be here.

I am a member of Kibbutz Ashdot Ya'acov Ihud, teaching, and studying and living. And seeing how the family grows up. I have three boys. The youngest is twenty-four. The two older ones just happened, but the youngest one was planned. One is married with two grandsons; one got married last year and just yesterday a new grandson!

This year I decided not to be as involved in the Ashdot community as I was before, just keeping the contact with my friends. My time now is for myself; before my time was for the community life.

I think the parents shaped my life, of course, but actually, very little. Since I was six, I didn't like my mother. I admired my father, but my mother was never satisfied and angry all the time and complained about me. I was not a girl who went in a straight line. I was outside all the time with friends. When the girls went to the bakery here on the kibbutz with their mothers, I never went. She always said, "This girl is better than you." I said to my friends it is lucky that I managed. I should have been without confidence. When I was young I was pretty and I think she was jealous.

When she was old I took care of her. I did it out of my duty. I went to her every day at about 6:00. If I told her I couldn't come because I was going to a wedding or something, she asked, "Why do you do this?" She tried all the time to give me a bad feeling. When she died I had spare time.

I have a brother who died in the '73 war, but when he was young she wouldn't let me touch him. I can't think of a moment of her telling me something nice, or kissing or holding me. I heard from people on the kibbutz that she used to tell my father to leave and he would find another place to sleep.

Our generation was expected to stay on the kibbutz. I didn't think about it. Everyone had to be the same level — like the level of well mowed grass. They killed our dreams and what we wanted. Now when I teach, the children have a dream.

After I finished the army I worked on the kibbutz and then decided I would study. I had to get permission from the kibbutz. They needed teachers. In the beginning, I wanted to study landscape architecture. But when we finished the school in the kibbutz we didn't get a diploma so I couldn't apply. High school was supposed to be to study interesting things, not for a diploma. I didn't know what I wanted to do so I went to study to be a teacher.

I educated my children in one way differently. Every day at 4:00 I took my children out to the fields — all around by bike, until sunset.

I planned to have five children but I couldn't do it. I came from a big family and I like it. If I could, I would stay all my life in the university, studying. Meeting clever people, traveling all week from the border in the north to the south and resting on the weekends. Just two weeks ago I went to Jenin. There is a group from here who helps children. We wanted to give the chance for a group of children from Jenin to go the hospital. A journalist asked if I wanted to come along.

In Thailand, I was kidnapped by Palestinians to release terrorists. They kept us from noon until the following evening in the Israeli embassy on the second floor. This was December after the eleven Israelis were killed at the Olympics in Munich. I can't forget.

When I was nine years old, my teacher said that I did some drawings in the copybook of another girl. I didn't do it! She didn't believe me. I did not do it. She was a member of the kibbutz and when I grew up I wanted to tell her that I didn't do it — but she died before.

When I am teaching I do something that is important. I educated a boy who came to the kibbutz from Herzliya. He didn't want to be here. I cared about him for one year. I went to visit his parents. In that year I did many things. I don't know whether it was him or me but I felt I did something important for him.

Because I had experience, I saw that a student had sclerosis of the spine. It was the last minute to correct this. They put him in a brace for four years. My work is important.

For me, every spring there is a big difference between summer and the beginning of spring. I am excited every year about the flowers and the nature here in the spring. In Thailand there were a lot of orchids — but it was not mine. No smell. Here it is three weeks. If you miss it you must wait a year. I expect it, and enjoy it, and wait for the whole year.

In my profession as a teacher, I think a lot about how to educate the Israeli children. I am disappointed. When my first son was born I thought he will not know what war is. Even now I worry about my grandsons. The people in the government don't really want peace. I am worried about my children, grandchildren, and that still there are soldiers who are dying. I am so disappointed. I have no influence.

And now in the last few months, I have been reading about if the religious and secular can live together here.

I would like to include about my two brothers and one sister. They are so good. I know that everything I need, my brothers would do for me. More than my children, who don't have time. They are good brothers with a good heart.

I love to laugh! I love the life! I like to see movies, and go traveling, and see my friends — I hope I have enough time to do as much as I want. Friends are important.

Last week I had a feeling of being really happy. And then I went to work and did everything as usual. It flowed over me that I am lucky and am happy. I told my friend I am happy but I don't remember why!

Adi (Adiel) Amorai
Rehovot, 1934

One name given to me by a member of the Daniel Freeman Hospital board where I had been working in Los Angeles was all I had when I came to Israel. This Israeli family was very welcoming: a Shabbat dinner and then an invitation to a party of their hevre (long-time peer group). Adi was at the party. At the time, he was Deputy Finance Minister. He was very welcoming and to help me find work, gave me the names of many people he knew for me to contact.

During all these years he has been a good friend, sharing his stories, offering advice, commenting on the local political situation, inviting me to some events, and attending parties I have hosted.

Adi was the first person I interviewed and he encouraged this project. It was nice to see him surrounded by his books and projects, in his family apartment in the residential neighborhood near Tel Aviv University.

I suffer from the political situation today. I am ashamed of the Knesset and the behavior of the members of the Knesset in the government. However, when I ended serving four and half years as a deputy minister, and twenty years in the Knesset, I promised not to interfere. I read Ha'aretz and Yediot every day and it steals my heart.

I was born here! My parents and older brother arrived to Hadera and they suffered with malaria, but their generation built the country!

When I was in the kindergarten we lived in the last house in town, between the *pardess* (orange orchard) and an Arab village. From 1936-39 our home was attacked many times from this village. But I feel that we must withdraw our forces from the West Bank, not for the Palestinians' sake, but because I care about what the Occupation is doing to us — our soldiers and us.

My parents came from Russia. My father spent a year as a prisoner in the time of Lenin. Later, the wife of Gorky, who was the president of the political Bolshevik Red Cross, arranged for three hundred Zionist leaders to be kicked out of Russia, instead of being prisoners in Siberia. They were sent out of the country to Palestine. My father was among the prisoners. He came to Palestine, to Jaffa, at the end 1924, with my mother and my three-year-old brother, who later served in the *Palmach*. My father was the fourth president of the teachers' organization and became principal of the evening studies of Levinsky College. All the members of the family were teachers, except me.

I grew up in a Zionist family. I was in the Pioneer Youth Movement. Everything we did was connected to building the country. When we lived near Sheinkin Street, I saw posters from the three underground organizations. My brother, who was twelve years older, influenced me to participate in the left wing of the social democrat movement. I come from a political home.

I was educated by the home, by my parents, and the underground Zionists, by the youth movement, and by my brother and sister, who were members of the Palmach. Some of the young generation was educated by the Pioneer Youth Movement. The others were in the "salon," the bourgeois generation.

I decided to become an economist in 1950 when Israel was suffering from very difficult economic problems. When Israel left the sterling zone, there was drastic devaluation, and I was deeply affected by the government's task. I was still a Marxist, and I moved to a kibbutz to settle the northern border. It was only later that I became a social democrat. I wanted to keep democracy, not to have a dictatorship of the proletariat.

At that time it was the British Mandate. I won a stipend for a Zionist school. There was only one Jew on the High Court at that time. According to the test to earn the stipend, I could choose to either follow that judge, Weizman, or Einstein. I chose Weizman. I dreamed of being an MP (Member of Parliament) in the Israel Knesset! A friend from elementary school recently reminded me of this.

Now I am on the board of an investment bank, as the chairman of the investment committee. Until recently, I was chairman of the public assembly of the Philharmonic Orchestra and also on the board of the Israel Documentary Film Fund.

All my children are worried and are more left than I am. My oldest daughter is in the organization of Mothers Against the Occupation. They also grew up in a political family!

We Jews have no chance to leave; this is our home state, where we can continue to develop our culture, and to be free. This is in contrast to what existed before and there is still anti-Semitism that emerges from time to time (But notice that in the case of DSK in France that there was no mention that he is Jewish!).

I choose to live here — all my family is here, but worried. Herzl knew that without international support we would not survive. Once, the Zionist Ya'akov Hazan sat beside me in a boring meeting in the Knesset and asked me if the Jews around the world would follow the call of Chaim Weizman. If the Jews had come in 1917 with money we would have avoided the Palestinian problem. We could have been the majority. If we had missed 1948, and waited another twenty years there would be no state, because of the anti-colonialism atmosphere. In 1968 it was clear we must be a bi-national state, but the Arabs said "No, No, No." The result was to begin the settlement of the West Bank, as there was no chance for peace. After the Yom Kippur War, many of us, including me, changed our minds.

My wife and I had economic difficulties. We spent two and a half years in *Nahal* (soldier/settler part of the army) and then two years in the kibbutz. We lived fifteen meters from the border. We left Kibbutz Misgav Am after five years, and married three weeks later. I had twenty-two Israeli pounds in my pocket, the equivalent of a teacher's salary for three weeks. We went to Jerusalem where I studied economics and international relations. My wife taught and I gave lectures in schools for Zionist leaders from abroad. In 1957, I was appointed assistant to the Ministry of the Interior.

I regret almost nothing! I was lucky. I have done my hobbies as a profession! When the minister changed, who came from another political party, I stayed with the job because we had a child at the time. My former minister became the general secretary of my party and he wanted me to be his assistant and spokesman. But I wanted to have only time off without pay. Ben Gurion, the Prime Minister, who was responsible for the civil service, was against civil servants becoming political workers. But he obeyed the Minister's request. He agreed and I worked in the party. Later, General Yigal Allon, the winner, asked me to be an assistant. I decided not to be in a political *hamama* (incubator). I tried in the open market, was rejected by Israel Aircraft Industry because of my politics, but was accepted by Paz, and was the head of marketing department of Paz Chemicals for seven years. At the time, I succeeded in exporting to Iran. Before the election of the sixth Knesset I took a break for three months to be a co-spokesperson of the *Ma'arakh* (political party) with Yossi Sarid. I left Paz when I was elected to the Knesset, coming with both theoretical and practical experience.

I have a strong memory of the time Sadat came. I was a member of the delegation to the UN Assembly. I came back to Israel carrying the *partitura,* the music score, and the equipment for the concert master, and a small Egyptian flag in my pocket. Walter Cronkite, sitting next to me in the airplane, asked many questions. I saw Sadat's appearance in the Knesset and met him in the Labor faction. At that time we believed more Arab countries would follow Egypt's lead. We waited for Begin to make the next step but he didn't follow up with more peace efforts with the Arabs. He didn't achieve autonomy for the Palestinians. When I was fourteen, I remember the night when we waited for the UN vote to establish Israel.

The good things I have done in my life — leadership in the in the youth movement; we kept the border and settled the country. As an economist, I was active in the Knesset, as the head of the Labor Party in the Finance Committee. And as Deputy Finance Minister I participated in reforming the financial structure, initiated and handled stabilization, and ended the years of hyper- inflation. In 1985, I began the reform in the capital market. Later, I prepared the banking system for privatization.

What else would you like to include?

The idea of social security was started by Bismarck, who enacted labor laws in Germany to prevent the success of the labor movement. E. Bernstein, the ideologist of the social democratic movement, encouraged the labor unions to develop in the parliament the equality for the workers. First, it was the non-democratic socialists who believed in the dictatorship of the proletariat. During the time of Lenin, it was the dictatorship of the Communist Party, and then it was Stalin for himself.

I remained a student of Lord Keynes. Unfortunately, Milton Friedman and his followers ruled the economics world, especially during Thatcher/Reagan times, and then during Bush times. I am one of the few in Israel to believe and to realize Keynesian theory, as do Paul Krugman and Ben Bernanke, in the US.

Natalie Rubenstein

Santa Monica, California, 1988

WHEN I WAS VISITING MY SON CARL IN SHORT HILLS, A FRIEND OF HIS DAUGHTER SARAH came to visit. This was Natalie! When she said she was planning to come to Israel for the summer we arranged to meet. The following December she came with her brother, Sarah, and my grandson David to spend a week in Israel. We hiked the Yehudia Trail in the Golan, walked in the desert, and did meditation in Kfar Hanokdim. Following her plan, she came to Israel to do an internship for her studies in social work and was thrust into the morass of South Tel Aviv. She is finding a better situation, here for good.

I just arrived — one week! I am an *olah hadashah* (new immigrant) looking to build my life here. I did a nine-month internship for a graduate program in social work last year. I could go back to finish my degree or take a year off. I decided to come here when I applied to the program.

I must learn the language! I have to find a job! I have to grow as a person here!

My grandpa was very Zionist. He brought my uncle here when he was ten and he fell in love with country. He still is. My uncle suggested I go to Israel one summer because I had nothing to do/no established plans for the summer. Prior to coming here, I knew nothing about Israel. The weekend I arrived we went hiking in the Golan and immediately I fell in love with the country. Things I have learned here: how to be a friend, the importance of family, and looking after others — and how nature and people can touch you and open your heart. I grew up in Short Hills in a "jappy" neighborhood, being Jewish was just part of your identity, but it didn't have meaning. I went to regular public schools. I have a sister and two brothers. I think my life was ordinary and privileged. There was no work ethic. I learned about material things, like who had what designer bag, how much designer clothing items cost. A lot of my friendships throughout high school and college had very little substance.

Mom grew up Jacksonville, Florida. My Dad in South Orange, New Jersey. My father is an MD; my mom played tennis and pissed her life away. Dad's happiness is from his children — he worked hard for us. My uncle taught me how to fish! He has given me important life messages. He speaks to a person's heart. My uncle is really remarkable. He is clear about what is right and wrong and he only does what he thinks is right. He is brilliant, and speaks several languages. He is so inspiring. Maybe he will come here, too.

When I was young, I was idealistic. I thought I would be in psychology. I wanted to be a doctor, a psychiatrist, but I hated science in college! And I thought I would find someone and fall in love. I figured one thing would lead to another as long as I did everything I was supposed to: as though life followed an equation - this plus this will equal stability and happiness. Everything was rainbows — all would come along. All I had to do was to follow the right steps and it would happen. Never would I have expected to be where I am now.

My parents' divorce really changed my reality. It was a real wake-up call. Although, in the end the outcome was quite positive. It helped me to become more realistic. Also, the Wurzweiler's social work graduate program was an astoundingly awful experience. It has been disappointing due to a lot of internal politics. They are not working for the students. Social work is based on helping others, but they don't. My experience currently has turned me off from social work completely.

I should have paid more attention in Hebrew school. If I could go back I would have surrounded myself with better people. Also, I would have tried to discover/get involved with things that I feel passionately about. I would have traveled more as well. When I graduated from college in Ohio no one came for the graduation so I didn't go through the ceremony. I was really sad. I packed up four years into my car. I was crying and stayed for the night with a friend in Cincinnati. We went to a performance of friends who were dancing to the music. It was a ray of sunshine in the rain. I was so low and so upset and it was amazing how she could change my mood. She is now here in Netanya, and I see her.

Now I feel like a clean slate. I gave away my stuff. Being in Israel will change me. I let go of who I was before. Really, coming here has been the best thing that I have done in my life.

Living here, I feel like I'm already a better person! It's easier to be a better person here. There is something magical here. The important things I learned here: how to be a friend, the importance of family, and looking after others — and how beautiful nature can touch you in a way that looking at cathedrals can't. I feel safe here, that I can really be my true self. When my girlfriend broke up with her boyfriend I insisted she come to stay with me. You don't even think of it — you do things from within. And you don't have to make excuses about not wanting to do something. My heart feels more full here. Very often I think to myself that I am so grateful/blessed to be here. It is a wonderful feeling to have such a beautiful thought. I live a five-minute walk from the beach and try to go for a run along the water every night at sunset. The food here is amazing-fresh fruits and veggies. I have met the most wonderful people here who I often sit with at cafés and bars. All over Tel Aviv they have these green bikes which you can rent for the day and they are so much fun to ride. Also, I have recently fallen in love with an irresistible Israeli gentleman. The way that I think about my life here, I have bad moments, not bad days or bad weeks and those bad moments don't last very long because the good moments produce an indescribable feeling of peace and almost euphoria. This is a country with a lot of soul. It is hard to not get swept up in the energy of Israel.

Since coming to Israel almost every experience has become a cherished memory. The way that on Yom Kippur the country is so quiet, time spent with loved ones. I suppose it is a bit of a cliché to say but I genuinely feel as though I really discovered the feeling of true happiness in Israel.

Shai Ariel

Tel Aviv, 1956

I JOINED A SUNSET HIKE FROM NAHSHOLIM TO HABONIM, ORGANIZED BY FRIEND SUSAN
that concluded with a swim and barbeque on the beach in the moonlight. Ishaya
was among her usual group of hikers. As we ambled along, he told me stories
of The Land. I was intrigued by his accounts of the history of the very place
we were walking.

I visited him and wife, Malka, in their village/kibbutz, Sha'alvim. The
village is on the site of an Arab village, previously a Jewish settlement going
back two or three thousand years. We saw the mosaic floor of a wine press.
His wonderfully strong, prehistoric sculptures of STONE, FIRE, LIGHT are
in the garden. Malka was her usual warm and welcoming self, with offers of
pomegranate jewels and shakshuka. I was entranced with his knowledge and
love of the Land.

When I asked about his situation today he laughed and said, It was best
when I was born and it declines—but I don't complain.

The answer is problematic, like asking what is the situation of Israel
after sixty years. If I look from outside, I am working on this every day,
every minute you have a new situation — takes you down or takes you
up. Back, forward — I am optimistic.

I have a very good family. God helped me to succeed and have good
children. I am surrounded with very good people: wife, neighbors,

friends. I have some anarchism inside me, a non-conformist personality, seeing freedom as a necessity and an important value.

I think that homogeneous communities where everyone tries to live and act like everyone else, behaving in the same format, are problematic. It's better when you put different ingredients in a pot and cook it together. This can be called a peace pot. Practically, it's not easy to live like that. It's a dream. I think this dream is not less important than living in homogeneous groups aiming to preserve the most important values.

For work, I am a tour guide and I also work with computers.

My father came from Poland, from a Zionist family. They came to Israel in 1935. In Poland where my father grew up, in the *shtetl*, the yeshiva students didn't have a place to eat so they were sent to families. One of them, who later went to Warsaw and became a politician, was a regular guest at my father's family. When he got a certificate to come to Israel he gave it to my father's family remembering they were anxious to come to Israel. In 1935, my father and his friends had a hard time here earning a living. He went to an evening high school and during the day helped his father as a painter. He finally became an engineer and was also an artist, a painter. Later on, he volunteered to the British Army in the war against the Nazis.

My mother came from England in 1951. The first night she came everything was stolen from her room and she was left in her pajamas. Israel was a burning issue for her. In spite of her mother's thoughts about her leaving London and coming to the desert, my mother made an aliya. Not long afterwards, a friend she knew from England introduced her to my father.

My life was shaped by my family, my Mother and Father of blessed memory, my wife, children and grandchildren, good teachers and not such good ones, the special places that I was privileged to pass through, the hikes, the Yeshiva, the army, my students, and my artistic friends.

I can point to three significant events in my life:

A. Creativity

This began in my head at a very early age, expressed ideas, imagination, and writing from a young age. It featured poems, painting and sculpture in my adolescence. This transpired without a plan or formalized learning. It simply poured out.

B. Hikes

This started when I was young, together with friends. I immediately realized I had reached the real thing. Ever since then, I hike. In my young days, difficult hikes of many kilometers in heat, rough surfaces, with no marked footpaths, they consisted of climbing, descending mountains, without a hat, water, or sticks, with no maps, almost without any information about the area, only to experience, to breathe, to smell, to make love to the earth, the nature, and I hope I will not blaspheme if I say, with God. Now as an adult I hike in a more systematic fashion, along paths, on the layers of history, with plants, birds, cultures, and people. When I was young and even today, I still think that the hikes then at the basic level, without advanced knowledge and study, were much loftier.

C. My studies in the yeshiva

Total Torah studies with no compromise, with no exemptions, no exams and no grades, through complete freedom. In Judaism, Torah study at a yeshiva is the holy of holies. One who is privileged to taste Torah, knows and experiences touching something of pristine purity and glory that sometimes is the root of love. It is a secret, impossible to reveal or to describe.

There was also the experience of war, where I received back my life as a gift a number of times, and of the friends who did not.

I see living in Israel as a great privilege, incomprehensible, to be the first child born in Israel after 2000 years of Diaspora. In fact, I represent the realization of the dream of my grandfather, and his father and his father for a hundred generations. Every day they prayed and wept over this dream to return here, to the land of Israel, the land close to God. They have fought for this; many killed for this. Only my sister and myself and a small number of the family have been so privileged. It is a great honor, a gift, and also an enormous responsibility. We represent them. We are committed. It is difficult even to think about it.

However much it sounds trite, we have returned here, and we must be better. To bring redemption to the world, nothing less. Our sages taught us that the salvation of the world depends on the little man.

In the Land of Israel these things are felt, they are not clichés, it is in the air, if wanted or not; we are surrounded by them. We aim to be better, by the work of the individual and by the efforts of the most ancient nation that is establishing the youngest state.

The life in Israel is a dialogue between man and God. There is no rest in Israel; there is a constant search for consolation. "And from Zion will go forth Torah."

I have never set up defined goals. I want to believe and to dream that everything can be much more than a definition. I think that from an early age I knew that the conflict between the reality and the ideal, between the reality and the dream, would accompany me all my life.

There is always the thought that accompanies me that perhaps I could be better, could learn more, pray better, love more or be loved more. Today I think that we do not have a choice in everything. What we have done was always good. Disappointments and failures have their goal. We call it trials. The trials can also deceive a man, and they have a decisive role in his life.

I remember as a dreamy child that I once tried to check how it was to run at a high speed with my eyes closed. My head struck a stone fence with great force. I woke up in the hospital. Was that a disappointment? Did I learn not to run with my eyes closed? Or did I learn that real attempts are also worth the price of losing consciousness? I don't have an answer even today, perhaps because my head is "screwed up."

Even today I take uncalculated risks. Heaven help me, so that there won't be any harm. Doesn't this precise and calculated world often bring upon itself disasters? Perhaps a little use of imagination and walking along unmarked trails might prevent them?

I grew up in a modest home where the main values were peace and integrity. Loving water and not so much fire, my burning issue is finding the middle way between them.

I would like to see the different groups in Israel listening to one another, learning from each other, respecting the others' feelings and ideas.

Connie Azulay translated parts of the interview from Hebrew.

Ofra Ben-Zion

Shkhunat Hatikva, Tel Aviv, 1953

SOME TIME AGO, I ATTENDED A SERIES OF LECTURES SPONSORED BY MIT FOR SMALL *businesses. Among the mostly young men, we were two or three women. One was Ofra, who gathered us women together. That is her spirit. I have enjoyed family events at her house, relaxed in the garden that she uses for coaching, and watched as she developed her meditation facilities. She and her husband, Amir, go on wonderful trips to Argentina, Sri Lanka, China and we get to hear about it.*

I live in Nes Ziona, and enjoy living there because I have my garden, and work from home, consulting and coaching. I live with my husband, Amir, whom I love. My children, Inbar and Ido, are both married and each has one child. They live very close to us. Everything is OK except I miss my mother, who died last year. My father died six years ago. I study Buddhism and like it very much. I belong to a group and we study together.

Today my burning issue is my grandchildren. One is one year and the other is ten months. I am very busy with them. Also, I have my meditation room in two hospitals: Hadassah Ein Karem and Sheba Tel Hashomer. We have seven volunteers who do meditation with the oncology patients. It was my idea that each hospital should have a meditation facility to help the patients deal with their serious illnesses, because when I had cancer nine years ago, I had a spiritual teacher who taught me meditation techniques and it helped me to deal with my situation.

My grandmother was born in Sfat. Her father came from Persia. My father's family came from Poland in 1923. My parents were both born here. Both parents were studying in the Bialik School in Tel Aviv. The teachers there were all famous, like Tchernikhovsky, and Raziel Naor, who was an MK (Member of the Knesset or Parliament). My mother was chosen to attend the Dizengoff birthday party.

I grew up in Holon, and went to school through high school there. When I was in the army, I was in Ein Gedi, (a nature reserve in the desert) as part of the *Nahal* (a part of the army that developed settlements in the land). When I was sixteen I met Amir, and since then we are together.

I don't think there was some one person who shaped my life. My mother wanted me to be a teacher, but I didn't want. My grandmother, who went to school until the age of twelve, who studied in Alliance Sfat in 1905, always told me that a woman should have a profession. I thought I would go to university and be like Marie Curie, a scientist. In high school I studied biology.

When I was sixteen I went to the kibbutz and met Amir, who became my husband, who was in the *Nahal*. He was older and lived in Ein Gedi. When it was time for me to go to the army I decided to go to Ein Gedi with a group of my friends and join Amir. I was in high school, and went to work in Kibbutz Ein Gedi. Amir was a friend of the guide who went with us in the Nahal. I *knew* at that time. It was mutual. It wasn't love at first sight, but I liked him and he liked me and we decided to go together and it developed slowly, but surely.

And then I got pregnant. We loved each other so we decided to get married. In those days, it was difficult to study and live in Ein Gedi because Ein Gedi is far from any university, so we came back to Tel Aviv. We got married.

I wanted to study biology but I had a child! They wouldn't let women with children study if they were not going to teach. It was difficult to study with her but I got a lot of help from my parents. Amir was working. I decided to study economics and accounting. Instead of going into science, I went to business school. Then there was the Yom-Kippur War and Amir was in the army. He had been serving for six months in the army. It was very difficult. But I was very lucky that my parents could help me. So now I am helping my children. But it is little compared to the help I got.

Today I don't know if I would choose to be a scientist. I like business! I work with small businesses and it is very interesting. It's entrepreneurial. I help them in the first steps of creating a business. Ten years ago I worked for a big company as a CFO. When I met you, I had just quit and planned to raise money for start-ups, but the dot-com market had just exploded and there was no money for start-ups. This is when I decided to go into consulting. There are two kinds of businesses I help now: the food business, like cafés and restos, and I work with women who have their own businesses.

One day a week I am in the meditation rooms that Tamir Masass and I established in the hospitals. Tamir Masass was a Zen Buddhist monk in Korea and he is a specialist in meditation. I knew him from when I studied coaching. Now we are seven people who do meditation with the patients. We started at Hadassah Hospital with a pilot program in the emergency room with the staff, because they work under a lot of stress. It was part of my Buddhist studies. They say if you want to get something you need to give it first to other people. We wanted to do meditation with sick people so we helped other people who work with sick people. Then I suggested to Prof. Peretz, who was my oncologist when I had cancer, to let me do this meditation room in her department in Hadassah Hospital. As she is very open-minded, she agreed and we started there in 2009 and in 2010 we started in Sheba Hospital, too. Our next goal is to enlarge our volunteer staff and get donations to build our own meditation rooms in hospitals.

I like Israel. But it is very complicated to be in Israel when I don't agree with the situation of occupying lands or people in the territories. I like the people in Israel. In general, the people in Israel are warm and take care of each other. We have very good friends. I hope peace will come soon with my contribution to it by doing meditation with everybody, no matter what their religion or nationality.

Connie Azulay

London, 1932

THE HEAD OF THE ISRAELI AIR FORCE FOUND A JOB FOR ME IN THE EDUCATION DEPART-
ment to prepare the Israeli soldiers who were working on the Patriot during the
Gulf War to manage with the soldiers from the US. In the course of this work, I
met Connie, who was in charge of English for the Air Force. She organized work
for me: preparing candidates for the English interview for El Al, later engaging
me to do English interviewing for El Al, and as part of the team testing English
for Israeli pilots and air controllers. When she had time we went on some ram-
bles. We even had lunch at the Golf Club long before I moved to Caesarea. We
share our travel experiences.

I am still working freelance on everything connected to aviation in English with El Al, the Airport Authority, the Civil Aviation Authority, etc. I am still a working woman, with a lovely family of two children, nine grandchildren and three great-grandchildren. My niche is air-to-ground communication for pilots and air controllers. I am also teaching and on the selection board for accepting El Al flight and ground attendants. I love walking holidays and trips abroad.

Since I was about thirteen I wanted to come to Israel but couldn't for family reasons. I did come when I was married with two children, after the Six-Day War. It was then or never! The influence on me was the Holocaust and belonging to the youth movement, *Habonim*.

When I came I went to *ulpan* (Hebrew language school) and also began teaching English. I was asked to work in the Air Force by someone who gave my name to a deputy commander of a flight squadron who needed English. This was at the end of 1973, after the Yom Kippur War. I was in the Air Force for twenty-six years teaching, supervising assistants, preparing delegations going abroad, writing booklets for teaching English to different units for different missions.

I was born in London and grew up there. I spent the war years in London. We children were evacuated at the beginning of the war, taken in by families who were not that happy to have Jewish children. My sister and I ran away and were billeted with much more pleasant people. My parents stayed at home in the East End of London and we joined them just in time to be bombed and for a short time buried in the blitz of London! If that wasn't enough, in 1944 we received all the rockets – V1 and V2 but never had another direct hit.

I was twelve when the war ended and only then did I learn about the horrors of the Holocaust that have really influenced and molded my life. It was then that I knew I wanted to be part of the new Jewish state. At sixteen, I had wanted to run away and join a kibbutz but didn't have the guts.

Long before I could realize my plan I went to high school, and at the immature age of nineteen got married. In those days it wasn't automatic to go to university. I studied to be a secretary and after my marriage I studied to be a commercial teacher in a local comprehensive high school. I had to wait until I was almost forty before I obtained my BA in English Literature and Linguistics in Israel.

I was quite a fervent socialist in high school – my schoolmates called me a "connunist" – not quite a communist!

When I was about ten or eleven, during the war, I discovered culture. We lived in the East End with no opportunity to imbibe culture. When I went to the local youth club, the woman in charge took us to the Sadler Wells Ballet to see Swan Lake. This opened a curtain to a world I didn't know existed. Reading and the radio were the main activities. I read three or four books a week, some from the adult section of the library, and especially for some unknown reason, books on Egyptian history. Maybe I knew I was going to end up in the Middle East!

As a result of an undiagnosed peritonitis when I was five, I couldn't have children. I don't know if the doctors told my mother, or maybe they didn't know. So when I was married it took six years and miserable tests and one operation before I knew. I remember the day I adopted my two-week-old-daughter and the day the adoption became final — I only had a one-day notice to leave my job and to stock up with everything needed.

My mother came from Kovna in what was either Poland or Russia when she was six months. My father was lucky to be born in England of Polish parents. But poor. Father sold pieces of chocolate in the street. I knew one grandmother — she always seemed ancient, extremely religious and only spoke Yiddish. I never got to know her - a shame because I am sure her history before she came to England would have been interesting. My father and uncle set up a wine shop in the East End of London and by the end of the war we were able to leave our house with no bathroom and only an outside toilet and move to a town by the sea where I spent my high-school years.

My mother had a tough childhood, one of twelve children. She was orphaned at a very young age and she slept wherever she could among the family and left school at twelve to work in a sweatshop. She never wanted to talk about the past. Her twin brother disappeared in the United States during World War I and as far as I know he ended up in Sing Sing! That generation was the survival of the fittest.

Many people shaped my life - some teachers at school, the woman who introduced me to Swan Lake. I think the events I lived through had the most influence. After my marriage, I suppose I shaped my own life – for good and for bad! Coming to Israel as a Zionist totally changed my life. I would be a famous writer, journalist. I never dreamt I would become a teacher.

I have done a lot of missions connected to the work in the Air Force. Until my husband's deteriorating health, I used to enjoy doing voluntary work. There was a long period when we "adopted" a boy who came here from South Africa, but at the beginning of the Yom Kippur War his uncles took him back to South Africa.

My children and grandchildren are living and working in Israel leading busy and satisfying lives. My husband contributed to Israel as an engineer as well as having served as a reserve officer - while everyone has served in the army or did national service - so our contribution to the growth of Israel is probably more than I had anticipated when we made the decision to immigrate. I made the right choice, and have no regrets.

My burning issue is the situation in Israel, and the future for the grandchildren and great grandchildren.

Abu Hamed Hader, MA
Daliyat al-Karmel, 1958

I MET HADER AND HIS WIFE IN THE MALL IN OR AKIVA. HE HAS A VERY SMILEY DEMEANOR and we discovered we were both English teachers. He writes poetry. He guides visitors to Daliyat al-Karmel, the Druze village. It seems he is busy with family weddings all summer. Before I came to Israel, I knew there were Jews here. Now I know that there are many other people here: Moslem Arabs, Christian Arabs, Circassians, Bedouin, Druze, and others I probably don't know about yet.

Living in Israel is a mission — it is wonderful — better than other countries. I was born here and I will live here until my death. I have no other place. For me, Israel is my home. Maybe I could immigrate to the States — but I have nothing there — I wouldn't find myself there because everything for me is here — my family, my dreams. I and my children served in the army. We served as every Jew does. Therefore, Israel is my home that I have to defend, and educate my children and my pupils to do everything for the sake of Israel.

We are here in Israel since 1800. I'm here because my parents were here. I grew up here in Daliya, in the village. My great-grandfather, four generations ago, came here in Daliya. They came from Lebanon during the rule of El Mani the Second, a Druze from Lebanon. He ruled all the area to the Gaza Strip in the middle of the 15th century. He wanted to defend his southern border. He sent the Druze to Palestine, first to the Upper Galilee and then some families came to the Carmel mountains. There were sixteen villages around Daliya. All the villages were destroyed by the Arabs here, except Daliya and Isfiya. We still have a very big family in Lebanon. We met them in 1982 after the War. They came to visit us.

I love the country! We believe in reincarnation. Maybe in the next generation I will be born in Syria or Jordan or other places where there are Druze, only to Druze parents. It is all planned. You can't decide. It is different from the Kabala in Hebrew. It is not related to reward or punishment. We believe that when someone dies, his soul goes immediately to another person to a new birth. God decides. Reincarnation is a way to meet God, spiritually. It could be four, five, ten times of reincarnation to meet God. God gives you the opportunity to meet him.

I am writing a book about reincarnation. It is my real story. I have written many pages already. It is a story about a boy who was a shepherd, spending all day long in the fields with his goats. It is my previous generation, before 1958. The story begins when the British were here. It tells the story of the villagers, their relationship with the British, the Jewish, and the story of the Arab destruction.

I have given many lectures to many tourists who visited the country and arrived at my village and wanted to know about the Druze and reincarnation. The local council and other foundations in the village set this up.

I am married, with four children. The oldest is thirty-one. She got an MA degree from the Technion and is working in a medical lab at Carmel Hospital. She has one daughter. The next is twenty-nine. She also studied at the Technion in computer science and she works at Orange Mobile Company. She has a son, a year old, a four-year-old and a daughter three months old. Every day I bring them home from the kindergarten at 3:30. My third son is twenty-eight. He got married a month ago. He works as a medic in the prison. The youngest is twenty-two, studying interior design at the Menhal Institute.

I have been teaching for thirty-three years. School starts tomorrow on September 1st! My first year was in the Golan Heights. I was a soldier and I taught in the high school. After I got married, I came home to Daliya and started teaching in the same school where I am now. I teach English, and am an English trainer for Gordon College. I have a BA and MA from Oranim College, but not in English, in education. I have no free time as I am very busy with my writing, the children, my grandchildren, and especially in summer, because we have two months of weddings for many relatives and friends and for each wedding, it is a week of celebration. My brother's son just got married and we have been celebrating for two weeks!

My wife helped shape my life. We were married at the age of nineteen. Yesterday we talked about that. We had a coffee here on the terrace and we talked and she reminded me — we were young. She said, "I shaped you! I have to be proud of that!" I was busy with my studies. She was supporting, helping, and patient. She's great! She educated the children and the grandchildren. She gave me a wide space to learn and to work. I learned from her to read a lot. She is patient with me and the children and gave me the opportunity for reading and writing. She has self-confidence. She is very proud of her family. For me she is everything. Yeah! We had three children when she was twenty-one. We were young. At thirty, we had four children and were building a new house.

Once I planned to be a medical doctor, but it didn't come true. Instead, I became a teacher, perhaps because of our economic situation. We had a big family. I have eleven brothers and sisters. Only my father worked to earn a living and he couldn't afford to send me to a university to learn medicine. He said he would do everything, but he couldn't. Perhaps after I retire, I will do alternative medicine.

I have had no setbacks, except for the death of my two sisters. I take care of their children. The eldest daughter's husband died and then after ten years she died. They had twelve children and we had to help them. It was hard to do because my mother suffered for fifty years of cancer, but she survived to participate in my son's wedding. She is eighty now and my father is eighty-three.

Now I am busy in translating two of my writings – two books and a book of poetry. Here is a book of poetry I translated. This is my first published translation. The writer is a friend from Daliya. He wrote many books. We sent it to the States but they don't want to publish poetry. I am writing two different stories. One is about reincarnation and the other about a trip to different places in the world, but it is imagination. I write in English. This is how I spend my time: writing, reading.

I am still doing good things almost every day — being a teacher and helping — I am not religious but I keep the values and the traditions. I was educated to do good things. I am a member of an organization. Every year we help forty children by providing books, clothes, and 1000 shekels for each child. We have done this for five years. We call our fund Tamuz; it comes from the name of the month in Hebrew, but for us it means volunteering. Yes, we get feedback from the families. They are grateful.

I give private lessons without money — to help! After 3:00-4:00 I have five hours to do good things, including the thirty minutes in which I pick up my grandchildren from the kindergarten. Then I have free time to do many things.

I have a happy face. I always smile. I have a warm family, a happy house. A lot of love here. If you smile, they will smile back. Even if you are very sad, if you smile you cover it. My inner self is good and happy. I had many problems but overcame them. Once I had a factory with twenty-five employees. My two brothers and I ran the factory for five years. He had a problem in the factory and we needed 500,000 shekels to pay, but God helped us to overcome it. If you understand the problem you almost have the solution.

Florence Benhamou
Algeria, 1950

There was a very attractive pharmacy in the neighborhood where I lived in Basel Square in Tel Aviv and the pharmacist was a very pleasant, attractive French woman. After I paid a few visits to buy necessities, she asked if I could do English lessons with her. Of course! And thus started a friendship as she developed and changed. She not only works hard but is seeking her own true self with honesty.

Until I was twelve, I grew up in a little town in Algeria seventeen kilometers from Oran, Ain Temouchent. My father was a tailor, my mother at home.

We left in a hurry. Our house was above the main market. One of the agents of the OAS wanted to come into our flat and from there to shoot into the market. If my father refused they would kill him. If he allowed it the Arabs would kill him. So on the thirteenth of May at four in the morning, the driver took us to Oran and we went into the line. We took a plane to Marseille. We stayed in Marseille one night and then went to Toulouse, as my father's sister had a flat there. We stayed for a week. Then we stayed in a hotel for a month. After, the French government helped us with money to rent a flat. We just ran with one suitcase. My father also had two cafés and a hotel. After ten years we received some money for this. The house belonged to my mother's first husband and went to her children. I stayed in France until I was twenty-two and then met my husband and came to Israel.

My family was from Algeria for at least four or five or six generations. We spoke a dialect of Arabic, Jewish Arabic. My mother only spoke French to me. My father died when I was nineteen, about three months after I met my fiancé. This was the cause of my life — it was a way for me to not accept, to deny his death to come to Israel. Everything was against my wishes. Israel was not my wish. It was not a good economic situation then. And I was away from the family. I avoided the suffering of my father's death.

I thought I would have a princess life. My mother was dreaming with my fate, and colored my expectations. I never saw my friends again after we left. I could find them now maybe but they were not Jewish. There was a secondary school near me, but the school in Oran was better and we were five girls, ten years old in boarding school. It was very strict and not Jewish. Until I was eighteen I was ashamed to be Jewish.

I married my husband on his condition that I come here. He was from Strasburg. We met in Toulouse while he was studying for his Master's in engineering and I was a student in pharmacy. I was living in Toulouse since 1962 after my family came to Toulouse escaping from the Algerian war. We married and one year later we came here and I had my son four months later.

I was only with my husband. I was so young. I was dying — I couldn't be alone. So I did everything to be with him. Now at sixty-one I am shaping my life. I didn't have the self-confidence until now.

I have had an interesting life. I feel much more serene and contemplative of myself, looking after the positive things that I have. I feel very positive. I am working; I have my own pharmacy twenty-one years! And I have grown sons. One is going to marry in a half year. I am expecting good years! I can't think other. Maybe in one year I will be a grandmother!

Just to have day after day not suffering, pleasant. And turning the pages of life. I am just trying to find my best life with my relationship with a man who loves me. He is good for me, but I don't want to live together.

I would do nothing differently! The articulation rolled out. I have been observing the flow of my life that makes me evolve. I am not passive. I understood the understanding. I have had psychoanalysis and this has helped me.

One special memory is a Friday evening when my mother had prepared everything for Shabbat. I can smell the couscous and see the house lit with many lights. She wore a special robe made from the sheep of the Pyrenees. We were waiting for my father. I was lying on her and smelling good smells.

A good decision was to make the decision to divorce. I just want to keep what I have — nothing else. Living in Israel now is very nice. Like a fish in an aquarium — *gan eden.* (Garden of Eden) Here I can be European, mystic, Jewish, Ashkenazi. I can do it all here. In another country something would be missing. I have made peace.

Tali Yadgar Benzvi

Israel, 1974

BEFORE I DID INTERVIEWING FOR CANDIDATES FOR AIR AND GROUND CREW FOR EL AL, I prepped applicants to improve their English. When Tali came for lessons, she was nineteen. After some sessions she decided we would be friends. She passed the El Al interviewing process, and then spent a year as an au pair in London while her boyfriend, Ziv, was studying law. We have maintained this friendship until now, including a recent visit to her in Bangkok, a bike tour in the Mekong in Vietnam, and a bike tour in Taiwan.

Once we went to the desert for some dance workshops and one of the participants asked Tali, "Is that your mother?" "No, she's my friend!" I have become friends with her whole family.

One of the revelations for me here in Israel is the lack of social boundaries of gender, age, social class. At the tennis courts one time, the court matchmaker said, "You can play with Yossi." I said, "Yossi is only sixteen; he won't want to play with an old lady!" We played, then two of his friends joined for doubles. I was laughing: I told them this would never happen in Los Angeles! They didn't know what I was talking about!

Sawadeeka! When Lori asked me to participate in her book I was very thrilled. Why me? What is so special about my life? Then I realized that I do live in a movie. My husband repeats the mantra: Your life is like a movie. I laugh at him and respond: How many tickets do you want?

We live in gated community outside of Bangkok, The Bubble. I am a yoga teacher for kids and love to see the little ones practicing yoga. Sometimes it is challenging — I see them as big souls in little bodies. Working with kids and practicing yoga makes me joyful and keeps me balanced. To connect with grownups I started an Israeli cooking class. I tell stories about my grandmother's Iraqi food and my grandparent's Eastern Europe Jewish food. I have a good life here in Nichada, the suburb of Bangkok — although there is a big longing for all my family in Israel.

When I left Israel at thirty to live abroad, it was a great gift to spread my wings — I had felt like a child under my parents. It was time to move on and grow up as a wife and a mom. For my husband's work, we moved to Washington, DC. It was winter and snowing and so cold, but I loved the snow. It was so uplifting and opened my heart.

I grew up in Tel Aviv in the protected neighborhood of Tzahala. During the 80s it was a quiet place. I went to the Tzahala elementary school and went twice a week to the scouts, and to ballet school with the Israeli ballet. It was the most wonderful time. There were lots of green fields around my house. We walked across the field to our friends' houses. While I was in my army service my parents moved to Ramat Hasharon so I can't tell anything special about this place. I met my honey in *Zahal* (the army) in Tel Hashomer where I was working for the medical officer. Later, when I became a medic and went to Mizpe Ramon to the cadet school I fell in love with the desert: the unending space, dry weather, and the colors of the sand.

Every summer when I am on vacation in Israel I must go to have some quiet time in the amazing desert. I have a dream to live there one day.

My mother was born in Germany and came when she was one year old in 1948. My father was born in Baghdad. When he was five, he came to the Holy Land. I am a mixed-culture child. When I was young I was not connected to my Iraqi side. We spent weekends with my mother's parents and lived in an Ashkenazi neighborhood. My grandfather will be ninety-five in June. I like to take Saba to *Shuk Hacarmel* (the Carmel Market) to see how he manages. He has great resilience. He was in the Russian army. My grandmother went through the Holocaust. My parents met in the army, just as I met Ziv, my husband.

My father, my grandfather and you, shaped my life, my dear muse Loretta Lulu!

I always admired that my father came from nothing, and because he wanted to succeed in life, he continues to work very hard. He worked late every day. He was very dominant on the weekends — we traveled only in Israel. I love his stories from all the wars. My mother was at home and took care of us and I felt it was not enough for her in her life.

My father always gave me the right advice when I came to him. He was very strict and old fashioned about my boyfriends. He got liberated when he got older. When I was fifteen, I wanted to bleach my hair. He said, "No, keep your nature!" And I will always keep this advice.

Another person who left a stamp on my life and my desire to study English was Mr. David Gordon. I took an English course in London after my army service. David was the principal of the school. He was like a father; he was a great story teller. I wonder what is going on with his life.

Also, my dance teacher in the ballet and the international dancers in the company. I was very eager to meet these people and talk to them about their culture.

You are my great inspiration in life! I admire you that you are honest to yourself. I admire your enthusiasm for seeing the world. You are an open-minded person. You taught me how to do my nails at the age of nineteen! And your book about traveling.

I knew I would have two kids, a girl and boy. Even when I was a child I knew I would live out of Israel. My grandparents took me to Europe for my bat mitzvah. I discovered the big world and I was eager to learn about other cultures. I knew I would explore the world. I worked for El Al and explored new places. I had a dream that my kids would know English as it would give them the tools. I knew I would do something with movement, dancing, then a passion.

I wanted to be a geisha for one year in Japan. Then I met Ziv and went to England while he was in law school there. I'm still waiting to go to Japan. When I want something I try very hard to get it. I will get it! I believe we can do what we want as long as we work hard and put all our heart into it.

I would have built a career when I was young. Like studying for a Master's in something. I am too lazy and get nervous in the university. Maybe one day I will go back to school and finish my Master's in Hospitality Management.

My most precious memory is dancing in the Nutcracker ballet with the Israel Ballet in 1985. I was in the fifth grade. I was born to be a ballerina. It was amazing to be on the stage and to perform and great to be part of this production.

I am a giver and a player person — I try to satisfy everyone around me and to be in the world and do something meaningful.

When I was thirty-five, living in India, I did sun salutations in a group of many people on a day dedicated to peace. I decided to donate money to build schools for orphans in India. I am an organizer. I give to the community. I organize the International Day, Israeli parties, and celebrations of holidays. In India or Thailand, I host foreigners at home and present my Israeli traditions. I am a good listener and a good friend — supportive, loving. I support my husband in his career, but sometimes I am upset that he spends more time with his Blackberry! I try to stay content as a mother and with my yoga. I try to be content in what I am doing and not to complain.

I miss Israel and I do pay the price, but living in an international community makes my life colorful, diverse, and so much fun. I am giving my kids an opportunity to be citizens of the world. My eight-year-old daughter told me today that she was born to change the world. The most difficult time in my life is during the holidays when I want to be with our extended families. So you build a family here. I have domestic help and won't have it in Israel. It will be hard when I come back. I don't have expectations about the country, but it is in my blood. I hope to have a soft landing. I would like to create a different lifestyle when I go back and not live in the city. Maybe some day I will open a movement/yoga spa hotel in the desert.

What is your burning issue?
Sex!
And how to be nice to my kids and my husband. And what I will do when I go back to Israel.

What else would you like to include?
I want to go skiing!

Yair Dalal

The small village Kfar Ata, now Kiriat Ata, 1955

WHICH WAS FIRST: FALLING IN LOVE WITH THE OUD OR BECOMING A FAN OF YAIR DALAL? I have followed his soul-satisfying, rousing performances with his fellow musicians. He emanates a message of peace and integration. We met for the interview before a performance with his students at the Third Ear. As always, wonderfully lively! Too bad that Israeli music went into rock.

I am fifty-seven on July 25. I live in a very special place, a vegetarian village called Amirim. I am an international artist and a teacher and I perform all over the globe with a lot of joy, and try to do my best with music. I can say that I don't have any property. I can move from place to place. I live a very modest life, you know, as an independent musician life is not so easy. Because I lived many years in a kibbutz I don't have much savings. I am creative person so I hope my music will spread. I have the hope it will be all right. I love Israel, I love the Middle East and the people and the culture.

All that I did came from a good intention, anyway I tried. Being a musician is a good thing, working for nature, being a teacher, working for peace. Being involved is a good thing. Trying to be honest. I don't succeed all the time. There were some incidents when I was lying here and there. I don't consider myself a *tzadik* (righteous one) — but I try. I give myself a report about my behavior — to be positive. Not to feel a victim. It's a struggle.

My parents came to Israel from Iraq. The Jews were in Iraq from Babylonian times. They came to a young country. All of us felt like one big family; we were spontaneous.

I was born here. I grew up in Ramat Gan. At that time it was lower-middle class. My father was working for the train; he was working class. We were four children in a small apartment. My three sisters and I shared the same room — with a lot of love. I don't think we had something missing. We had everything. I studied music. My mother worked taking care of children. There were some rich people but we didn't know about them. The banks belonged to the State and there was a lot of solidarity. In our neighborhood there was one television and it was open to all the kids. Our neighbor had a car and offered to take us to the beach. Then my father bought a '54 Chevrolet and took us ten kids to the beach. It was a big community and even though it was not easy, there was no materialism and people were helpful.

I took everything slowly. I took my time. I was working. After the army I took a camel to the desert for a year. Then I worked for the Nature Society in the desert. I got married when I was forty and had my first daughter at forty-three and started my career as a performing artist. I don't know if something kept me — I don't know. Maybe my own rhythm. I am very active; I am not lying on the beach. When I was working for the Nature Society I was active from 5:00 in the morning! Also milking cows, and picking dates in the desert, and now practicing music.

Sometimes I am sorry I don't have any property. Maybe I should have bought an apartment in old Jaffa. Or maybe I should have gone to India; I haven't been there yet. I don't know — I am quite happy. I have a very rich soul. I lived in Sinai, Ein Gedi, now in Amirim, Jaffa — the most beautiful places, and I don't regret.

I was in Oslo when they signed the peace document and there was a big concert. I have a lot of memories about music. When I was six,

I bought my first violin here in Tel Aviv. It was my idea and I had to convince my parents by force. Almost every memory is precious for me.

I find it not easy to live in Israel now. I can see things now because I have been touring and performing. I didn't leave the country until I was forty. But living here is a challenge that never ends. For me, still it's the best place to live. It is possible to have a better life other places. But something above that is important for me to be here.

We have a lot of problems but I never think of leaving. I could go and live in San Francisco or other beautiful places in the world, but we have a lot to do here.

I have dedicated my life to music and peace. I am a peace activist and try my best to work for that, especially with music. I am against any violence and also how capitalism is now. I am always for sharing, supporting, love between people, not using each other. I read about the history of slavery in the US and read about how the Blues music started and it has a lot of influence on my soul.

Now the current demonstrations are burning in me. It is important to share the ideas of the '60s; Gandhi, Martin Luther King. In Israel it's very important. Israel started as a socialist country, the young pioneers that came to Israel from Russia, building a new society. When you read the Bible it is there as well. In the last twenty years it has become the most capitalistic country; it doesn't suit us; it is not close to the religion. All the prophets spoke of helping and honoring each other. It is forbidden in the Bible to use money interest, but it has happened already. Some of us are against it and we are waking up. When I was young it was about wars, but this generation doesn't accept that any more. We couldn't avoid the wars — now there is the possibility. The young generation can question that and avoid it. It is not necessary to make war on Iran, Gaza. We were the victims, but not now.

I can say very loudly that I don't like the political situation. I don't agree with the Israeli government. There is a lot to be done. We must make peace — we missed it. I have an idea — but I can't tell you because no one will accept it. If you want peace, forget about justice. Give up justice or you will never get peace. My justice is not yours and not the Palestinians. Justice — maybe it will come. Peace is more important. You have to give up for peace, to give up justice, property and more. I know it is not easy, but in the end this is it; we can live like angels if we will learn to share. Jimi Hendrix said, "When the power of love overcomes the love of power the world will know peace." I believe in that.

Tal Medvezky

Hadera, 1961

SOME YEARS AGO, WHEN TAL WAS AN AIR FORCE PILOT, HE CAME TO STUDY WITH ME TO improve his English so that he could fly for El Al. I was charmed by his gentle, humored, humanistic manner. Later, when he was working for the bank selling commodities, he decided that he would rather fly than work at the bank. As he had small children at home, he chose to pilot for Arkia locally. He is now captain and trained on the new Embraer aircraft. To celebrate the bar mitzvah of the son of friends of ours visiting from Chile, Tal flew the youngster in a small plane over Tel Aviv — and was disappointed at his low level of his enthusiasm! I was enthusiastic when I sat in the cockpit on a flight he captained to Eilat!

I am married, three children, captain for Arkia Airlines, happy. I grew up in Pardess Hanna — it was the center of the world. Where was the rest? I went to regular school, and then high school and then to the army. It was the usual. We went to the Scouts. Before the army there was supposed to be a supervisor, but there wasn't any supervisor, so I took care of everything. I ordered the trips, organized the treks — all before the army. Now I live in Ramat Aviv Gimel, a fancy neighborhood. You read in the paper that the people from north Tel Aviv don't take hard jobs in the army. When I check the children who are in the

Scouts, they try for the best, the hardest group in the army — but just the youngsters who go to the Scouts.

Both of my parents are from Pardess Hanna; both are *sabras* (native born Israelis: bristly on the outside and sweet on the inside). They knew each other from youth. I went to a meeting some time ago when all were asked, "Raise your hand if you are both sabras." In a hundred people they were the only two. When my grandfather came, he left everything from what is now Ukraine. He was about twenty. They never told us stories. My father doesn't know either. My father grew up with one or two people, not a family. He didn't learn how to be a grandfather because he had no examples. But my father is an excellent grandfather! He is a friend to my children. The family meets at least once a week. My father comes every Friday and after dinner the youngsters go out.

In the middle of the week I ask my ten-year-old, "Did you call your *saba* (grandfather) this week?" My grandmother was in the same aliya. My grandfather on my father's side was a very intelligent man. He didn't know English at all but they sent him to the US to develop a machine to take water from the ground with a meter to count, but the patent was with the company. He was an autodidact and read a lot of stories.

I try to be a good person. I try to follow *don't do to your friends what you don't want them to do to you. Don't do to others what you hate.* I'm teaching this to my children. When you do something you must not only think if it is just good for yourself. My children maybe act a little differently than their friends — they think about them too much! It's a bit hard to live like that.

For example: A lot of times when the pilot says "I'm not coming today. Put another man in my schedule." When I do that to think how does he think — will it be convenient? Or will he say, "Oh, that Tal made me have a bad day." I never do it! But when someone who has done that asks me, I say, "Oh, I have a lot of things to do."

I try to think if there is a future and if I am a smart man and if I educated my children with what is good for them. When I look at the past I think of my grandparents and all the people who came here and worked and died here for us. Even those who didn't care about being Jewish, it didn't matter to the Nazis. But about the future, I don't know.

My parents shaped my life. And the environment. My mother educated us. She didn't work until we were in high school. Then she went to university and then worked as a librarian.

If you ask me, why do you want to be a pilot? I didn't want. I just succeeded. I went to the navy as a commander. I passed everything. The priority was for flight school. I am not a strong man with a lot of power, but because I wanted to succeed I did. My older brother is also a pilot, but it didn't influence me. I just succeeded. My brother and I try to coordinate *miluim* (reserve duty) together. We are in the same squadron for one week a year. We try to start early and finish early and make a trip together.

Suffering with my English was a setback! When I went to the States to get my pilot's license I managed. We were four and I was the best — even though two were American.

I wouldn't do anything differently. When you are on the right politically you always know you are right. If you are on the left you always have a question if you are doing the right thing.

I think in the small part I did good things. I took my kid's class to go to for a trip so that they love the country. Yes, I trained pilots in Ethiopia, but that was my work! And I was in the *va'ad* (the house committee). I went to miluim and gave the young people in the army a presentation about how to fly, but it was because I wanted to. Usually they say thank you. I took this mission because I don't think the younger pilots bring the same understanding as we had.

I am worried about the future, but my head is in the sand. The political situation and the conflict between the religious and not religious. If there will be a future! I am not worried about the nuclear bomb in Iran. The problem is inside. I used to read Ha'aretz, but I couldn't stand Gideon Levy anymore! The security after September 11 was very severe. I am on the left. It is not good for us to control another people. I don't believe they will leave us alone — it won't be forever.

I did the Night Run last week. I am not a person who can run a lot; I can walk a lot. I could run 100 meters. I started practicing with 2 kilometers and a month before the run I had a back problem and couldn't train. Two weeks before I did 6.5 kilometers. When I did the run, I did it with all those people, I just did it with my daughter, who is nineteen and she is an athlete in the army. Running with the group gave us power.

Doreen Mervish Bahiri

Cape Town, South Africa, 1937

When I first came to Tel Aviv, several people told me I must go to the Dervish gallery and meet Doreen and Miriam, sisters who specialized in ethnic art and who had an extensive social network. We became friends, which meant many parties and celebrations on their roof, trips to their house in Sfat, travel stories, hiking, and interesting eating adventures. Doreen is carrying on the traditions, after the loss of Miriam.

I learned that here you meet new people, you like them, it is mutual, and then you are in each other's lives for the long term. No sniff and wag, getting-to-know-you time.

I grew up in Cape Town. A wonderful childhood, a close and warm family and a vibrant Jewish community — but also very stifling. My mother's family had a blanket factory. The first members of the family came from Poland and the family grew sheep in the Kalahari Desert. It used to take them three weeks of travel to visit Cape Town by ox wagon, so all my mother's generation was born either nine months after Pesach or nine months after Rosh Hashanah. My father came to South Africa in 1908 from Lithuania and his father was head of the *beit midrash* (house of learning). They were very poor but he was the first

Jewish doctor to qualify in South Africa — all the other doctors went to Edinburg or London.

My mother was born in South Africa but her parents came from Poland when one of the family won a lottery ticket in 1880. My father and family arrived in Cape Town *erev Yom Kippur* in 1908. My father was ten years old. I often wonder what their first impressions were of Cape Town.

Cape Town was getting very boring. I thought I would live in Cape Town, get married, have children, etc., etc. It is astonishingly beautiful, always changing, but boring. When I visited I was always overwhelmed by the beauty. A lot of people came here, and Miriam was here. forty-seven years have passed since my late sister Miriam and I tossed a coin — *etz or pali* (heads or tails) and Dervish was born in the Old City of Sfat. In those days it was a fascinating place to live, full of characters, stories, legends, myths. The trash was transported by donkeys with huge sacks on either side of them, one still saw people carrying ice from the ice factory with special holders, people rolled the roofs with cylindrical stones of Ottoman origin to strengthen them against the rain. At the start of Lag B'Omer the Abu family's home was host to a small group of musicians who played haunting music on saxophones and clarinets and then carried the Torah and danced through the *simtaot* (alley ways) of Sfat all the way to Meron. It was a genuine folk festival. And on *Simchat Torah* we accompanied Moshe and Sarah Pearl from the legendary Herzliya Hotel to all the ancient synagogues, getting drunk on arak. I loved the intricately worked Damascus brass lamps in their hotel. After all, Damascus wasn't so far away. On the walls hung paintings of the best of the Sfat artists. Sarah once suggested that we start our shop on her ping pong table in her courtyard with its 1,000-year-old olive trees.

Our family legend was that our great-great-grandfather walked from Lithuania to Sfat to be buried there. We never found his grave. That was all a long time ago. Today I don't know anymore. I am not happy about a lot of things happening here, the way people have become callous towards others, the whole Palestinian scene. But there are a lot of wonderful people here.

I'm still married, still working, still running around the world. I want to travel more. To eastern Turkey, Malaysia. I just read a book by an *amazing* English woman, Isabella Bird, who in the 1890s travelled alone in China, Afghanistan, Persia, Malaysia in areas where no European had been before, under the most extreme difficulties, travelling by horse, mule, elephant, whatever, sleeping in caravanserais with the animals and hordes of other travelers. That was real travelling. Simcha and I travelled in India the hard way, seven-rupees-a-night hotels, endless bus journeys, fighting to get a place to sleep on the deck of the boat that used to go from Bombay to Goa.

My family shaped my life. Working with my sister Miriam for forty-three years in the shop. My husband, Simcha, changed my life! Living with someone with whom I could share everything and laugh a lot was, and is, great. The first time I met Simcha was in Nuweiba, in Sinai. I went with friends and he was there. We just clicked from the beginning.

I have faced a million setbacks. Living in Israel, with all its plusses and minuses.

I have taken wonderful hikes. The most amazing was a three-week hike in Nepal. Now it is very common, but not then. At that time it was truly different and totally exhilarating. And at times very difficult.

I haven't lived anywhere else for fifty years. I love my friends, the way of life, and hate the politics — the constant war mongering — *hate* it. The shop is a big part of my life — social — traveling to buy things for the shop and making friends, like in India. I am now an amateur belly dancer; everyone there is thirty or forty years younger than me! I get great pleasure from my silversmithing — and creating jewelry with my big collection of beads.

Yair Kenner

Ramat Gan, 1955

WHEN I FIRST STARTED WORKING WITH SOME MEMBERS OF THE DEPARTMENT OF ORGA-nizational development at Bank Hapoalim, Yair was about to go to New York to participate in an organizational review. He needed to ramp up his English and I took the opportunity of preparing him for the culture in the States. We have stayed in contact over the years of his career development and recently had additional sessions to improve his written English for the international role he now plays. I knew we had succeeded when he had to send an important email to his client with no time for my approval. I read it after it was sent and realized he had totally succeeded. I learned a lot from him. He said, "Grab the good stuff, because the bad stuff can grab you."

In my situation now, I feel today very good and very comfortable with myself. I think I got to a situation that I am satisfied both in my personal life and the work I am doing. I also feel I succeeded in developing my spiritual side. I have a positive approach. I always look at the full part of the glass.

I found a woman who I love and like and we have a good life together. We are together for the last nine years. In the recent trip to India I got the feeling that we will get married. Even though we live together, I think it is good for Edna. Instead of being in a "divorced" status — to be "married" — the formal obligation for long term. I understood and accept this to get married formally. Not religious — maybe in Cyprus.

I also can support, with my experience, to guide my children and my family. I am beginning to plan my pension. Formally, ten years from now I have to go to pension but maybe I will go earlier. We have a lot of ideas — maybe to live in Toscana for a year, not as a tourist but to live in other places. And other plans to develop my hobbies — to do wood carving. To develop my skill in alternative medicine, healing, bio-energy, like reike, all this kind of treatment — I feel I have talent in this area. I spent time in the past doing this and will develop it further.

I have two burning issues: one, at work to balance the work demands and the things I like to do and the things I am good at and try not to work too much and enjoy what I am doing.

Second is the family. We have five children between us. I try to guide my son. One just finished his Master's and maybe he will get married next year. The young one is confused lately about his direction and I am trying to help him find his way, in life, and studies. He is diabetic so he has to stabilize his life style to be healthier, do more sports and eat more healthful food. I am trying to balance these two issues and to enjoy with friends, and trips.

I grew up in Ramat Gan and went to regular elementary school but high school was professional. My parents came from Europe and thought I should learn Work. I learned to be a technician. I have high skills in technical things. My mother saw me dissemble a clock and try to put it back. After the army, I decided to go to university to be an engineer.

My mother came to Israel when she was twelve years old. She fought for the State in the underground, *Lechi*, the most extreme of the three organizations, led by Abraham Stern (whose underground name was Yair) who was caught and killed by the British. She promised to name her child after him. I grew up in a house where I was educated to love and serve my country. I grew up here and all my family and friends were in Kfar Moladeti — the village I was born in. I did the army, served my country. I feel very strong about this. Although I want to experience living in other countries, I am not going to leave Israel — my roots are here.

When I was young, my mother had a big influence on my approach. Although she came from Europe with old-fashioned views, she had good instincts of how to raise her children. She gave me confidence. "You're nice, clever." As an example, when I decided to divorce when I was thirty-nine and had two children, I came to her and she tried to understand. After five minutes she understood it was final and from that time she encouraged me. She didn't try to lecture me. She tried to support me. Although she was against divorce she was flexible.

After the army I established a business in carpentering with a friend. I made a lot of money. We thought to continue with this, but my mother pushed me to study — like a mantra. In the end I went. I also learned that way of how to convince somebody to do something. Repeat the mantra again and again. In the end it influenced me. I am doing the same with my children — a lot of talking — I don't push but I don't let up.

My parents came from different places in Poland. My mother from a village very close to Russia. She came here in 1932. My father from a city in Poland. She was dominant in education for the children. When we were young she stayed home. She made fresh bread sandwiches to take to school, picked me up from school and made sure we did our homework. When we were grown, she went to work in a company as a clerk. My father was an accountant in a government office. His parents came with seven brothers and sisters. Some of them went abroad. My father's sister and husband went to Mexico and established a business. He was the only rep of air force military — he became a billionaire. They are still there but own a lot of property here. This is the shelter for them; they come once a year. Another brother is in Florida and one in Los Angeles. My father was also a Zionist but not as strong as my mother. My mother passed away three years ago. My father is still in good health at ninety-three — I hope I get the long-life genes from the family!

After I was divorced and living with a woman I loved very much, she got cancer and died. I experienced the pain of losing someone who I loved. I had to be supportive while she was suffering. I tried to take from this experience the lesson learned: A day that passes will never return. You must enjoy every moment. If you are angry or bitter, your life will pass and never return. This also opened me to the spiritual world. I tried to get out of this situation as well as I could and not break down and feel self-pity.

In my work: most of my life I have been working in Bank Hapoalim. One of the most challenging positions was when I built the internet activity for the bank, from the beginning through to achieving awards for the best site. I expected the organization to promote me after ten years. But I experienced the political situation and was not promoted. I experienced frustration. I went through this and decided to move on and look for another position in the bank and got to the international division.

For a person who believes that what happens in your life has a reason, you learn to accept that. I don't have any regrets. In each point, I decided what the best is. When I finished university and looked for work, I got three offers: Bank Hapoalim, Scitex, and an industrial company. I had to decide which way to go. Like the movie "Sliding Doors." So I accept what happened in my life.

I think Israel, in the last few years, changed not for good but for bad. The country lost a lot of values that it had in the past. The new leaders are not good — they educate the people for bad values. The President raped somebody and he is still fighting in court. And the previous Prime Minister stole money. Even though they catch them for corruption, they don't have shame. They don't resign. Here the leaders have no shame. These values are going down from that level to the business leaders to the people: less concern about the country. I don't like this atmosphere. Lately, the social movement tried to fight against the high prices that are controlled by the major families/businesses. We are on the wrong track. Still in the same relationship with our neighbors. I don't like it. I hope things will change. The social movement will influence our country, too. In the meantime, it is not good.

I would like to include a few words about Lori. I met you over twenty years ago in the industrial department to make an assessment in the US. It was my first job abroad. We used your advice to know how to dress and behave in the US. At that time our knowledge was not enough to know about the US and Israel. For instance, wear dark socks, and not to put my things on the other person's desk, and about Time, that I still carry from that time we worked together in culture training and teaching English. We like to be friends and talk about everything. I like your approach. I admire your way of living and sport, culture, your connection to Israel. I am carrying a lot things that I learned from you. It helped me as now I am doing most of my work abroad. The basic skills of how to be open and sensitive to differences. For example, in Switzerland I had to get used to them; to be patient to their methods and thinking. I developed the skills to be sensitive to different ways of thinking, talking, working. I am using this opportunity to thank you.

Thank you, Yair.

Annette Samuels, MM, OTR

Houston, Texas, 1934

JUST UP THE ROAD FROM OUR HOUSE IS THE ARCHEOLOGICAL SITE OF TEL DOR. I JOINED the summer excavation season by working for a week, starting at 5 a m, digging with a little trowel, hauling dirt-filled buckets, and eating watermelon at the break. Annette, from Ein Hod, joined in, and we had a good time sharing the experience as local participants with the young people from Washington University. She was expanding her many activities. We enjoyed her recent family concert at Ein Hod.

I hope I will take part in another dig. Years ago we rode our Lambretta over what is now Caesarea, before it was excavated. There must be a lot more to be found still today.

My husband Bob and I were students in Jerusalem in 1956-58. My father was a Conservative rabbi and a Zionist leader, one of the pioneers. Instead of Palestine, he went to Texas and I became a Zionist as a youth, but my husband's family was not Zionist. We fell in love with the country and its people. We traversed the whole country by foot, bicycle, scooter, and hitch-hiking. It was just right for us. We were here two years without children and came back in '62 with three children. We made aliya without extended family. No one could understand how we could leave a comfortable life. But we loved the challenge and spirit in those early years.

I grew up in Houston, out in the country. My father had a little plot that he gardened. I spent many hours in the garden helping him. I had a bicycle and was free to come and go, exploring new places, as it was not dangerous in the '40s. Just having fun — driving my mother mad by not practicing enough.

I was the only Jew in my elementary school and experienced anti-Semitism: I had my hair pulled, and face scratched. Hard to believe! My mother was an orphan and from age sixteen supported herself, even while studying at Julliard. She thought I was a child prodigy at the violin. From age four she kept me out of school for three years to study violin. She was an excellent and ambitious pianist and with my sister, who played cello, we played together as a trio. In high school, I had a great social life, dating and dancing and was a majorette on Friday nights. Dancing is my second love. I was a member of Jewish organizations. As a teenager, I had only Jewish friends, and after fifteen, I didn't ask for permission for anything.

I got a full scholarship to Radcliffe. Harvard and Radcliffe were becoming one institution while I was there. I think my musical ability as well as being an A student helped a lot. My original plan was to go to Rice as pre-med. My sister was one of the few women in medical school in the '50s and I idolized her. But at Harvard I decided to concentrate on musicology. I was the concertmistress of the Harvard-Radcliffe Symphony Orchestra. Chamber music was and is my first musical love.

My dad came to Ellis Island with ten brothers and sisters in 1900, when he was five, from Lithuania because there were pogroms. His mother came some time after their father and brought all the kids in steerage. My paternal grandfather was a Talmudic scholar and he was run over by a carriage as a young man. My paternal grandmother had to support the family running a poultry farm in New Jersey. She decided that one son had to be a rabbi so they chose my father. He went off and worked in a grocery store in Brooklyn while he put himself through high school. He earned three degrees between 1915-22: a BA, rabbinical ordination, and a law degree. He was quite a scholar.

My mother lost her mother at two from diphtheria. She loved music and at sixteen went to Julliard and earned her way as a secretary. She studied all of her life, taking college courses, reading voraciously to the last year of her life. My parents met in Freeport, Long Island in New York. He was thirteen years older, and was a rabbi when he met my mother. He was a founder of the Student Zionist Organization. He took a congregation in Houston in 1929. After the crash he got no salary, lived on credit for two years, and had to make a living by selling insurance, but continued with his rabbinical and community work. He fulfilled his Zionist dream with us.

We came to Haifa because of the Leo Baeck School, a very small school founded by Rabbi Max Elk, who came before the Holocaust. With my husband Bob's vision and great leadership he raised money and built one of Israel's best high schools, a community center and a sport center. The school is now a full K-12 grade.

For my career, it would have been better to be in Tel Aviv, but I am not sorry that I spent ten years mostly at home with the three kids. In those days most women's careers were secondary to the husband's. In 1969, I joined the Haifa Symphony Orchestra and began teaching in kibbutzim. I have introduced over a hundred young people to the violin. What I really loved was our women's string quartet, performing especially for children all over the country.

My violin teacher shaped my life from age four to seventeen. At Radcliffe, it was the whole community of Harvard - professors and students alike. Those four years undoubtedly were among the most important in my life. In Israel, it was Zev Vilnay, who adopted us. We were always invited on Shabbat and he took us on his trips as a guide. My love for music and nature from my mother, and gardening from my father. My sister was always my ideal and today we are soul mates and best friends.

I have always been interested in medicine. In '78 I resigned from the Haifa Symphony to study occupational therapy. I graduated in the third class from Haifa University. I loved the studies. We learned medicine, anatomy, physiology, psychiatry, psychology, child development, and crafts. I loved working with children and ended up working with immigrant Ethiopian children for several years. It was a wonderful experience, both challenging and rewarding. In the first meetings, I had blocks and pencils and colors to test the children. The mothers were as excited as the children as they had never seen these things. Another group I followed through Leo Baeck was from Quara, a remote area in Ethiopia. We started with holding a pencil correctly and writing, caught up on physical development through exercises, learning to swim, and sat with them doing math, English, and other homework. They are now graduates of the army and I am still connected with them. I have also worked with the elderly living in *moshavim* (collective farms). I analyzed homes for safety and health issues, connected them with other health workers, introduced craft projects and other enrichment in their lonely lives and led an exercise group in wheelchairs for fifteen years in Kibbutz Naveh Yam. While working as an OT, I continued my playing, especially in the Kibbutz Chamber Orchestra. This was my favorite group, not only as musicians but as great friends.

Now I'm retired. I still play in and coach several chamber-music groups, teach violin, travel extensively, and spend time with nine grandchildren. I don't spend much time in the kitchen. I love to work in the garden and swim in our pool. I go out to pick a rose and spend three hours — there's a little dust in the house! I play golf four times a week with my husband and son, and a few times a month I have our family of seventeen people for dinner or brunch and organize chamber music "happenings" in my studio in Ein Hod. That can involve anywhere from four to twenty-four musicians. A third of my time is with music, a quarter with family, and left over time for sharing my exciting life with Bob.

He and I have deep concern for the future here. We came as students in the '50s full of idealism. But now Israel is moving towards a fanatical orthodoxy and an undemocratic, ultra-nationalism. We long for the Israel of social justice and pluralism. We need a strong leader to bring back democracy here in Israel. We are among the few liberal idealists left, I'm afraid. Our government has made so many terrible mistakes with the Ethiopian community. We failed to make knowledgeable citizens, a once-in-history opportunity lost.

On the other hand, Israel has been good to us as a family. Our personal life is fine, the children and grandchildren are wonderful and successful. Music gives me that extra inspiration that makes life beautiful. My three kids all play string instruments. They graduated from the Interlochen Arts Academy in Michigan. We play together as a family string quartet. We perform one concert a year in Ein Hod, where I have lived since 1985. My son, an investment banker, is the cellist, the second son crafts violin bows and plays the viola, and the daughter, a music and dance therapist, rounds out the quartet. This string quartet is non-verbal communication that is very moving and fulfilling for us as a family. It's amazing when we all get together. Tonight we are playing a Dvořák piano quintet.

Bishara Naddaf

Nazareth, 1960

I MET BISHARA AT A PARTY AND I REALLY LIKED HIS GOOD NATURE AND WONDERFUL music. For a summer solstice celebration in our backyard, Bishara came with twenty darbukes and got everyone playing and dancing! He has kept me updated on his music activities: teaching at summer camps in the US and running classes here. I am hoping to attend more of his music performances. We sat on his balcony in Nazareth.

My grandfather was Palestinian. He was born here in Nazareth. And also my father. In 1948 they didn't run away. If they had run away I would be in Lebanon or Jordan. Many Nazarenes didn't run away as there was no war here. On my mother's side, too, from here.

(See the film, THE TIME THAT REMAINS.)

In Nazareth I went to the Silesian school. We can see the school from the balcony. I started music as a child; my grandfather played the oud. Salim, my brother, played violin and oud. He started on Israeli radio in 1973. Many musicians came to the house. I was drumming on the table and my cheeks and he said I was a drummer. I studied in Egypt to learn *darbuke* and learned for ten years for two weeks every year. I studied with one of the best drummers in Cairo. Some of the other musicians were from Saudi Arabia and other Arab countries and didn't know there were Arabs in Israel. They thought Arabs were just in the West Bank and Gaza. They were amazed that I worked in Jewish schools. My parents raised me to see people as human beings. My oldest brother's wife was Jewish and sang with him, but she died last year. It was no problem for my father. They each had three children from before.

My model was my oldest brother — he is very charismatic. I wanted to be good and famous like him. My head was saying I would be the best musician. But I was sporty even though I was short — soccer, basketball, gymnastics — I was good. But I wanted to see beautiful women at the parties where I played. Now everything has changed!

Today I am focused on many things: I am married with two grown-up kids. The younger one, Amir, is finishing his BA in English and working for a hi-tech company in Yokneam. Feras is working as a musician playing guitar and composing. His band is *Chaos of Nazareth*. It's on YouTube. They perform for the big bands; they do the warm- up. He also teaches guitar and works at Radio Ashans as a sound engineer. Amir has work now, but what about in the future? What about teaching the guitar? It is very small in Israel — he needs to go out of the country. Who knows?

My wife is the best housekeeper! Her name is a musical name So La Fa — she is the best cooker — because of her, my belly! She makes Arabic food, Palestinian food, and also food from Lebanon and Syria, but she uses her own "pilpel" (pepper). On Facebook you can see So La Fa's kitchen.

I am teaching darbuke in Jewish and Arab schools. I teach teachers to play the darbuke. In the summer I travel to the US and do workshops in Jewish camps. I am on Facebook and YouTube.

I also play with the Israel Philharmonic Orchestra. We have an Arab-Jewish ensemble called Shesh-Besh. The last performance was in March, at Tel Aviv University. I love my work. I work very hard but I love my job. Because of that I succeed and am happy, smiling, and optimistic.

As a human being I don't talk about Arabs, Muslims, Christians — the culture in every religion is going down. The respect is going down.

For example: Once upon a time if we saw the teacher in the street we said "Hello" with our heads down. In the class we stood up for the teacher. Now — if an old man gets on the bus who needs a seat — it's all over.

I am asked to play when others come and why offer any of them? They say, "We will work for half." They are jealous. I say God is God — I feel God is with me. I don't go to church but I pray every day. Maybe I go once a month. I am grateful for my family and my health and success. Now I have a trio. I need to know how to promote myself. Maybe if I would have learned the computer …

The good thing I did was I got married to So La Fa and have two kids. And I am a musician and decided to be a teacher, and work with the Philharmonic, and work at Jewish schools. They respect me as a human being not just as an Arab. They acknowledge my work. This does good things in my heart. In Arab schools they say, "We have this at home." If you want something good you must pay. It's not like buying cheaper tomatoes!

That I bought this apartment — I have the best view in Nazareth. I took a loan even though I could have lived with my father. I have lived here ten years.

I honor my father and my mother. Mother's day is March 21 here in the Arab area — all day there are songs about the mother on the radio. And my father.

Working is good. I am happy with my kids and my wife.

Thank you for coming! I am glad to see you after so long! I have photos from the workshop at your house.

I am happy in my life. Just all the time I am thinking how to arrive to sixty-five! I want to have a respected life. I want to remain famous, wanted! I look for the bright side: maybe I win *Lotto* (The national lottery) so I can work less. Once in a while I put ten shekels in the Lotto place.

Today is Sunday. As it is my Shabbat, my wife is going out of the city. We usually go visiting on Sunday. All the other days I am working.

ASKAR
exclusive fashion items

Ashkar Sandrine Canella

Blois, France 1975

Yes, Ashkar is my neighbor. How lucky to have such an elegant, charming neighbor with a fashion boutique right next door! Ashkar is acclimating to Israel with gusto. Her kids swim on our pool, we love to chat about Life! From her, I am learning to be more "spontani." She is full of good spirits and heartfelt enthusiasm. I am watching as she finds her way here. Maybe this will be an opportunity to continue lifelong efforts to improve my French.

I am here because the father of my kids is Israeli. The real and only reason; I would not be here otherwise. Moordan lived abroad for twenty years. When I was pregnant the first time he wanted to come back. I was not ready — it was a big trauma! I left my job to come to Israel — no job, no work. He took a flat in Tel Aviv but I knew I could not survive with my baby in the tummy. When we came they checked me at security, asking questions for an hour and half. I could not stand it. When I arrived I was sick. We went to the hospital right away — the macho doctor. It was raining all the time. When I recovered, we sat at the beach and some soldier with a gun came to sit next to us — a military plane overhead. Everything was telling me not for now. Moordan was intelligent enough to understand and to come with me. As I was moving from Paris anyway, and we had the dream of Provence, we moved there. We stayed in Provence, in Cadenet, where we found a house we liked, doing babies and eating good food. When I was pregnant with the second, I felt a change and was ready to experiment and come back again to Israel.

We came here on holidays so it matured. It's about momentum. The sister of Moordan, who was living here in the house, moved out so everything came together; the house was empty and Moordan wanted to come back. I felt I had the openness to come. I was ready. It was too long with making babies and eating good food. We were ready for the next stage.

I grew up in the Loire Valley — a little village, Pont Levoy. It was a special place. Although it was in the middle of nowhere, artists, designers, Americans, Parisians — a lot of friends from all over the world came there — a lot of taste!

When I was sixteen I moved to the big city! To Tours, to continue school. I was independent already, not living with my parents. It was very natural, there was no option. I was looking for that for a long time. My parents were ready, too! They trusted me a lot — they gave me the power for this. They sustained me — I came home on the weekends. I stayed at school with all the girls the first year. The second year I had a room in a big house, and the third year I had a flat. I was working, but they supported me, too.

My mommy is French, born in St. Etienne, close to Lyon. And my father is from an Italian family, born in France, not far from where I grew up.

From the past, my mother shaped my life. She was always there with huge space, and lots of love — lots of freedom. And yoga. That gives me the sense of my life. I started yoga when I was nineteen; my sister recommended it to me. She is in Tours. For me, it brings meaning. Hard to verbalize this.

Now I am living in Caesarea with my kids and husband and managing my boutique and taking care of my family. My burning issue is to find myself. I was always looking for wisdom. This is first. And then I was very attracted to traveling and fashion, to design, to be with color, to do fabric — from my mother — she has a great taste — she was always so beautiful — she had It! I don't know if I got It from her but I played with her clothes, jewels. My playground was her big closet. She was an inspiration for me. She is still! My parents worked together for fifty-five years. She had a shop in the village for electricity. She sold all the stuff around that. She did all the accounts. They had special connections in the village because of her.

We were in France because my grandfather could not stand Mussolini. First he ran away, built a business and then the wife and two kids came. He wanted a son. My father was born. My grandfather died two years later and left my grandmother with two big girls, and the little boy in the war in a foreign country. Because it was a place where Germans came they had to move to the free part of France in Angouleme — the free zone. Everything was robbed from them when they came back, not from the Germans, it was the locals. The Germans gave chocolates to my father as a little boy. My grandmother punished him for this. There are many stories. They were not Jewish. My father was more French than French — the first at school. My grandmother was in the survivor mode to protect everyone. She had two big girls, one eleven and one thirteen. She was very strong. She got flour and eggs from the farmers and made pasta for them and for her family. One soldier in the resistance protected the house and some years later married one of the daughters.

Maybe I am facing my setbacks now? How to realize oneself — to be free when you have a family, kids, when you get married — what it means — to run your business — how to harmonize everything and be happy in the picture now! Even though it's tough and we would like to do everything, I know that everything has a reason.

Maybe the good things I do is to bring beauty — I feel like I am becoming a channel for beauty — a type of magic. It was my heart, and it became my business, like a magnet, my mother was an inspiration. She could listen without comment — all the magic is coming when you are totally free, when you are waiting for nothing.

I love English — my greatest love story was in English. Moordan and I wrote in English when he was living in Canada and I was living in France. We met in India and both went back to our respective homes and started to communicate. For one year. Then he moved to France to be with me. We still speak English at home.

Living in Israel is very interesting. First of all, it's a very warm country. We are very lucky because we are living in a type of bubble: Caesarea. I decided to protect myself from the politics and all those issues. I think people are very curious and generous. And it is one of the most interesting places I have ever known — the intensity of life here and openness of the people. I meet a lot of different minds. It's not obvious. People are looking for meaning. I like the weather. Of course I am missing some things from my culture. It's very different to raise kids. Kids are the only priority here — I am finding my way with this difference. I like it!

There is a lot of energy here — things move very fast.

When we live abroad from our birth country, it is always a challenge. To recreate yourself all the time and redefine yourself. For me this is like I am like a little kid because I am not speaking Hebrew — you are a part and you are aside. There is something there — I don't know how to treat it. When you have kids in a different culture they talk to you in a language you don't understand. They become Israeli. I want to feel that my life is a life!

Munther Fahmi
Jerusalem, 1954

SOME YEARS AGO WHEN RAMBLING AROUND JERUSALEM, I WENT TO SEE THE FAMOUS *American Colony Hotel. Yes, it is very beautiful — built by a sheik for his wives. And in the courtyard was a great bookshop with a comprehensive collection of American books. Munther was the smiling bookseller and his warmth and humor drew me in. It still does! It was painful to see him struggling to regain his status as a resident of Jerusalem.*

How is it that you are in Israel?

How is it that Israel is in me? How did Israel come to me? My parents have been here many, many generations.

I am a bookseller of Jerusalem. Even though I was born here, I am not allowed to live in the country. According to Israeli law, Palestinian residents who have lived abroad for seven years or more, lose their right to live here. So my situation is in limbo at the moment. I am divorced and hoping that my situation will result in granting me residency so that I can do what I like best, traveling and finding great books to sell in my bookshop.

I grew up in East Jerusalem in Wadi El Joz. Middle class. My parents were both educators, teachers. Because my father became a school principal, we moved around to different neighborhoods so I have a lot of friends who remember me because of my father. At that time, the teacher was respected. I went to regular government school in Arabic. I went to high school in Egypt to stay away from trouble here. It was a private boarding school in Cairo. Then I went to America to study business in upstate New York, in Albany. I got used to the winter. I was there one year and then went to work selling insurance successfully for seventeen years. During that period, I got married, had a baby, then moved to St. Louis, ending up in Lincoln, Nebraska.

The Oslo agreements in '93 made me want to come home. I was no longer married. I fell in love with a Jewish woman from Holland. After living together in Jerusalem for one year, we moved to Holland. She loved to read and it was contagious. I got sick with the reading bug and the idea of having an English bookshop was born in Holland to be implemented years later in Jerusalem at the American Colony Hotel.

My father was born in Acre and my mother come from a Nablusi family but was born in Jerusalem's Old City. My mother married at age fourteen. By the time she was twenty-eight she had been pregnant ten times and only six survived. She is now seventy-three. We are really good friends. I am fifty-seven. My father died about five years ago at age eighty-three. I have two brothers and three sisters. So we are six. We have regular meetings. At one point we were all living in America. Now my siblings live in five different countries and except for one brother who lives here in Jerusalem, the rest have been stripped of their rights to live in Jerusalem by the Israeli Ministry of Interior because they have lived abroad for more than seven years — so we meet in Jordan. They are too dignified and have too much pride to beg the Israeli embassy in Jordan for a visiting visa!

My father, and an Iranian-American guy, Mahadi Fakhrazadeh, helped shape my life. He was Mr. Insurance, according to Fortune Magazine, the top Met Life insurance salesman in the world. He invited me to his house in Hoboken, New Jersey to stay for a week of coaching. He wrote a book titled *Nothing is Impossible*. When he was in Iran he received the news that he was accepted to study at Brigham

Young University in Utah. He flew from Teheran to New York, got out of the airport and was so innocent that he asked a cab driver to drive him to Utah!

I have no memories of when I was young — not as a whole picture. I was very spoiled, as I was the first-born after three who died prematurely. I was like the *Messiah!* I was the only one who went to English kindergarten and learned English at seven. In the British Mandate most people spoke English — but no memories as a child. I don't know why.

Most of my setbacks have been with women. I am the most helplessly romantic man and women take advantage of me. I give too much and too fast.

If I could change one thing, I would never, never, ever touch smoking. I have quit some time now. I would have ten children by the age of thirty.

When my first daughter was being born I was watching. It was a miracle. When I used to sell insurance and be in people's houses and there were babies I thought they were just a nuisance. But after I had my own, it made me look at children in a different way.

I think I am comfortable supporting humanitarian cases and organizations. Those are good things I do.

This legal situation is my burning issue — my fight with the Interior Ministry.

Now, I am in an alien country. The only thing that keeps me going is the love of my bookshop and coming to work in the morning. It's been fourteen years. The bookshop is like a passion. And the desert — I get to go to the Dead Sea often — but I don't know how to swim. I go in the morning at 9:00, do exercises in the water and can be back here in the shop at noon.

Dear Friends,

The Government of Israel has accepted the Israeli Supreme Court recommendation that my residency be reinstated. I have been granted 2 years' residence on the basis of a Jerusalem Identity

Card, and pending good behavior, shall receive permanent residence thereafter.

I am deeply indebted to all of you and extremely grateful for your kind support during this year of particular uncertainty. There is still much work to be done for resolution in line with international law for the 130,000+ Palestinians whose residency has been revoked by the Government of Israel.

With Best Wishes,
Munther Fahmi
The Bookshop
at American Colony Hotel

Talmon (Moni) Haramati

Hadera, Israel, 1950

MONI CAME FOR ENGLISH LESSONS SO THAT HE COULD APPLY TO BE A PILOT FOR EL AL. He had been a helicopter pilot in the air force, and had started his own aerial photography company with his partners. Yes, he passed the English test, but chose to continue with his own business, Albatross. As I had limited space for lessons, we decided to meet early mornings at the beach. It was a real treat. During that time we reviewed the instructions for his aviation GPS! He has shared his many publications and videos with me. Many of the aerial shots in the news and documentation are by Albatross. He has hosted my grandchildren in his studio. He has helped me through some personal crises and enjoyed some celebrations. Even though we are not politically aligned we are good friends.

I was born here in Israel. I was raised here. When I was eleven to thirteen I lived in Antwerp in Belgium with my parents when my father was sent to teach in a Hebrew school. I realized as a Jew the anti-Semitism and that we don't belong to that country. During the holidays our small family- my parents, with my brother and me- toured all Europe 1961-63. I decided I would never leave Israel again.

I grew up in Jerusalem. All my father's family was in Jerusalem. I went to regular school and high school. During high school I did gymnastics, played the accordion and guitar, and was in the youth movement. I was very good at gymnastics! I went to learn how to build airplanes and all about aeronautics. Even at that age I dreamed to be a pilot in the Israeli Air Force.

During the Six Day War, I was seventeen. I realized that Israel was surrounded by Arab countries like Jordan, Syria, and Egypt that wanted to destroy Israel. During this war a helicopter crossed very low above our school. I thought to myself: I hope I will be a helicopter pilot.

When I got the notice to go the army I had just come from vacation. It was already 9:00 and I saw the note said 7:00. With my long hair, short pants, and in slippers, I ran for the bus that was waiting for me. They thought I was going to run away from the army! The bus arrived at Tel Hashomer. The people around me didn't look like the air force guys. I came to an office. "What do you want to be? A driver or a cook?" They laughed at me when I told them I want to be a pilot in the air force. So I chose driver. I spent a year as a truck driver, making an effort to understand how that happened. I was a good athlete. What had happened? Three times I went to a doctor to ask why? The third time he said, "You are serious person but you have a low profile, which means no air force." Flat feet made my low profile! "You don't have a chance!" but he sent me to get a review from an orthopedist who raised my profile.

It was a long way to become a pilot. It took me a year driving all over Israel and in Sinai till the exam to be a pilot.

I was persistent. I went to the helicopter squadron, to the place I belonged. This led to my present career.

After I left the army, I became a crop-duster pilot in the Chem-avir Company that also did some filming of police missions, oilrigs, and aerial films. Because I loved to film I went to learn about this professionally. Parallel to my crop dusting, I opened an aerial photo company with a partner from the same course. After we separated, a friend from my squadron, Duby Tal, who was a professional photographer, joined me to form Albatross Company and we are partners until today. www. albatross.co.il

My mother is from Hungary, near Romania. She came with her family in a special train that saved Jews from the Holocaust. She was a fighter in the *Palmach* and was captured by the Jordanian army during the fight at Gush-Etzion and was sent to prison in Jordan. She was a fighter! She is a good Jewish mother, a giving person with a lot of humor.

My father was raised in Jerusalem in a religious family. His father came from Russia, but his mother and grandmother were born in Jerusalem, third generation in Israel. Now they live in a very nice place for older people. My father still teaches the weekly portion, *Gemara* and *Chazanut*. At eighty-seven he is busy. My parents are getting old. I'm proud of them.

Set back: my flat feet! The compromises you must make for the people around you — the army, your family, your partner — you can't do exactly what you want. Bottom line — myself! We are our own self! Every day!

I did a lot of tours. I skied every winter. I did a lot and liked it, but you always want more — now I am quite satisfied. We have to be satisfied and thank God every day for the family, our health, the business. I was very busy — I am so sorry about not giving enough attention to my children.

I would like to make the business better, to improve my family life, and to learn more and more about Jewish tradition and the Bible. The meaning of what we are doing here — the purpose of our life. I am concerned that each of my children will have his/her own house. In the tents now, the young people show that they can't do it now.

I don't know about some of the good things I have done — Maybe to learn about Israel, the Bible, and the purpose we are here for and to become a better person.

In our company, Albatross, we did a lot of good books and films of Israel that show the good side and the beautiful side of Israel.

I will be sixty-one in July. I have my profession. I'm lucky to be alive in Israel, to be alive in a country that didn't exist for two thousand years. I am proud to be an Israeli, Jewish, with a family and the work I am doing. I am lucky to do the work I do. It is the dream I had to be a pilot. What I am doing is exactly the work I want to do.

When I fought in the Yom Kippur War I escaped being harmed or killed! Later I found out my father was praying for me every day.

Rachel Ann Gambash, MMS

New Jersey, 1969 after the moon landing and
during the Notre Dame/Michigan football game

SOME YEARS AGO *I RESPONDED TO THE CALL OF THE DESERT AND WENT TO LIVE IN* EILAT. *Hiking in the desert and swimming in the Red Sea were great, but selling jewelry at Stern's was not. A job doing development for the local college did not happen. When I decided to return to Tel Aviv before my rental contract expired, I looked for someone to take the apartment. Rachel came to look. She had been working at The Red Sea Sports Club. I said, "Rachel, you are too young, too smart, too beautiful to bury yourself here in Eilat. Get yourself back to Tel Aviv!" She did. And she found good work and more. I have witnessed her life unfolding according to her plan — except for the latest addition of twins, which means she now has five adorable, full-of-personality, children.*

I first came to Israel when I was a teenager. I came on a high-school trip — these youth programs really know what they are doing. Coming at sixteen is very impressionable, a very powerful time and the youth programs instill a sense of belonging. On the trip they take very good care of you. It worked!

I really loved the country and felt a rootedness here. I spent my junior year abroad in Haifa and then I went back to Rutgers to finish my bachelor's and then I came back to Israel when I was twenty-two. I came when I was in my late teens and twenties because it was an appropriate place for a young Jewish woman. I loved my family but I wanted some space. They supported my decision to come here.

I think it was a natural progression. I don't think my parents raised me to come here even though my grandfather was born here pre-state.

I grew up in South Orange, New Jersey. I went to a very typical high school. I think it was very good. There were five hundred in a graduating class. I still have friends from there who I love very much. We had a good education: Latin, and languages and art history and wonderful teachers. I enjoyed school. We had good sports programs and girls' sports were strong. I was on the lacrosse team and the field-hockey team. We had a softball team, and swimming, and a chess club. It was an idyllic American high school in a metropolitan area. That's how I saw it, maybe others saw it differently. It was not mostly Jewish. I didn't feel like I was in a minority, although I was. The part of town I lived in was mostly Catholic. We lived near a Catholic church, but the student body was very diverse.

My mother, Barbara, is from Rochester, New York, and my father, Isaac, from Cairo, Egypt. My great grandparents on my mother's side came from Russia and Lithuania. My mother's family is very American. My maternal grandmother, Sarah, was born in Buffalo, New York and my maternal grandfather, Izzy, was born in Rochester.

My father was born in Tanta, Egypt, but raised in Cairo. His father, Leon, was born in Palestine and his mother, Rachelle – my namesake, was born in Egypt, I think Alexandria. My paternal grandfather was born in pre-state Israel and was involved in the creation of the state. He was thrown out by the British. Through family connections my grandfather studied agricultural engineering in Germany and then made it back to the Middle East, but couldn't enter Palestine so he settled in Cairo.

My mother shaped my life. She wanted me to be independent and to be loved. She wanted me to be exposed to different cultures and to culture. We didn't grow up with a lot of money, but when there was money saved she would take me to the ballet. My sister loved opera so she took us to the Met. We never saw movies. She would rather use the money for other things. I think it was a hard and good decision to do that. She worked hard and during my middle-school years had three jobs: as a teacher, a real-estate agent, and a phone operator at Lord and Taylor. I missed her very much and at certain times she would do special things with us. She was in charge of the children's community theater in our town. Later she told me she did that so we could see the shows — even the shows that she previewed in New York. This was the only way for us to go. She also worked in summer camps so we could go.

My father also shaped my worldview. He loved Egypt. He grew up a privileged outsider in a country that he loved and was then expelled for being Jewish. He taught tolerance and gave me and my sister an appreciation for other cultures.

I knew I didn't want to live in suburban New Jersey. I don't know why because it was great to go to New York. I never thought I would live in New York. I enjoyed New England, Boston. I had never been out to the West Coast, but of the places I was exposed to I liked the Boston area and Vermont. I had gone on some trips with my aunt and I felt at peace in those places. Maybe because I felt at peace with my Aunt Lois.

I didn't expect to have twins; I thought we were having a fourth child. I need more time! I would call them challenges.

The recent death of my father-in-law affects my husband. I will have to deal with my own parents getting older, and they aren't here. It all ties in. It gets harder to be away from my family as I get older. I am close to my sister, Claire, and my aunt, as well as my parents; I see them for very short, intense periods when I go to visit or when they come here. They miss the day-to-day of my life and I miss them.

I am aware that each choice was built on the previous one. Not that I haven't made mistakes! I didn't plan to have five kids. I didn't plan not to work outside the home, but at this time it is still a choice. There are things I would like to do that we can't afford. We make choices within the constraints. With my first child, Eden, the birth was life threatening for both of us. When I finally got home I felt like I was kidnapping my child. I remember lying on the carpet with my husband and my baby on my stomach. I felt total happiness. It was an instant of pure bliss.

I loved going to school and learning new things. I have my master's. I worked in advertising and as a copywriter. I published several articles and I liked to write. I opened a marketing company at a very young age and it was successful. I am a board certified lactation consultant and am very good at it. I am a good listener to my friends. I love a lot of people. I chose a great partner to be my husband, Nedim. We have wonderful, creative kids: Eden, Ella, Sahar, Ben and Keila. I think I am a good mom. I always want to be better but I think I am good.

I like living here, I like raising children here. I haven't lived anywhere else with children so I can only compare with what I see and my own childhood, so I don't know if it's a good gauge. I feel it's a healthy atmosphere. I think there is a general consensus on the feeling of concern for others. There is a disconnect with the establishment but there are concerned citizens who act in ways of caring for others. It's personal and not institutional. The cultural personality of the country is very giving towards children. I don't think that happens in the States. I think that runs strong here; it's different.

I haven't touched on negative things because I am trying to be a positive person. I hope things are better for my daughters and my son. I have always felt I have to protect myself as a woman. I don't know how it will be for them. I hope it will be better and that I can help them with the skills it takes to make it better for them and for others.

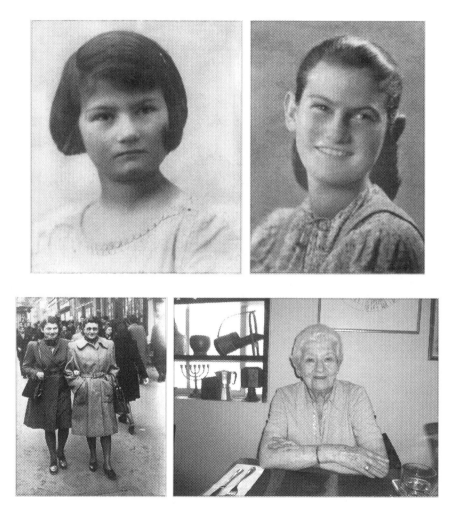

Erika Peitzer Miron

Lwow, Poland, 1927

WHEN I LIVED IN SANTA MONICA WITH MY SECOND HUSBAND, LILY LIVED DOWNSTAIRS *and we would often meet on the rooftop swimming pool. Her husband, Bill, was a doctor and was connected to the hospital where my husband was professor. Later, when I was ready to leave for Israel, and after Lily had helped me sell my belongings, she told me about Erika, who was related to Bill and lived in Tel Aviv.*

I looked up Erika after I was settled in Tel Aviv. She helped me with opening a bank account, often hosted me for lunch in her apartment, and gave me good, friendly advice about how to negotiate my new environment. When I was laid off from my first job, she told me not to deposit the check but to go immediately to the bank to cash it. Of course, it was not covered so I had to use some strong techniques to actually get my salary. She was very loving and caring, as is her nature. She has continued with her friendly assistance in every case that I needed. We lunch in Tel Aviv on a regular basis, exploring restaurants and the unfolding of life.

During the Second World War, my father was deported to Russia for over a year but he was allowed out by the Polish army in Russia. He came to Palestine through Tehran.

Being a pediatrician, he brought some Jewish children from Tehran. After the war he sent an affidavit to my mother and me in Poland provided by the British Mandate to get us to Palestine. In 1946, we came in a closed train from Poland, through Prague and Paris, and then by boat from Marseille to Haifa, organized by the Jewish Agency. I originally intended to go to Italy to study as I didn't know Hebrew. I had started studying chemistry at the University of Krakow, hoping to become a pharmacist. But first I had to face the difficulties of my parents' divorce. So instead of me, my mother went to Italy and married a man she knew from Poland, who, incidentally, I had helped to survive! Subsequently, my mother went to the US. I stayed with my father in Israel, began to learn a little Hebrew and English, and found a job in a button store.

I met Moshe on the beach where he was working as a lifeguard. He invited me for a ride on the *hasaka* (a flat raft that the lifeguard stands on and paddles). Moshe's family had left Armenia in 1918 by escaping over the mountains. They lost everything, including a daughter. Moshe was born in Jerusalem, one of eight children. He didn't have the chance for an education, but he had intelligence and both feet firmly planted on the ground. As a lifeguard he saved many lives. He was completely unlike the Jews I had known in Eastern Europe. He was tan, athletic, handsome, and kind. He taught me Hebrew. I felt very comfortable with him and his big family. They were not like the survivor Jews, nor like the native Israelis, who didn't want to know or hear anything about the Holocaust. Moshe's family came from a different background and this was comforting for me, in contrast to the European immigrants who didn't want anything to do with us. Their transition from living a dangerous life to living a "normal" life was very difficult. We married in 1948. I learned accounting and worked for a leather company for about twenty years; I eventually helped manage its closure. I then worked as the bookkeeper for a travel agent. We lived in Tel Aviv on Ben Yehuda Street. During the War of Independence some other families lived in our apartment with us. Many years later, we moved to Afeka, and now have a spacious and pleasant apartment.

I grew up in Lwow, Poland. We had a very comfortable life, as my father was a doctor. We had a big apartment and a housekeeper who helped raise me. After the war, I located her daughter.

When the Germans came, everyone had to go to the ghetto. My mother worked in a sanitarium and hid on the roof. They took my grandfather from our apartment; some people told me he was shot. I decided to leave but I didn't know where my mother was. In Lwow, I went into hiding, and then fled to Warsaw. A Polish friend had a certificate that said he was half German. He was able to take me by train to Warsaw to friends who lived as Poles. My mother also had the same boy bring her. I came with a birth certificate that identified me as Sofia Fritz. A friend of mother's took me to a school. When my mother arrived they found an apartment for us. We had to be very quiet to remain undiscovered, while they arranged a certificate. It took several days. My mother's certificate said her name was Stanislava, so I couldn't be her daughter; she was instead to be my aunt. For three years during the war I called her "auntie" and never made a mistake.

When Mother arrived in Warsaw, the ghetto was burning. We were in one apartment and then another; we were on the run. I was in Warsaw when mother brought a dress for me and sewed a diamond ring into its sleeve. She sold it in the underground and we lived on that money until the Russians arrived. They delayed until the Germans had killed almost everyone and then appeared, claiming to be liberators.

After the war I continued with school and my studies. In 1946 when my father found us through the Jewish Agency and sent us an affidavit, we made it to Israel. After the war, it was clear that there was still anti-Semitism in Poland.

My parents were born during the Austrian-Hungarian Empire. My mother spent her younger years in Vienna in very comfortable conditions. My father got his MD in Vienna and later specialized in Berlin. He was the head of pediatrics in the leading Jewish hospital in Lwow.

I think I was shaped by the good education I had in Poland and my loving family.

During the war I was not identified as a Jew; I was living as a Pole and had many non-Jewish, Christian friends who helped me run away from Lwow to Warsaw. I had already changed my name to live as a non-Jewish Pole. I was dreaming of the end of the war - that I could continue my studies and lead a normal life in Poland. I wanted to become a doctor or a teacher.

Now I am a pensioner, taking care of a husband who is in okay health, but his mind is gone. This is very painful for me as we used to share everything. Now I am alone, trying to enjoy life, remembering the past. I miss him because he is here yet not here. I have someone who helps, making it possible for me to go out — and also will teach me how to use the computer! I enjoy reading, and being in touch with my grandchildren and friends. I must be able to deal with the current situation.

The most critical setback in my life besides the war was after it, in Israel, when my parents divorced. It was difficult: living in a new country, not knowing the language, having to adjust to such a new and different culture. Now I feel I am firmly connected through my grandchildren. I wish I could have studied and had more friends, because I lost so many in Poland. I had many Christian friends, which made it possible for me to help provide money to Jews in hiding during the War. I even saved the life of the man who became my mother's husband! I also saved his sister. My childhood was very good and full of love perhaps because I was an only daughter. As was my marriage, and the birth of my son.

My son is now sixty! He is working as general manager of a hotel in Armenia, so I don't see him often as it is a long trip. He is happy with his work.

I am at home, this is my country — the only one there is for me. I am optimistic. My roots are through my son and his family, my grandchildren.

Zvika Crohn

Natanya, 1951

In a meeting with the chief of the Israeli Air Force, I told him that I do cross-cultural training. He proposed to Major Zvi Crohn, who at that time was in charge of education in the air force, that I do a program for the Israeli soldiers who were going to be working with the American soldiers on the Patriot missile. I did! Zvika was most kind and generous: inviting me for a Shavuot celebration at his wife's kibbutz, and for Pesach, too. We went to see the air force museum in Hatzerim, and I had the honor of attending an air force graduation. Later, when Zvika worked for RAD, he made it possible for me to attend conferences. He was in charge of all the communication systems at the new Ben-Gurion Airport.

I don't think I have "a biggest success". Maybe to retire from the air force. I am proud of whatever I have done. I look at my CV in the air force. The young people now will never do what I did, because of my behavior, the challenges, and the times. For example, when I took you to teach the soldiers English. Before me no one was thinking about this: the language, the behavior. If I was not there it wouldn't have happened. And if not, maybe it would be OK. There would be more time, more money but in the end it would be done. For me, I enjoyed it — I just met a guy from the Patriot in Tel Aviv — Do you remember???

Now we have internet, cell phones — information immediately. You can choose — amazing!

I asked Esther, "Let's take a tent and go to the beach." She said, "No, no it is dirty." I told Esther, "I just have twenty more years to live — I want to enjoy." If I need I need, and if not — not. If people see me in my old car they will think I don't have money — but I don't care.

When I dive, sail, fly — I check everything — check the tank. I am diving forty years and I check everything. You need to know how to minimize the risk.

In Angola where I worked, the people don't understand the money or the life — if you need to die you will die.

I am in the third part of my life, enjoying myself, making fun. I completed the course to be a skipper and have a timeshare yacht in Tel Aviv harbor. I am also sailing my kayak. I am doing business in Angola — you remember I was there — now I am selling to them. And I have some property in Romania. It is a lovely place — you should go there! And I am looking for my next job!!!

I have two granddaughters, one from each son. I retired from the air force many years ago!

I was born here. I grew up in Herzliya Petuach. After I was ten, we moved to a farm in the Negev. Ben Gurion asked people to move to the desert to build the country. We moved to Moshav Sde Moshe. We grew vegetables and cows. My father was an electrician. He came from Germany and my mother from Hungary. My father was sixteen when he came here alone before the war. He wanted to come to Israel. He never told me the whole story. I knew his family in the past but there is no connection now.

My mother arrived when World War II started. I had three cousins who I see for weddings, bar mitzvahs. I think at that time the parents didn't talk about the past. My parents spoke German to each other. My mother knew five languages; she was very educated. I have one older and one younger brother. I am not in touch with them. We had a fight when our father died — about the money, twenty years ago. It doesn't bother me now.

My father, the moshav, the army, the people all helped shape my life. The life on the moshav was very good; I enjoyed it — maybe I would stay — After my regular time in the air force I stayed on — action brings action. I wanted to learn all the time. When I was taking the skipper course we were asked who wants to climb the mast? I went up the mast.

I don't remember any setbacks, nothing special. I think whatever I wanted in the end, I did. I went to the US in '69 to train for the air force in California, Utah, Texas. This was a big challenge — one year. I went with Esther and Eldad, who was four years old. Everything was a challenge; the language, the life. When I came back everyone came to see me — WOW, you have been in America!

I like to do whatever I want in the moment. I don't know — I don't have dreams — I am in reality.

I like to help people. I do favors for people who ask me — I never say no. I will help immediately. Esther complains about it but I like to do. Yesterday I went to some family in the kibbutz where we are living and replaced a light and fixed something in the kitchen for a friend of Esther's. I like to help.

I could live in Romania. I live here because I have my house, my family. I want to build a farm somewhere in the world. Build a house, grow animals, and work in the earth — to grow things — I want good weather, a stream nearby. I found some place in Angola but it is very expensive.

What else would you like to include?

You almost know all my life!

But Zvika, you haven't said enough about how you worked on creating Ben Gurion airport!

Well, it was supposed to be Ben Gurion 2000 but it didn't open until 2004. Why this delay? If you looked at the elevator shaft you would see graffiti in seven languages! We needed to merge all the systems and we had people working from the US, China, Turkey, and Portugal in English and Hebrew!

The manager of the airport called the company Bynet, and said "Save me!" I was assigned the job. We had to connect all the video systems, the internet, telephones, audio, television, and the security system. I had seventy people working for me. It was a complicated contract with the companies involved. If you look at the airport you can see that it is unique.

Bat-ami Melnik
Haifa, 1955

Bat-ami and I have common interests - interviewing and writing. We are intrigued by the many stories of everyone around us. We attempted to do a business project together that unfortunately did not work out. Given the right geography, time, and focus we would cook up another project together. She and her husband, Oded invited some of us to tastings on Friday mornings at a local winery.

About fifteen years ago I volunteered for the Steven Spielberg project which involved my interviewing Holocaust survivors. The interviews were very difficult, weren't edited, and the interviewees were old and frequently didn't remember clearly. I wanted to further develop their stories so I contacted a magazine explaining this idea, and the journalist responded. She wrote in her column, "If you have a grandfather and you can't stand hearing his stories anymore — then call Bat-ami." At first, not many people did, but I continue to write based on a steady stream of replies. It was like being a ghost writer for ordinary people. I found it very interesting, and still do. Here in Israel everyone seems to have a story to tell. Some are amusing but most depict the human will to survive against all odds.

I am married with three sons and two granddaughters. I studied social work in Haifa University, and also in California, but I am not now working as a social worker. For ten years I worked as a probation officer employed by the Welfare Ministry. I no longer want to get involved with the seamy side of life, meeting drunks and criminals. Though I must admit that some of them were delightful characters!

My burning issue is my kids. Always. If I could worry less I could help them more. Also I am very much interested in the problems of Israeli senior citizens. Many of them are able to remain in their homes, often with a Filipino to care for them. Most of them have adult children who also visit and help care for them. But still, they are lonely. There are projects here for youngsters to interact with the elderly, but they can never give enough of their time for they are soul-yearningly lonely. I wish I had an idea or a plan that would provide more adequately for them. Every day I listen to the news and worry that we Jews are an endangered people that either through war or intermarriage will vanish.

In California I wrote my thesis on intermarriage titled, "When Love and Tradition Meet." I interviewed people who tried to combine two religious cultures. The creation of a "Hanukah bush" is an example. It is both an existential and a personal threat.

I was born here in Israel. My parents came here from England after the '48 War. They arrived in Haifa and were taken directly to Moshav Habonim, having been members of this movement before coming to Israel. At that time, Israel was a very poor country where food was scarce and rationed. They settled into Habonim. They had not been persecuted in Britain but they were Zionists. That's why they gave me the Zionist name *Bat-ami - Daughter of My People*.

I grew up in Habonim. It was more like a kibbutz in my time, but we didn't have a collective dining room, nor children's houses. There were wonderful plays and festivals for children. It was a *meshek shitufi*. This means the land and various agricultural branches were communal, but members lived in their own houses and the children lived at home. My mom was a librarian and my father worked with the subtropical plants. He was one of the first to grow avocado, mango, and lychee. He was given an award by the marketing association for his contribution.

My parents were very fulfilled and even though we had little money, they were happy. Mom cut the toes out of our shoes so we could use them longer and announced, "Now you have sandals." I was drafted into the army when I was eighteen and served my two years like everyone else. I enjoyed most of it as it was a relatively quiet time in Israel. After my army service I went to Haifa University where I met Oded, who was in the Navy, so I never went back to live in Habonim. Oded didn't want to live even in a semi-collective community.

My paternal grandfather escaped from Vienna to Argentina in 1938. We sometimes wonder if he was escaping from the Nazis or from his wife, as they never got back together! My grandmother was able to take my father, who was born in Vienna, to England in 1939, as her sister had arranged for them to come from Vienna to London. My mother was born in London, so my parents met as members of the Habonim Youth Movement. My mother's parents came from Poland to England after the First World War. This is where their children were born. My mother's father's parents remained in Poland and together with nearly all their large family perished in the Holocaust. Both the Viennese and the Polish sides of the family were murdered by the Nazis.

My life in Moshav Habonim shaped my life. Afterwards I found university life so fascinating in Haifa and at California State University at Fullerton. A few years after I was married we enjoyed three years in California, when my husband was sent by the Israeli Navy. But I'm not sure how much these institutions actually shaped my life. Volunteers came to Habonim from abroad and it was exciting meeting them but I never wanted to be like them. I was sure I would live in Israel.

My horizons were not too narrow because although we did not have television and lived in a little village, it was quite cosmopolitan and I read a lot. We children lived in a very protective society which by European standards was incredibly poor. Most of the members of Moshav Habonim had a reasonably good education, some even with university degrees; they listened to the BBC Radio, read Time Magazine and discussed everything. They worked on the land but were not peasants. My friends and I thought we would grow up, get married and have children. Most of us did just that. As I studied social work I knew I could, and would, work. I needed to be able to earn my own living. I felt that if I worked hard enough I could manage. I had economic security as a probation officer, but I decided instead to start my own business, thinking that if I were diligent and did accurate work, I'd succeed. So far, it has worked out as I expected.

If I could, I would find work that took me out of the house, as writing is a very lonely occupation. Maybe even now working with colleagues would be better.

My middle son was born in America. While I was in the hospital a non-Jewish friend came to visit me. I said that it was hard for me to think about the fact that one day this sweet and precious baby must join the army. My friend turned to me and said, "For goodness sake! What new mother thinks like that?" And I had to answer, "Every mother in Israel. Except Arab and ultra-Orthodox Jewish ones."

I feel very good that a few times in our life we fostered Ethiopian and Russian kids, to help them settle into Israeli life.

There are a lot of annoyances living in Israel, but it is home and the best place for us. I would feel like a second-class citizen any place else, as if I did not really belong. Though I do admit that living in California was great.

During The Six-Day War my dad was in the army and my mom was left alone with my sister and me. We heard on the radio that the Temple Mount was once again in our hands. This reminds me of the story about Chaim Weizman, our first President. He was asked by a member of the House of Lords, "Why do you Jews insist on Palestine when there are so many undeveloped countries you could settle in more conveniently?" Weizman answered, "That is like me asking you why you drove twenty miles to visit your mother last Sunday when there are so many old ladies living on your street. "The peer responded, "But the old lady who lives twenty miles away is my mother!" "Exactly." said Weizman.

Oded Melnik
Petach Tikva, 1953

SOME TIME AGO, A FRIEND OF MINE RENTED SPACE IN THE OFFICE OF ODED AND HIS *partners and offered to share it with me when I needed to meet with clients. Oded was very generous with the office space and it was a pleasure, as we had lively conversations and found many common interests: skiing, wine, travel, the good life. We enjoyed a fabulous brunch at his home with his wife Bat-ami and friends after biking from Tel Aviv up to Reut. And we have enjoyed other times with good wine.*

My most significant memory maybe the '73 war. I graduated from the naval officer course two months before. I served on a missile boat as a bridge officer managing the ship and reporting to the commanding officer. During the whole war there were missiles firing on us, us firing back, sinking enemy ships. Our boat was OK. This was through the whole war. Each day when we came back to harbor I went to Rambam Hospital, in walking distance from the harbor, to look for wounded friends. They all survived. When the missiles are fired at you, it could be the end of you; you just function and do your procedures that you were trained for. Only later, you do think about it.

Today I am married, three kids, two granddaughters. I consult for business valuations and compile business plans. I also compile expert witness reports for court cases. In addition, I have entrepreneurial activities in real estate and an innovative structure of financing mobile homes, containers, or mobile storage units. It's like car leasing, but for mobiles. I'm the managing partner of these activities.

Until 1964, I grew up in Kiryiat Shalom, a southern suburb of Tel Aviv, populated mostly by low to medium income families. Then we moved to a northern suburb of Tel Aviv, Ramat Aviv. I went to the Alliance high school and learned French as a first foreign language.

I learned English by myself by reading.

When I was fifteen or sixteen I built a sailboat. Later I had a thirty foot yacht, I had the yacht even before I had a car! I used to hitchhike to the Marina. We sailed to Cyprus, Turkey, and Greece. I had the boat from '75 to '85. It was built by a friend of mine, but he got seasick and gave it up. I also gave it up when we went to the States.

I did my first degree in mathematics and computer science at Tel Aviv University in 1977-81. Before that I was in the navy and graduated from the naval officer course in 1973. I served in the missile boats in the Yom-Kippur War and after.

After graduating from the university, I switched to developing combat systems for the navy and applied my skills as a naval officer and my BS in computer science. I was stationed for three years in California, 1985-88, as a project officer in Rockwell International. It was great — that's where I learned to ski. We went to Mountain High or Big Bear or Mammoth Lakes.

We had a good life there. It was quite a culture shock to go there in the '80s: big cars, big supermarkets, big everything! And we could afford to enjoy it! We even managed to make some American friends, who are still friends. I had the chance to go sport fishing on party boats for bass and mackerel.

My parents came here as pioneers. This is my homeland. My father is from Poland and my mother from what used to be Poland and is now Ukraine. My father came in 1931 with his wife and my brother. He worked in construction of buildings and roads. After his wife passed away he married my mother, which explains why my brother is sixteen years older than me.

They spoke Hebrew, sometimes Yiddish, or Polish, when they really didn't want us to understand. My brother was drafted when I was two years old. My mother was born and raised in Dubno in Ukraine. She came via Russia and Turkey. She made aliya in 1942 by a fake marriage. Both my parents were active in the *Shomer Ha-tzair*.

About seven years ago we visited the town where she was born. I go to the memorial ceremony of my mother's home town here in Israel every year. They both passed away. My father in 1985, and my mother 2003. They had no regrets for coming here.

In my professional life, Professor Amir Barnea, at the University, helped shape my life. I apprenticed with him and worked with him for several years and we are still good friends. He did company valuations.

I served twenty-one years in the military. Four out of my five best friends served with me in the navy. I learned to stick to targets. I learned about loyalty. I am good under stress and uncertainty. I don't panic.

Marrying Bat-ami was a good thing. We had three children. Each one is different. Each one with his own areas of interest. The older, Leor, was in the navy, and now serves as a career officer. Boaz is studying economy for his first degree. He is also an entrepreneur. Gil, the youngest, is serving in the army. He is the one who loves opera and writes stories.

I taught all of them to ski. Boaz is the only one who skis, but now he switched to snowboard, after his girlfriend. I feel good about each one of them.

I have some hobbies, like growing Koi fish, jogging, and skiing. The Koi are about 50-70 centimeters and are very beautiful. I breed them and give away the small ones to friends. I have had aquariums since I was a kid. I jog about three or four times a week between 5-12 kilometers each time. I did the Nike Night Run last year with 15,000 other runners. It was a 10-K run and it took me an hour and ten minutes. I have another "hobby"- doing *miluim* as a volunteer with the navy.

Israel is my home country for good and for worse. I am not worried about the future for my children. The economy is good. I have a fair amount of business. What is not so good is the rate of unemployment. I am not referring to the "official" figures, which are low, but to the real figures. It is now about 20-30%, when taking into account the people who are not registered as workers and who live on some grants or whatever and don't contribute to the economy. It's a heavy burden on the country. There is an effort to get the Arabs and the ultra-religious to work, but it is not sufficient. The government should address this properly.

We are a young country; 50% of the population is twenty or younger. They will all grow and become consumers. The trend is positive; not like it is in the United States, with baby boomers who are now retiring, not like Europe with a negative birthrate. We have to solve the problem of the undocumented economy. In 2003, when he was Minister of Finance, Bibi reduced the child allowance but then there was a recession.

Noa Suzanna Morag
Tel Aviv, 1988

WHEN I FIRST CAME TO ISRAEL, I TOOK THE COURSE FOR CREDENTIALED TEACHERS TO *teach in the public schools. Maya was the master teacher I was privileged to observe in the classroom and we have been friends since then. At that time, her daughter Noa was two years old! It has been a treat to watch her develop her many artistic, musical, theatrical talents. Now she is grown up! I don't know how she did it, as she only ate salads.*

My writing is my burning issue. I have never written more — I have been waiting for that. I have been writing diaries all my life and always read a lot. But I never wrote a single story. The first one I wrote was to get into the course for creative writing — this last year I really found "my voice" in writing. I had two stories published.

I don't know where to begin about Israel. It's easy and unbelievably hard at the same time. For me, specifically, it's rather easy, because I live in Tel Aviv. But terrible things are happening — this country is like a pot full of boiling water. I'd like to think that we are living in a time of change.

I am between two degrees, my bachelor's and my master's. *(She applies some lipstick the same way Maya does.)* You know me; I am my mother's child.

I feel like I am happy with all that I am doing: working, writing a lot, starting my research for my thesis on my own. Next year I will begin my master's in The Cohn Institute for the History and Philosophy of Science and Ideas. My research revolves around narcissism, and a sociological phenomenon called *moratorium*, which means "to delay" in Latin. What interests me about this concerns the stage in life in which I'm in right now. When you were my age you were already married! Your generation perceived things like a job, marriage, having children, or in other words: adulthood, as desirable achievements. To my generation, these things are merely obstacles separating them from really "enjoying their lives to the fullest." They usually get to these achievements (which are now perceived as heavy matters) in their late thirties. Today's *thirties* are the old *twenties*. The twenties years are the odyssey years devoted to traveling, finding yourself and using drugs (among other things). Unlike most of the people I know, I know what I want to do with my life, in matters of profession. I want to do research and be in academia. The fact that I'm not lost makes me happy, having this passion for what I do.

I was born here. Right across the street. *We are sitting in a café in north Tel Aviv.* My mom is from Prague, but grew up in Hadera. And my dad is from Haifa. His mother is from Lebanon, Beirut, and his father is eight generations in Israel. My parents shaped my life even though it's a cliché — I am just beginning to realize how each of my parents is unique and both of them are so close to me. It's not like any other parent-child constellation I have seen.

I can't really remember what I thought what my life would be like when I was ten to fifteen, but I do remember the action of *thinking about it*, but can't remember my fears or wishes. The only thing I can really say is that when I was younger – I was a lot less AWARE of TIME. At this point of my life, I'm extremely aware of the time passing and of my status in society, what is expected of me right now. I'm even conscious of types of emotions that I'm *supposed* to be feeling at this time of my life — I despise this feeling. I miss the time when it wasn't like that.

Music has always been a huge part of my life, although I have always wanted to keep it as my playground, free of rules and compulsories. I can't read notes and I insist on playing only when I feel like it. I recorded six covers with a good friend of mine, and they're on YouTube, just for fun.

For the last year I have been mourning about how I'm too scared to study abroad. I am afraid of being abroad on my own even for a day. It puts me in anxiety. I think that my parents over-protected me, being their only child; I think they wanted me to be able to protect myself from dangerous situations when they are not with me. I was afraid of taking a taxi by myself until I was sixteen, even here!

Even though I am optimistic and open, I still miss a lot because of my fears. A lot of people I know are doing drugs — all the time. I can't bring myself willingly to a position that may cause me pain or fear, without having a way out. I tried it twice, and it made me feel so caged in, that physical feeling that most people enjoy - to me, the fact that I couldn't control it - frightened me.

I aspire to be less ego-centric and do more for others. I volunteered briefly in the beginning of the year, visiting an old man just to keep him company, once a week. I have a very strong sympathy to the elderly, and what worries me the most is the solitude of the elderly. After just one month of visiting him, I started doing a studies program in Ben Gurion University, while also organizing a really big conference for one of my professors in Tel Aviv University. That old man, his name is Michael, lives in a very posh old peoples' home called THE PALACE (nothing less) — he has people around him, so I know that he is somewhat OK, but I still feel bad for leaving him. I would like to get back to volunteering. Modern Western people, including me, are unbelievably self-centered. I also want to act out of hope — not fear.

My most precious memory is the hardest question because I am very nostalgic. I dwell in my memories. I have lot of memories of traveling with my parents, traveling in the desert and the Kinneret, and around the world. I had a really good childhood. Plus, memories to me are even what happened yesterday. The mere act of taking the trip down memory lane is indulgent, yet painful to me. People mock me for remembering every single thing.

To me, the only act that is truly worthy of the word "good" is benefiting other people around you, and the earth, nature. I think that my mother and father have unconsciously taught me how to be compassionate to others.

I want to say how much I love you and happy that you are in my life. I have always thought of you as one of the most inspirational people I have ever met.

Thank you, Noa.

Maha Zahalqa Massalha, MA
Kufur Qara', 1977

I HAD THE IDEA THAT I WOULD LIKE TO TEACH ENGLISH IN THE ARAB VILLAGE OF KUFUR Qara', which is close to where I live. I asked a doctoral candidate from the town whose application I had edited, who to contact. He gave me two names. One was Maha, the coordinator in the municipality for the department of culture and informal education. We met in her office. She is a very active and ambitious producer! And a warm and welcoming person. The English classes have not yet come to be.

Maha told me about her dream and her vision to make a crucial change in the Arab Palestinian community to change the way they spend their leisure time from ten years ago. She wants the people of the triangle of Arab towns to be addicted to cultural festivals in the spirit of multiculturalism, different identities, the gaps of nationality, gender, and job market, by producing theatre, book evenings, movie evenings, and other cultural festivals for adults, children, and the whole family. Maha studied sociology, anthropology, and education at Haifa University, where she was the administrator of the multiculturalism center and assistant to Professor Majid Al Haj. She was also the coordinator of the Arab Jewish center.

My work is the main factor of my life, reflecting on my family life with my three children Eyas, Mayar Alsomow, and Loure Yafa. The

157

support of my beloved husband is very crucial to my career. There is always a conflict between the needs of my children and my career. It is not easy, but it is very interesting to lead these two worlds.

I think about my work all the time, even when I am cooking, or taking care of things at home, it is always on my mind. I want to convince people to leave their busy lives to enjoy theater, poetry, and to enjoy culture in the evenings, in their leisure time.

My son has a great imagination and is very creative and so clever writing stories. He is in fourth grade and I worry about him being in an environment that might not encourage his creativity. He wrote a story that Love is the solution for all problems. He says Love and Peace are important and not money. This must come from Allah, inspiration for a child when he was six years old.

I was born and grew up in Kufur Q'ara, went to school here, and then to Haifa University for my degrees in sociology.

My parents are from here; my father's family lost their lands with this occupation in 1948. They taught us to respect our history and our past and to struggle for our academic ambitions. They told us that the investment in the people's education replaces the occupied land and we must cope with this fact. It is very difficult to feel discrimination in your homeland when you are forbidden to visit your lands. Since my mother died about nineteen years ago my father has been alone; we respect that.

My mother was illiterate, born in 1934, but she had ambitions for me and my brothers and sisters. She wanted me to be a PhD. She said I was the nicest of her ten children, I was the last. One day she took me to the mirror and said, "Look at your beauty, I dreamed to see you as a bride. Be strong and study until the last day of your life!" She died before I was married and didn't see my children. She worked hard, helping my father with the land. She was my friend and I really miss her. My mother, her last look when she was separated from us. She died of cancer, exactly when I started my academic life at the Haifa University. I'm proud of my dearest mother. I made some of her dreams come true,

I think!!!! I want to be a lawyer, and I will be. I will do it! In about five years, when the children are older.

There is an obvious influence of the poet Mahmoud Darweesh on my way of thinking and my vision. I respect and admire him and use his sayings as inspiration, such as "On this land what makes life worth living" and the "the butterfly effect is not seen, the butterfly effect does not disappear."

Zev Wanderer, PhD
Brooklyn, 1932

I MET ZEV AT ISRAEL ALIYA CENTER EVENTS IN LOS ANGELES, AS WE WERE PREPARING to depart about the same time. What a sense of humor! I visited him and Rita in Tel Aviv, and in Eilat when we all lived there, and joined their wedding celebration in the forest. The re-establishment of his eyesight is amazing! I am a recipient of his personal advice. He is happy he found his place.

I am here in Israel as part of my religious revival. The big story is that the people of Israel belong at home. When I made aliya, no one in Israel could believe that I could leave a good clinical practice, a professorial position consulting doctoral students at UCLA, a house on the top of a hill in Malibu, where I also did my private clinical practice and published many articles and four books, a wonderfully rich life, and come here. One local journalist wrote it must have been because my eyesight was bad, or that I was too fat for California. No one can believe — but I am happier here.

My first thirty years were lived in Brooklyn and Manhattan. Growing up in New York City was a gift. On a Saturday night, you got on the subway and you ended up in Carnegie Hall, stood in the back to hear Yasha Heifitz, or Isaac Stern at the YMHA, Wagner at the Met, or you went to the Museum of Natural History for ten cents. There is a giant dinosaur Rex in the entry hall who knew me very well. And of course, there was The (Greenwich) Village. People of all ages doing their homework on the subway. That's how it was growing up in Brooklyn, where there were many artists, writers, performers, cartoonists. The question was not will you go to college, but which college. It was an intellectual environment.

After a BA at Yeshiva, and an MS from the City University of NY, there was an MA and a PhD in clinical psych from Columbia. Then postdoctoral training at Temple University Medical School under Joseph Wolpe, the father of behavior therapy. I then started my trek West. First to Chicago (I can see where Obama came from). I spent two years in a marvelous job as a research director for an Illinois state facility for autistic children. And then twenty years in California — it was an adult playground. I went to visit Berkeley — that was serious, but LA was fun. Although an ex-yeshiva student, I didn't feel alien there. I was leading movements: the behavior therapy movement, the sexual freedom movement, and other experimental activities. All the while an active member on the psychological association's ethics committees. I was invited to lecture all over the country, Canada, even Europe. I was welcomed and didn't have to change my name and I always wore my Star of David. Royally welcomed, but never really "at home." So in 1985, I started thinking about Israel again. No more Zionist summer camps: this was going to be the real thing!

My American friends questioned if I had any relatives in Israel. Not really. But, yes, I have a few million relatives who tell me what bus to take, what hospital to go to, what I'm doing wrong; this feels like family.

Mom came from Ukraine; she said Austria because she thought it sounded better. My father was a cantor, born in southern Poland, Galicia, Novo Sandz. It was a shtetl. We visited there recently. Now all the non-Jewish Polish population is happy to show you through the Jewish cemetery and the synagogue is now a museum. The local Polish didn't recognize that the war was over. They just continued killing Jews.

My father left home as a teenager because he loved music and went to study music in the Vienna Conservatorium. When he was a youth, Europe was artistically fabulous. Dad could read and write music and also wrote cantorial music. We had a little pump organ at home and he would sit and write all the parts: tenor, bass, solo. When he would get a letter from another cantor with an original composition he would open the envelope and start whistling what was written. Our home was Orthodox. But many of the great cantors sang in Conservative synagogues. The Orthodox could only support a rabbi, hardly also a cantor. So we were never rich, sort of lower-middle class. I was nineteen when he died at age fifty-five. When I was a kid, he used to take me for a walk in the park and say to the old men sitting there, "Tell them what you learned this week."

My brother was eight years older than I. He had juvenile diabetes and as there were no special foods then, only saccharin and sawdust, my mother spent a lot of time making him sawdust cakes. She dedicated a lot of her life for him. He died in his forties after an injury from a car accident that didn't heal because of his diabetes.

My wise, disciplinarian mother helped shape my life, no question. And some teachers. I had funny, urbane, sarcastic teachers. To this very day I treasure that sarcasm. I studied for two years with Rabbi Joseph Solovetchik, who was recognized as a colossal Talmudist and philosopher. When I went to Columbia I continued with this. I am now reading what he wrote and find it mind-bogglingly rich. Some people are gifted and can make a quantum leap way beyond us simple folk.

My mom wanted me to be a rabbi. I knew I wasn't going to be; I found too many flaws in pulpit rabbis. Then maybe a doctor. I saw movies about doctors but my mom said she couldn't afford medical school. And at that time there were quotas against Jews. And besides, you have too many body parts to memorize. So I went into psychology. This was a great choice as it was stimulating; a cross between science and philosophy. At fifteen, I knew I would be a doctor of something. My mother wanted me to be a rabbi so I could marry the daughter of the usually well-off *shul* president to fall into the honey pot and to have an easy life without getting my hands dirty. She knew my choices and was OK with that. Even when I left my religion and she came to visit me in LA, and I offered to find a kosher place to eat she said, "Don't bother, eat what you normally eat." She was very accepting of me — as an adult. I like to think I am an eighty-year-old, married, American expat, Israeli Jew. I am mainly retired from clinical psychology practice and teaching.

I am on a journey of religious discovery. I came from an Orthodox Zionist family. At about age twenty I had a great disappointment. I found out I couldn't have children. In those days, women were barren, but men were never sterile. What did I do wrong to be punished? I became sort of an agnostic for about twenty years and then a devout hedonist. And then after twenty years of that I decided that this wasn't going anywhere. As I was involved in philosophy and science, I discovered that science also made assumptions and harbored beliefs. So I went back to take another look at the religion of my childhood. It was fascinating, way beyond what I had been doing. And that has been my gradual inclination over the last thirty years— reading and learning about that is exciting. I occasionally have doubts, but that's all right. This is a major part of my life.

I spend many hours of my day and life on email doing advocacy for Israel and the Jewish people. We have been very bad at presenting ourselves. David has become Goliath. So I spend a lot of time forwarding choice emails to about 135 contacts. Many are prime ministers, foreign ministers, media writers, friends, and some people who disagree with me. I guess I am doing a blog. I enjoy it very much and it is very challenging.

My wonderful wife, Rita, is reading Eric Hoffer's *The True Believer*. She tells me that my cyber work is not going to convince the convinced. One response I received recently was "Fascist Pig!" I replied, "You signed your name but there was no message!" (Not original — but I love it!) I think I'm addicted to my email project, like for cookies — I can't wait to get to it, even when I'm tired.

I lost an eye when I got a punch in the face as a freedom fighter in Beverly Hills. I had to have the eye extracted. The other eye got sympathetic opthalmia. For many years I walked around with a white cane. So from a book worm I became a tape worm. Just a few years ago I had two surgeries at Johns Hopkins and thank God my one live eye improved. I don't think of it as a handicap. But now that my eyesight is better my hearing is going, even with the best hearing aids. It is a problem when patients whisper or adolescents slur their words, or mumble.

When I got divorced the first time, in those days, in my circles, it was like suicide, not acceptable, failure. The second time I got divorced I felt I was a total failure and that I would never live with a woman again. Turns out that's not true.

A serious setback came from a young woman I was living with, who said, after four years, "I need some space to think about us." This meant goodbye. That led to my writing *Letting Go*, which was a best seller, had foreign editions in several languages, and then a Hollywood film, and is still a soft cover in book stores, after thirty years.

I think I was excessive in my hedonism in that I hurt some feelings and betrayed some Jewish norms. Beyond that, no regrets. Life is very good to me. I came on a pilot trip here. The day before I was to fly back to LA, I was invited to join a faculty meeting at Tel Aviv University. "You are the one who wrote the film *Letting Go*? It's available here with Hebrew subtitles!" They were looking for someone who was involved in, and could teach, behavior modification. So I got a job at TAU on a silver platter even before I came. After a while, I missed Malibu so we moved to Eilat. I now believe that we are here, not primarily to have fun, but to understand and fulfill a mission. That's what makes me happiest. To aspire to leave the world a little better than we found it. I think I've shown a lot of people how to be happy. I am pretty sure of that — a mistake here and there, but by and large good work.

Living in Israel now is challenging! People are sure on the right and the left. No one is totally wrong or right. We must compromise and be patient. Among ourselves and with our adversaries. I learned this in

Talmud. There is strict judgment or compromise — like in small claims court. The judge says, "You two, go out in the hall. Come up with a deal and I'll see if it's fair." Justice is the truth. Compromise is never the truth, but it brings peace. So true justice must be bent for the sake of peace. Here, in Israel, too. The trouble is we have adversaries who don't want us around. Period. And that creates a big, unusual problem. Because we're not leaving home again.

I liked meeting you. You tried Israel and came back. I wanted to encourage you, your stamina and resilience. I admired how you zinged along on a shoestring but were determined and you made it.

Thank you, Zev!

Shirley Raphaeli

Caesarea, 1979

I MET SHIRLEY SOON AFTER MY PARTNER AND I DECIDED TO BE TOGETHER, AS SHE IS HIS daughter. I have seen her mature from being a college student, to a swimming instructor, to a beach enthusiast, to a married woman with adorable twins. When I went to visit her in the maternity hospital when the twins were born, she looked as if she had just walked in to visit! She has shown organizing skills and competence in her demanding role, with patience and good spirits.

I want to see people give more importance to values of kindness to each other, not taking advantage of other people and considering others' wellbeing. Here in Israel, it is chaos — it's a global problem but here in Israel it's a burning issue. I was born here. I have had opportunities to live in other places, but the truth is I am drawn to Israel, in spite of its chaotic temper. I have a strong connection to my family and friends. I grew up in Caesarea. I lived there until I was twenty. Back then it was a small community, everyone knew everyone. It was a very safe and nice place to grow up.

My father is from Staten Island, New York, and has lived here forty-two years, but he is still very American. My mother is from Rehovot. Her father's family has been there for several generations and her mother's family ran away from Poland before the war began.

I have been in many environments in my life. I like to change. Even when I was in high school I moved to different schools. Also, when I was in the army, I moved to different camps. As a college student and a young woman I lived in Tel Aviv for ten years enjoying the city life — and today as a mother I have many friends with young children like myself; we raise them and ourselves – together. So I can't say there was some one person who helped shape my life, I guess constant change shaped my life. I wanted to know all there is to know about life, and there was more to it than just plain curiosity; I needed to feel it; I wanted to explore life on all its aspects. I travelled to South America and to India but the truth is, although I had a very good time I didn't find there what I was looking for. Shortly after I met Eattay, my loving husband, I realized we are very similar when it comes to this point. He also was driven by something that made him go through a lot of changes.

I can't think of any setbacks. I wanted to be famous but that changed as I grew up. Reality has changed so much in the past twenty years. In my wildest dreams I couldn't imagine myself working from home writing marketing materials for websites or working on social media because back then I couldn't even imagine such a wild and gigantic network like the internet. Modern Life has changed dramatically and I am glad to change with it. I like my job and I am glad things worked out the way they did.

I'm glad that I have twins — that's my good deed! It was a surprise! When I first learned I was going to have twins I was ecstatic/hysterical. When they were little, it was a lot of work — now not so much. And raising them I give a lot to attention to the values I give them. I make an effort to teach them to be considerate of each other and other people. I teach them the importance of connecting and cooperating with other people. To be sensitive to other people.

I try to set an example for them (which is not always easy) with my husband, with my friends and with the world. My ambition is to raise my kids in a warm and loving family — not just me, but Eattay, too.

Our goal is to build a considerate environment — ready to set aside our personal interests for the good of the whole.

In Israel now, on one hand is the reality, the way people treat each other, taking advantage of each other, the growing gap between rich and poor, the political mess, and the problems we have with the Palestinians, the problems of Israel with the world, which is turning its back on us. This is painful for me.

On the other hand, I see people in Israel who are working very hard aiming to bring some kind of change in spirit. I see people who care about what is going on here and are working to make a difference, traveling all over Israel organizing round-table events and educational seminars. And in the bottom line that is all there is to it – education.

Change is about being aware, and I see people are becoming more and more aware of that. Once you know what is not right it is very simple to fix it. The fact is change will not come from the government but from the people. Building a strong society that's dependent on mutual responsibly could change our reality as a nation.

We have to educate ourselves, to decide we have had enough of current values that measure one's success by counting the amount of dollars he has in the bank. We are ready to restart our society, to go through an educational process that will shift our values from pure materialism to caring for each other and live a community life. Experts are already talking about it and the sooner we will hear them, the better off we will be. But, I cherish the present!

Doron Bar Chen, DMD

Iasi, Romania, 1962

*S*OON AFTER *I* ARRIVED IN *I*SRAEL WITH MY SUITCASE AND MY BICYCLE, *I* STARTED RIDING *with a friendly group on Shabbat mornings. We met at 8:00 at the train station, decided which way to go and usually did a nice ride of 60-80 kilometers. Shlomo, Moshe, Yossi were the regulars and Doron would join from time to time. Not only was he a friendly rider, he was a dentist. He became my dentist. Having had only three dentists from California, I appreciated his high standards. Photos of his specialty of implantology show that he provides a life-changing procedure.*

The whole family made aliya in1964. Many came. They put us in Katamon in Jerusalem, as a concept of the Mapai party. They wanted to mingle the different groups of aliya, the Moroccans and the Romanians at Rehov Bar Yohai in Jerusalem. This was a very problematic area — there were protests about the uneven attitude. It was like Brooklyn in the '40s and '50s. I had to fight for my place.

The opportunities in Romania were closed to everybody. There was no food. The Jewish community was brought out. The Jews were never discriminated against in Romania, aside from when the Germans were there. I speak Romanian even now.

My father was a truck driver, my mother worked in a restaurant and then as a counter in the National Statistics, in publishing the consumer index. She had been a housewife before, and my father had been involved in transportation. They made the change. My brother lives in California. When he finished his studies in Jerusalem in computer science he decided to give it a try in Silicon Valley. He lives in Orange County. He is happy. I see him on Skype and visit occasionally.

Nowadays I am married, happily married for the second time. Each of us brings two into the package: Tamar's daughters twenty-two and twenty-nine, and my daughter twenty-one, and my son, eighteen, in the army. He is lucky to be in a rescue unit. Usually people go to the army to take lives; he is going to save lives.

I am a dentist, specializing in oral rehabilitation and implantology. It's my passion, my hobby, my business. I feel lucky and gifted. Like a present from God that I must spread around and maximize the potential. I am happy to go to work in the morning. I feel I am creating something out of nothing. It's a big gift.

To maximize the potential I am involved with a company in the Chinese market, since 2005. I was actively running it until four months ago. We decided that we would come back to Israel. Now the company is run by partners and an Israeli CEO. My wife is involved in the design. She was the one who brought me to China. When she complains I am overworking she has herself to blame! Our paths came together in strengthening our religious belief. Part of the reason for coming back to Israel was because we were more religiously involved.

In Shanghai I asked the rabbi at Chabad — why do you argue? There were the first twelve tribes, so heterogeneity is tolerated. If more people would adopt this attitude we would live more peacefully.

I started to believe that the Torah was delivered to Israel by God. Until that time for me everything was didactic. It stayed in the back of my head for about fifteen years. It was very logical. I wanted to find out. I went to a conference that included a pilot and two scientists and learned that it was logical. It was a fact.

I came to two personal conclusions. One, that nothing happens by chance. It is too mathematically organized. Somebody or something is directing nature. Two, that if we are here with all the difficulties for seventy or eighty years, there must be something more than that— or it, is a waste. To just vanish? The effort should have more meaning than that. This brought me to the conclusion that there is God. I go into this because we know each other a long time.

It brings huge peace of mind. If we know there are reasons, order, not just chance, it brings peace. People who know me for many years say they can see the difference. I take things in order. I limit my professional life — not 24/7 anymore. Religion is love your neighbor as yourself. All the rest is decoration. If one does what he thinks is right, there are no other questions by God. Religion should come out of love, not fear. Unfortunately, here politics and religion go hand in hand. The religious may delay the religion — they know but need to act. The synagogue from Chabad was very open.

Tamar had a dream we must visit a rabbi's grave in Tiberius. So we went. I bought *tfilin* (phylacteries) but he sold me for the right hand instead of the left, as I am left handed. I wanted to give it to my son who was about to go to the army. He was working as a cook. He told me that at about 11:00 a Chabadnik came in and asked him to do tfillin. It was at the same time as I was buying in Tiberius! Since that day he does it every day — from the army it's OK. The biggest scientists think about this; even Steven Hawkins with the Big Bang theory believes something caused it — it is almost scientifically backed up.

I don't think there was one event or person that shaped my life. It is related to different stages in my life. I think I was shaped by the army. I was in the Lebanon War, the first one. I was in specific units and had life changing experiences. I was lucky to come out stronger in my character. You can go crazy or be stronger, lucky, or blessed.

The birth of my children and the responsibility is one more stair in the process. Meeting Tamar, who eventually became my wife, is a life changer for me. And now there is the belief, which brought peace of mind and new order into my life.

The reason I am a dentist: I was gifted. I did painting and sculpturing and didn't understand what I was doing it for. One of the reasons I got into dentistry was because of the army — I didn't even finish high school — my mind was on water polo. It was a big part of my life. The army brought the sense of order and responsibility. After the army I finished the *bagrut* (highschool diploma.) I wanted to be in medicine — by my character and talents I thought dentistry rather than medicine. It was a cold process to decide. I was committed to my targets. You may reach the target but you might miss everything all along the way. I paid for being so dedicated. Now I have proportion in my life. I have fulfilled my goals — not retired! I am lucky that now I see it in proportion.

I am blessed and lucky that all the difficulties are things I brought upon myself — with my stubbornness, my perfectionism, with my endless trying to swim against the current. All self-made! it's not that my path was a rose garden, but ups and downs and good times and sad times — this is life. I would do it again.

We spent the last two weeks in Italy and France. Tamar is half a witch! On Tuesday morning in the room in Paris I am doing my tfflin; I don't talk during it. "I just saw your grandfather." She said. My grandfather died thirty-six years ago. "You should go to see his grave." When I returned I told my mother and she said, "Tomorrow is the day of his memorial." He was a dominant character in my life — my guardian angel. I was seven when he died. I completely understand Yiddish because of him. With my father I have something long to go through. I am grateful and honored to the point of being overwhelmed to give health to other people. It is very fulfilling. I am doing good! I am trying to be a better person in many aspects. When I pray for health and wealth I am not asking to be rich — I am asking to be able to help other people. Very fulfilling.

I have just returned from Europe where modern society began. I started appreciating our prime minister. In Europe they are supposed be so cultured and advanced — I felt lucky to be here with all the bad things and frustrations. We are very lucky.

Living in the Holy Land, the Promised Land, where things will start and things will end. I was living in Shanghai for nine years - really living - with an apartment and all. I never felt warmer than a complete a stranger. This is home.

Chava Vester
Wuppertal, Germany, 1933

CHAVA CAME FROM GERMANY TO LIVE WITH STEVE. I KNEW STEVE FROM THE SUMMER *I spent picking apples on Kibbutz Ne'ot Mordechai. Some years later I produced a book of his photographs with my publishing company in Los Angeles, Mara Books. Chava measured and then brought a container from Germany with everything to make a cozy home. Steve was very proud of her and enchanted with her loveliness and efficiency. The situation radically changed when Steve went back to his wife. I stayed friends with Chava, sometimes spending a Shabbat or stopping by when I biked the Hula Valley. She made a life on the kibbutz.*

I am a member of the kibbutz. Now I am a pensioner as I stopped work when I was seventy-four. Since then, I look after my dog, house, and garden. For the last two or three years I am slightly handicapped. I am reading a lot, mainly in English, some German. I am writing for my files. I help people with translations. And I help people who are trying to be writers, instead of being one myself!

I made aliya when I was fifty-two. Because of the background of German history and because of the way I am. I cannot tolerate injustice and I cannot tolerate people not telling the truth. It was against all my principles and feelings to live among people who I was not sure had not been murderers of Jews. I started the process when I was forty-four. Why that late? Because I had two kids who were studying and financially depending on me. I was born a Catholic and I converted to Judaism the orthodox way, when I was forty-eight. I found out, at thirteen, what happened in the Holocaust and was not able to discuss this with anyone. After the war, I realized I couldn't trust anybody. In 1960, when I was twenty-eight, I met a person who had visited Israel, which was unusual at the time. I then tried to get hold of all information about the Jewish people. I came here for the first time for a visit when I was forty-four. In Germany, it was impossible to make contact with Jewish people and the ones who were there were survivors who I couldn't ask about their story; at that time I was on the side of the murderers!

My children were studying, and not so open to what their mother was doing. They were living on their own. When I finally came back from my final conversion with the certificate in my purse, I invited them for dinner and they were totally impressed. They were educated to care for the underprivileged, pacifists, and justice. My son refused to do the army and did civil service.

I came in 1985 to the kibbutz. I had an offer to be an English teacher and house mother in a youth village for Ethiopian orphans. I also had a job as a secretary in the new factory of Steff Wertheimer. Since I had met somebody on the kibbutz where I am living now, and since actually I wanted to live on a kibbutz, my new partner and I decided to start a new life together. In spite of my age, (the limit was forty-five) I was accepted as a member of the kibbutz. I lost my partner to his ex-wife, who returned to the kibbutz.

I worked in the landscape gardens of the kibbutz and did translations for the kibbutz. I did two ulpanim to learn Hebrew. In the first one I met an Australian journalist who was also trying to make his life here. It took him eight years of coming and going. He joined me working in the landscape garden. He died after fourteen years on the kibbutz; he claimed they were the happiest of his life. I was able to accompany him until the hour of his death.

I have inherited the dog from him. Since then I'm living as a single. My daughter died at the age of thirty-seven in Germany. My present hardship is that I can't see my remaining family more often. I have a sister a year and half older, but she gave up contact with me since I'm in Israel. I have a son and a grandson in Germany. We have regular contact by phone and letters.

I grew up in Western Germany in a small hamlet of two houses. I went to public school and high school, walking each way an hour — and also survived World War II there. My teachers thought I would be a high-school teacher in physics. I started writing for a newspaper. I wanted to get married and have kids.

At twenty-one, I moved with my parents to the town where I had been born. I went to a commercial school in the same town and started to work as a simple secretary, and afterwards as a private secretary and as interpreter in English in a big company. I had learned English in high school and got a grade as an interpreter.

Then I got married, and after a year my first son was born, and my daughter a year and half later. Since my husband worked for IBM, he was transferred every two years. When I was thirty, I got divorced. This was very unusual in a Catholic family, and the laws were not particularly helpful. I lived with my children in southern Germany, and worked as a language assistant in the university until two weeks before I came on aliya. When I was forty-seven I took a leave for one year and came to study in Ulpan Akiva and lived here in the country. That was the basis for my conversion — I never thought I would be accepted!

My parents were both German from the same area. My mother was a milliner. And my father worked as a technician in the water-supply system. My mother was still alive when I converted. But she didn't want to hear anything about Israel. She lived until ninety-two in an old people's home and I left instructions with the management when I was leaving, in case something should happen, I could not come to be with her. The day before I left, my mother collapsed and died two months later. The information about my mother's death was sent to the ulpan but was lost in the office someplace and I only got a message, "Your son Marcus called. Your mother died."

My concern about other people came from my father. He was a very correct person. It was amazing how people trusted him. When I learned about the Holocaust, I missed the correct attitude from my parents. When my father was in the air force on the Western front, he was taken prisoner by the US and British and was in prison camp for six weeks. The prisoners dug holes to protect themselves from the rain. His companion was Hans Frank, the governor of Dachau. He got information about the Holocaust, which he later hid in the house. Later, I realized the Polish had been responsible for the death camps in Poland. I learned about this much later — no one talked about it. The loneliness of that rural environment and the difficult circumstances of WW II shaped me.

To be here is my happiness, to find integrity and human relations. The people on the kibbutz have open relationships, they have a high intellectual level and to see them working in agriculture was fulfilling. They could have their feet on the ground — not like my colleagues in the university who were in their ivory tower. I have the feeling that I have really settled down, because of my age and physical condition and living among people I can be proud of. And I can still be helpful and useful to people living around me. We are members of a society that contributes the best it is able, and to give an example to the children.

Milton Novak
Chicago, 1941

MILTON HIRED ME FOR THE SUMMER SESSION AT SHENKAR COLLEGE TO TEACH ENGLISH and then asked if I would like to continue for the regular school year. Yes, Yes! I was out of money and really needed this job.

Some years later when I was recovering from pneumonia and did not work for several months, Milton came to see me. I was afraid he was coming to tell me he would have to let me go, but he just came to see how I was doing. We really enjoyed working with the engineering and design students, using the extensive library and creating material. On Fridays, Milton rambled in Tel Aviv to satisfy his curiosity. Sometimes I joined him. And I have joined the family for a bar mitzvah and a wedding!

I met Lori at Shenkar College where I was in charge of the English department and looking for a teacher for an English course. I was convinced after a short while that she would be the best person for the job. I was looking for a friend as well as a colleague, and I thought that we could become friends. I was 100% right in my determination. Our friendship has outlasted our connection at Shenkar, and has lasted to this day.

I had an adventurous life that lasted until 1980. Part of my adventures included traveling, music concerts, sexual relations with women, experimenting with drugs, and pretty much enjoying wine, women, and song. I would prefer to discuss the details in a more private conversation.

Now I live in Ra'anana, a nice suburb north of Tel Aviv. I've been married to my wife Amalia for the past thirty-one years, and we have four kids, and only one grandchild. I've been living in Israel since 1979. In the year 2000, I was diagnosed with Parkinson's Disease.

Milton said that he would do what he could as long as he could, and enjoy what he could as long as he could. I think he still maintains this attitude.

My father was born in 1910 in a shtetl named Makov, in Poland.

My mother was born in 1914 in a city near Krakow, Poland. They met in the USA, and got married at the end of 1940.I was born on Division Street in Chicago, and grew up in Albany Park. I am here because of the inspiration of Zionism from my father, which has shaped my life since 1979. My burning issue is peace in the Middle East. I enjoy being an Israeli citizen, and I have right-wing political views on our historic rights to be here.

I have precious memories of the birth of my children, and my grandchild and my parents' 60th wedding anniversary. Nowadays it's harder for me to get around, therefore my traveling alternatives are limited, and I don't get to see a lot of the country. I am struggling against my disease, which is affecting my abilities to function and communicate normally.

Yael Schutz Gavish

Uruguay, 1955

I MET YAEL AT PARTIES LIORA GAVE. DURING THE WINTER WE HAD ALL DECIDED TO GO to Kfar Hanokdim to enjoy the desert and meditate. The scheduled weekend there was a furious storm with danger of flash floods. We were advised to stay away. But Yael and her husband went to see the desert in its storm. Later, we made up for this by going on a hike in the desert guided by the editor and publisher of Eretz Magazine, Yadin Roman — a moonlight hike down the wadi and an early morning hike up the mountain.

I came to Israel alone from Uruguay when I was seventeen. I said goodbye to everyone and came to study, never to go back. I wanted to be independent, and growing up in a very Zionist Jewish home and culture, Israel was for me an aspiration I felt related to. We were not religious but we had a traditional home, celebrating the holidays, keeping kosher. I went to a Jewish school, Maccabi Tza'ir, a Jewish youth organization, and generally lived in a Jewish world.

My father was very dominant and had great influence in my life. He was one of the founders of the Hebrew school, active in the community, and didn't want me to "assimilate" and marry a non-Jew.

He wanted to make aliya when he was in his twenties, but due to medical problems couldn't fulfill this wish. For my father, my coming to live in Israel was a great realization. Of course, we visit. I have one sister who also came, but she went back as her husband didn't find his place here in terms of work.

When I came, it was a one-day transition. Because of the difference in the school calendar, one day I was on vacation on the porch of my home in Montevideo and the next day in school in Haifa and living in the student dorms. I got on the plane and the next day I was in class. I arrived in the evening from the airport, and went to sleep on the bright orange couch at my father's cousin's home. Next thing I know it is morning and I am in the car heading to Haifa, fascinated by the deep blue color of the Mediterranean. I didn't have one day to acclimate.

I had planned to come a year later. But Uruguay was in a crisis. Terrorist attacks by the *tupamaros* (a Uruguayan revolutionary movement) shook the country. Studies were suspended for months as high schools were on strike. The *shaliach* (emissary from the Jewish Agency) encouraged my father to send his children out of the country.

Three months after I quit the country, the military government took over, beginning a dark, sad period of repression and dictatorship in this usually peaceful, quiet, free, and democratic country.

My father was from Poland. He came to Uruguay with his parents in the early '30s. My mother was born in Uruguay. Her mother came from Russia and her father came from Romania. I remember these grandparents.

Now I am married to Eitan, and I have two wonderful children. A son, thirty-one years old, from my first marriage, and a daughter, twenty-five, with Eitan.

As Eitan is a Cohen and I was divorced, we couldn't marry in Israel, so we went to Cyprus. I went through a difficult time between the marriages, but this was a long time ago. Now I am in good contact with my former husband and his new family, and I am glad to say that as an architect I designed their house.

I feel also part of a big family, a "tribe." I have first, second, and even third loved cousins with whom we keep in touch.

In my professional life, I am an architect, and work occupies a large part of my day.

At this period of my life, I feel like "now it is *my* time." I always worked, but bringing up a family, trying to give the best to my children, and being the physical support for my closest family in Uruguay, I had to split myself between many different demanding tasks. I would like to take a year to find myself, to get out of the expected routine, out of the system, out of the usual environment — to be free.

Now that my children are grown up and are beginning to fly on their own, I can begin to allow myself to dedicate my time and attention to work and self-expression. Of course, I am lucky. I enjoy my work, and I can say that hobby and work go together. Interest, challenge, diversity, learning new issues and developing new skills, and other aspects of the practice, make it an everyday mix of business and pleasure.

Architecture was not an obvious choice for me. As I am a curious person I was interested in everything, and I didn't know what I wanted to do. Maybe I would be a scientist or maybe have a bookshop. I didn't know. My husband, for example, knew he would be either a painter or an architect, and he became an architect. But I didn't know. I wanted to wander around the world, find out about the world and about myself.

I considered studying literature, computer sciences, art, and maybe psychology. My father wanted me to do something professional. He was special, an intellectual, realistic and imaginative, interested in science and art, and he had a great influence on me. As architecture is a multidisciplinary profession, this choice allows for a wide range of experiences.

Today I am engaged in three main channels: design of architecture and interior-design projects, including housing, office spaces, and others, in my office at Rishpon, teaching at a school of interior design, and initiating real-estate projects of building renewal and strengthening.

When I first came to Israel I felt very alone. I got married at twenty-one and functioned as if everything was OK. I did what I should and didn't have time to find my way, to mature. When my son was little I had no family to help, and as my husband was a doctor and working nights, I was on my own. I worried that if something happened to me, no one would know and what would happen to the baby?

The years surrounding the end of my first marriage were also a difficult period in my life. And then, a little before turning fifty, I got cancer and that was like a brick on the head. Treatments lasted for a year and a half, and were tough. But difficult as it was, this experience brought a present with it. It forced me to stop. It made me look at my life.

Until then, I was like a little hamster running in its cage and can't stop. And then in the blink of a second I understood that life can come to a stop at any moment, so if there is anything I want to do, I'd better do it. It gave me the opportunity to get in touch with myself and allow myself to do things that I didn't even know I wanted.

The best part was three months in Greece, in a spiritual retreat in the island of Paros. Maybe this was the best gift I ever gave to myself! We worked three hours a day as part of the program. We had sessions with Zen Master Nissim Amon, workshops and meditations, yoga, tai chi, walks by the sea, music jam sessions. There were people from all over the world. There were music and dance and silence. I was un-plugged! I could go to sleep at 4 AM, I could listen to music all night, drive around the island on a motor scooter, I could do as I wanted. My husband came to visit, but most of the time I was on my own and time was in my hands. Above all, there was a space of acceptance, of "Everything is OK".

My burning issue now is financial. Our work is very rewarding in terms of personal and professional satisfaction, but it is lacking in terms of economic return that would be in accordance to all our efforts, skills, talents and experience. I find this very frustrating, and I think many of my colleagues would agree with me.

Nevertheless, I treat myself with things that are very important to me. I don't care about buying clothes or fancy gadgets, but I include in my life spiritual development, and activities for inner peace and growth. I do meditation, shiatsu, massage once in a while. I go to the gym, to *rikudei am*, (folk dancing) and have coffee and read a book in the morning. I watch the sun set into the sea from the terrace in the evening. And make some trips to the desert! We took the television set out of the house, and let books, conversation, volunteering, or whatever we want to do, take its place.

And of course, I keep in touch with my children, and I meet with friends. My children are my best project, the best thing I have done. When my son was born and the nurse put him on my chest, there was this moment when I *knew* this is an everlasting bond between us. Nothing could sever us, nothing could keep us apart.

Some good things in my life was going to Greece for these most precious three months, helping my friends, sometimes coaching or giving some advice when they ask for it.

Doing the Landmark Forum was a crucial turning point in my development. I followed my heart when I met Eitan, my husband, and he is the love of my life, but we used to quarrel a lot. The Landmark Forum and other programs gave a whole new level of understanding, communication and fun to our relationship. It also allowed me to create new possibilities in my work, family and other relationships, and in any area of my life, expanding my limits beyond what I thought was possible. This is why I volunteer as a Landmark Education leader. Doing this, I know I made a difference for the best in many people's lives. This gives me great satisfaction, and makes my world a better place to live in.

And there are the work projects that have accomplished my clients' dreams. It is wonderful to see how they enjoy the results of our work! Maybe the place is not always photogenic, but the people use it and it fits them like a glove. These are projects that support life!

Husam Massalha, PhD, MPA

Kfar Q'ara, 1961

A FORMER PhD APPLICANT I HAD WORKED WITH FROM THE TOWN REFERRED ME TO DR. Husam, who runs a school for youngsters to improve their studies. Maybe I could teach English in the school. I was intrigued with this effort and found Dr. Husam enthusiastic and energetic, as this is in addition to his regular work as Deputy Chief Scientist (acting), Senior Division Director, Environment and Agriculture at the Ministry of Science and Technology in Jerusalem. He and his wife are hospitable and welcoming.

My situation is good, excellent! I am happily married, with four exceptional children who show me how old I am. I have a good job as serving Deputy Chief Scientist at the Ministry of Science. I have been in public service for sixteen years. I am responsible for environmental, agricultural, and water research. This is a very broad position with scientific research at the local and national levels as well as in bi-national and international programs.

I was born here. I grew up here in Kfar Q'ara. Also, I spent four years in Rameh village, Galilee, as a high-school student. My big family is here. I was educated here in Israel, and my wife, too. After a few years in Germany, where I went to earn my PhD and do a post doc, we came back. I have been here seventeen years except for a year in Brussels, where I served as a Detached National Expert in Science Policy at the European Commission, Directorate General for research. My task was to consult the head of the unit concerning various scientific policy issues, especially in biotechnology. One of the major issues we have dealt with is GMO (Genetically Modified Organisms) which was toughly opposed in Europe.

My parents, now seventy-seven and sixty-seven, were born here in Kfar Q'ara. They are both healthy, active socially, and they are my neighbors.

They were supportive of my efforts for a PhD. When I was a child my father insisted that I study. He was born before Israel. His first contacts with Israelis showed him a life that was totally different from that of peasants. He saw doctors and lawyers and wanted me to be like that. That generation of Israeli-Arabs pushed their sons to study. If not for Israel, we would be peasants, farmers; not educated. Kfar Q'ara was a rural village. Maybe some were educated but not many. If you compare a village of three or four thousand people in Lebanon or Syria now you will see what would have been the situation.

In 1948, it was declared a military regime for Arab citizens, limiting the possibility of working freely. After the land was expropriated, the possibilities for the people were limited. They had to find other means to support their children, and not gradually. We had to meet the situation. Living in Israel is OK! It's my home!

The birth of my daughter was abroad. I was not aware of the danger. We took our time getting to the hospital. We took the train and came to the clinic. During the monitoring they lost the pulse. The nurse rang a bell and four people came: Sign here for a Caesarean procedure! They took my wife and I was alone. After a while the nurse came and said, "Your wife had a boy!" I cried heavily. Then she said, "Sorry, it's a girl." and I cried again! The first forty days when Bahaa, my newborn daughter was in the hospital, were very tiring, we were almost alone, only a few friends around us. I needed to go to the lab for my work. Maha stayed for ten days in the hospital following the operation. All this at once was too much to bear alone. Around the 40th day my sister, Ibtisam, joined us and we could rest a little bit.

Maybe identity is my burning issue. Success, to achieve my goals. My children need to go to the university. My wife, Maha, is to go to Hebrew University for a PhD in Arabic literature. Maybe I want to improve the financial level. My Cordoba Institute of Complementary Studies must fill the lack of manpower for so many children. Sometimes their parents can't, or have no time to support the studies of the children. We try to fill the gap to seventeen to eighteen-year-old-youngsters. It's a business officially, but I am running it as a "not for profit." It's enough to see the shining in the eyes of a child who succeeded to overcome one or the other obstacle, to solve this or that problem in his studies, to feel satisfied from the institute. It's never the money alone that satisfies me. Our policy at Cordoba is based on open door. We meet the parents from time to time for follow-ups. We want to learn from them about the situation of their children, if they have improved or not.

My father, by his encouragement to study, shaped my life and also many friends. One uncle wanted me to go into politics, which I did for a short period of time, until 1986. My wife was, and still is, influential, positively, most of the time. During my life, on the various stations and locations, I met many people. I am like a Bedouin; I don't stay in one place too long. I was in high school in Rameh and after that in Beer Sheva at Ben Gurion University and then to Frankfurt am Mainz in Germany, and then to Brussels. In every place I had friends who I enjoyed and I was active in various ways.

By sixteen, I knew I would be a PhD in biology. All my thoughts were to become a researcher in biology, maybe cancer research, or ecology. I was ready to move for my studies, but I knew I would come back. I have the feeling I belong here. I am connected to the community and the geography.

My dream now is to get another degree in the philosophy of science, even to study the origins of religions. In Germany I was very successful in my studies. I published ten articles. I took a cut to go to public service.

And then I took time for my Master's in Public Administration. I could not continue my research. There was an abrupt cut in my career as a researcher. I have adapted to my new position but I wish to be a researcher, an active researcher in cancer. I can't go back now to research. It would be very difficult to compete with the young researchers.

Setbacks did not influence me. When Maha and I wanted to get married, our fathers, who are in the same big family, were in a dispute and we had to delay our wedding for a few years. It was good for us to go to Germany. Then the birth of my daughter at thirty-one weeks was a shock of responsibility. We were in Germany with no family to help. I could go to the States either for, or after, my PhD to do research! I had good marks and could have been accepted.

One of my major achievements is the establishment of the regional R&D center here in Kfar Q'ara. It was my initiative and I have supported its establishment and the colleagues directing it. This initiative might prove to be very influential in the long range of time. Actually, it was the second research center in the Arab sector in Israel. Several researchers and educators are conducting parts of their research in the center.

The Cordoba School is one achievement, but not major. I try to empower the people around me. Ask me and I try to empower. The youngest sister of my wife was studying at Hebrew University. Her English was not so good, so I helped her write to get support from various funding agencies and programs. Very soon she had improved her English tremendously. In that time, one of my relatives was Deputy Foreign Minister, and to tease her we used to say that she is traveling abroad more often than he, MK Nawaf Massalha, who served as Deputy Minister in two governments: Rabin's government in the early '90s and Barak's government in the late '90s. She is now living in the United Kingdom, married to a Britain, getting her PhD in socio-politics at the London School of Economics. I think I was effective in this.

My sister was at Ben Gurion University when I was there. I finished my MS and went to Germany, got married, had children. After returning from Germany I asked her, "Where is your degree?" "Sorry, no English!" "So I will pay for you to learn English!" One year later she had her diploma, and now she is studying again. I think I influenced this.

From time to time I do something in local politics.

I just remembered to add. When I was a youngster my mother sat with me every afternoon with my studies and insisted I do my homework. It was only when I was grown up that I understood she could not read or write. I just thought all grown-ups could.

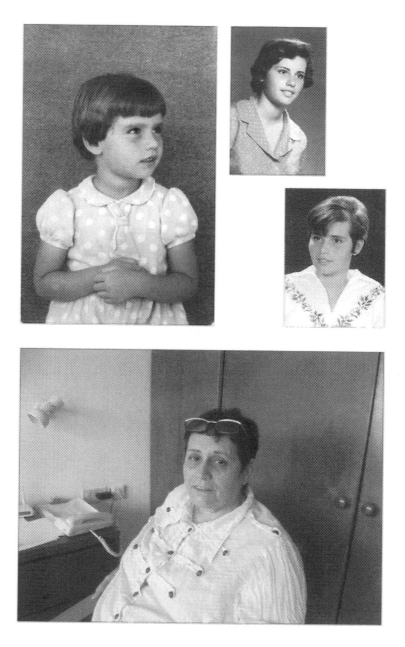

Vered Giladi
Moshav Bnei Dror, 1956

VERED CAME TO ME YEARS AGO TO IMPROVE HER ENGLISH WHEN SHE WAS WORKING FOR IBM. She developed her own company in computer technology. She built a website for my business. I accompanied her on business trips to provide feedback. She has a special way of looking at the world — she sees things in original configurations and can simplify complicated situations. She has given me good advice in difficult situations. As her name means "rose," I call her Rosalita.

I grew up in a moshav shitufi, like a kibbutz. The difference between this kind of living and a kibbutz is that the children lived at home, and not in the children's house. Everything was shared, but each family managed their own home and family matters. Every family got a salary from the moshav. My father worked in the dairy, my mother in export of roses. It was a wonderful place to grow up. We were very Zionist and worked all summer. This kind of life influenced me for the good and for the bad. The good is that you learned to always give to others, the bad is that I didn't know anything about money. This was a problem for me when I had a company. I didn't know how to measure the importance of money. In the moshav, we didn't know about any economic problems. In the city it was hard in those days, but we were OK. My parents were good at calculating the money. All our clothes were homemade, there were no restaurants. We had the simple life that was a good experience. For children and old people it is heaven.

I was born here! My parents made aliya after a thousand years of living in foreign countries, fought in several survival wars and established an advanced democracy and a strong army. It was all a miracle! I have the privilege and the honor to live here. I think this is one of the best places for the Jews to live. This is the place that you can say it's mine and I care about it. Maybe in other places the economic situation is better, but here you can care about it and feel part of it! It was destiny that led all the Jewish people to come and establish the state from the ashes of exile. We must save it for the next generation. You can't find any other country where people gathered together from all over to be a nation. Even with the many problems here, it is a miracle and we need to keep it.

My parents came from Turkey. My father came from a place that was sometimes Bulgaria, or Greece, or Turkey. When my grandmother was born it was Greek. It was a town with many middle-class Jews. My grandfather had a shop that sold the Turkish fezzes, but after Ataturk outlawed the fez, they started to make dresses for the rich ladies in town.

They ran away to Istanbul when the Germans came during World War II. The family in Greece was killed in Auschwitz. The family in Bulgaria was saved by the government. The Turkish government didn't allow the Germans to take the Jews. But they lost all their property. They lived there until 1950 when they made aliya and came to a kibbutz.

My mother's family came from middle Europe. Her parents died early and left five orphans, and she grew up with cousins in Istanbul. Some of her brothers were in an orphanage. She came to Israel when she was twenty-one and met my father on the kibbutz and they got married. My paternal grandmother studied in the Alliance, so she knew French. Her sister went to a German school and knew German and Yiddish. They made jokes to each other in several languages! The Turkish family spoke Ladino. This was my legacy — and when I hear

Ladino my heart opens. The stories I heard from my grandmother were that we were descended from Hissday Ebn Shafrut born about 915 and died about 975 at Cordoba in Spain, who was a Jewish scholar, physician, diplomat, and patron of science. He was a famous philosopher in Spain who was a personal assistant to the king. We studied about him in history so we knew our grandmother's stories were true.

Besides my mother and father, it was my grandmother who shaped my nature, because my parents worked and my grandmother raised me. She was a very strong person. I learned from her to work hard, not to waste time, to be professional. Along with my two brothers we are very professional. She keeps me on track. She influenced us all. She was wise, smart, and helpful until her last day.

When she made all the costumes for the annual celebration of the children's *bar mitzvot* everything was perfect to the last detail. She worked for 100%. We learned from her to go for 100% even if you can't do it. Because of this the three of us are outstanding. Not smarter, but dedicated to professional results.

I thought I would be a farmer in the moshav. Nothing else. Live a simple and secure life. In the moshav you have security that in the city you have to fight for; economic, social, and health security and there is always someone who will ask you how you are, and bring you cookies if you're sick — always someone to help. It is a protected environment that is worth a lot.

Now I am married with three children, and three grandchildren. I am doing freelance work in computers for several large companies. I'm fighting for my small place in history, at least for the coming three or four family generations. I am trying to make everything to be OK.

I am the kind of person who always passes setbacks. Some people know their way and don't bump the walls. The other kind, like me, cannot walk straight; they bump the walls, and don't see the map of their life in front of them.

The package of my childhood is precious to me. Also raising my kids until they are seven or eight is precious to shape their way. During that time they are dependent on you and you can give them a lot. You are their mentor.

I have two issues: one is to establish my own financial security, and the second is to see that our nation will do better for the people. The kind of democracy we have seen in the last 60-100 years is coming to an end. Now with Facebook, Twitter, smartphones, etc. the people will have more direct influence. Now the general public will change and make more national decisions. This is changing all over the world. You can see this in Europe and in Arab countries, and also in Israel. We are witness to the end of a period. I support the demonstrations that are going on now because I believe the situation must change. The young people are doing our fight.

What I did until now is the result of my character, from my nature. A fatalistic way of thinking! Not something I copied from another person. I don't know what I would do differently. I know that my mistakes come from my character, which I can't change.

The major thing I contribute is to help people. At work, when somebody needs professional help, I teach and help as far as I know. Most of the time people remember it long time; I think it's because of some small hidden help. They say, "You told me this and that and I did it and look at me now" — or "You helped me in my worst hours." People tell me years later! I can see someone and he says, "Hello, Vered!" I ask, "How do we know each other?" "You interviewed me years ago and suggested to me what to do."

In general, I try to enter deep into the other's life and heart to give them the right idea. I can put myself in the other's position and speak from that position to help. I just got a card for my birthday from someone who wrote, "You helped me in my bad hours." I can feel the need and try to help. And they don't forget me because of this special touch. It is natural — I don't think about it.

I thank every day that I live in Israel. Even with all the problems, the lack of equality that we have in society, and the gap between the rich and the middle class. We need to save the country with our soul and our body. As I see it, the problem with the Arabs is not solvable. There are here two nations that have the same rights for the same land and no side will give up.

I would like our children to have a better life here in Israel. Our parents suffered a lot and established the State. We, as a second generation, tried to establish customs, regulations and procedures. I hope that the result of all these efforts is a better life for our children. We have to be a strong and humane country.

Ziva Elgar

Petach Tikva, 1951

I MET ZIVA ON SEVERAL OCCASIONS WHEN WE CELEBRATED WITH LIORA. WE IDENTIFIED common interests in Greek music, the oud, travel, different cultures, and many parts of the life here! I was curious to know how she and Ilan managed living abroad for their diplomatic postings.

I grew up in Bnai Brak, in the outskirts of that religious city, in a neighborhood for the army officers, so we grew up together, although we did not belong to the army. When I was eight, we moved to Ramat Gan because my parents wanted to be close to the rest of my mother's family and to move to a better apartment. My father was working for a major health fund, in the lab in Beilinson Hospital because of his special training in bio chem. He got his PhD at the Weizmann Institute and later taught at Tel Aviv University. I think that's why I went on to study biology, to follow in my father's footsteps. He was a very hard worker as a scientist, but I don't think I have it.

I studied biology for the BS and a teaching diploma in Tel Aviv University, and then was teaching for two years in school, and then worked for two years in a lab in the medical school in Tel Aviv University. As Ilan started his cadets' course in the Ministry of Foreign Affairs we got married in 1976 and moved to Jerusalem. I worked for two years at the Hadassah Hospital in Jerusalem in the medical school in research. I did what my father did but on a smaller scale. I had to leave this when Ilan got his first post in Malawi; there I worked in the embassy. Later on, in Los Angeles, I studied history of art, painting and other subjects, with full exams, and from then on, I always studied something — Spanish, German, French and some Italian. In high school I studied Arabic. I like very much to study languages. Then I studied public relations and advertising in the College of Management in Jerusalem.

Maybe I wanted to be like my father to be a scientist; otherwise I don't think I had too many dreams. I heard Swan Lake at three and danced! But I didn't continue with ballet and I wanted to play the piano. We didn't hear music as we had no record player. I begged for a piano at eleven and I learned quickly and played in a concert every year. At about seventeen I stopped. I still have it; next week the piano will be tuned and I will start! I like too many things! Although I studied biology, I like music, opera, film, theater, art and painting, traveling in nature and different countries. I never thought I would travel and live in foreign countries and adjust to new places. Learning German was difficult, and living in Germany for two years was very difficult, because of my family background and personal history. I was brought up in French — that was my mother tongue. I picked up Greek because they spoke it between them, but not reading or writing. Later I had Hebrew.

I am looking back to my story. My parents came here from Greece after the Holocaust. Their roots are in Spain from where their fore-fathers were expelled in the 15th century. Many of them settled in the Ottoman Empire, of which Greece was a part. The Ladino Sephardic heritage is on our shoulders. My parents lived in Salonika. This big Jewish community perished in the Holocaust. My father's parents were taken to Auschwitz. My father studied chemistry in Athens; he was a single child and survived with the money and jewelry that his mother sent him. He was hidden in the chemistry laboratories in Piraeus by his professor. My mother had two sisters and a brother who were hiding in different places in Athens with their parents. That community had more connections with the Christian community and had more help. My mother's father was taken to Auschwitz. We have nothing — no pictures, no nothing. My parents survived. My mother was caught by the Gestapo but she survived posing as a Christian as she knew the prayers, having gone to a Christian school in Athens.

After the war, they got married and my father was drafted into the Greek army for three years. They immigrated to Israel in 1950 with the rest of my mother's family. My father was already a chemist in Athens so when he came here he could continue his career as a bio-chemistry scientist. He became a professor here. My mother started her studies in Athens, as the war started, to be a medical doctor, then a dentist, then an opera singer. She never continued her studies in Israel. I remember her singing opera pieces in my childhood; she has a broad classical music education, French and Greek literature but never fulfilled herself.

In the 1950s, no one spoke about what had happened in the Holocaust. We heard a little in school; you came to it little by little — My children heard more from my mother than I ever did from her. In school, my children did a big project about their roots for their bar/bat mitzvah. Now we have computer programs for this - family tree and genealogy. My mother remembered everything. Her mother had ten brothers and sisters, some are in the US and France. Because they had Spanish passports, they survived in the concentration camps as Spanish.

They went to ulpan to learn Hebrew. My mother worked and they managed to save some money. They had been well off in Salonika, but they couldn't take money out from Greece. They got some compensation from the Germans after 1950. My mother is now eighty-nine years old; my father passed away a few years ago.

Today, a year and three months after we came back from the last post in Switzerland, we are almost settled in our new home in Mevasseret Zion. We renovated an old house and that took a few years to finish. We started our diplomatic career in Malawi, 1979-83, then

Los Angeles, 1985-88, Norway, 1988-1990, Germany-Bonn 1995-97 and Switzerland, 2006-2011.

Now I am at a junction or cross roads, as that was our last post and we came back for good and would like to choose my own way, a new direction in my life — to be for myself and try to fulfill myself in different ways. I am trying to find places to volunteer, teaching students with learning difficulties in a school near here. I am looking to go back to my hobbies of playing the piano, painting, and to finding something different in the art.

I chose to start with a small group of women that aims to encourage social change for the status of women, the way women participate in life, in the business world, and in politics. We concentrate on the conflict between state and religion, the segregation of women in the name of religion. We are interested in who is suffering from segregation between women and men in the public sphere, like buses, medical centers, and the army. Women constitute 50% of society but only twenty-six women serve in the a hundred and twenty seat Knesset! The situation has worsened in recent years in some ways for the secular society. The religious coercion excludes and restricts women in the public domain more and more. The ultra-Orthodox women also suffer. I want the Orthodox to be part of Israeli society and not to be separate, to study science, math, and English and take part in the army and the economy.

We don't know if they want to. They don't go to the army because of an old political arrangement. The men don't learn general studies in the *yeshiva* and therefore don't contribute to the economy — Israeli society is quite divided. We have many different backgrounds! We don't need to be homogenous but minorities like the Arabs, Druze, and others need to be connected. I was aware of this for many years but as we were living abroad and I was concentrating on the family, it had to wait until now.

We have two sons and a daughter. The oldest is thirty-three years old, our daughter is thirty-one, and our younger son is nineteen, in his military service.

At the beginning, it was interesting and exciting to be abroad, to meet other people and encounter different cultures. The life of a diplomat looks glamorous with cocktail parties and dinners and big events, but that is not the essence. It is hard work. It is also dangerous. Israeli diplomats and their families are potential targets for terrorists and live in constant tension. It was not easy for me to adjust to new locations, climates and cultures, and I felt lonely sometimes. My children feel like citizens of the world. But my younger son was not here during high school so now in the army he feels not fully attached — the outcome of an international education.

To be abroad and take care of the family in a foreign society you are always an outsider. I tried to integrate in the way of culture, language, and to represent Israel. I was always helping the children to adjust to the new countries and trying to find my way, meeting people. I entertained a lot, prepared Israeli food and showed the variety of the Israeli culture, music, and art. When the children came back their Hebrew was not so good.

Today it is easier with internet and all the connections to keep in touch with Israel and family, friends — not like it was in Malawi sitting alone. There are some holes in my life: during the Lebanon War and the first Intifada we were in Los Angeles and Norway.

I met Ilan when I was nineteen, during my Army service. A friend introduced us. Then we went to the same university. We took a marvelous trip to the Greek Islands as students before we were married: seven islands in five weeks with hardly any money. When we came back we decided to stay together.

Looking back, I realize I sacrificed a lot — but I don't know if I would have given it up as I wanted to be with Ilan. Some women stayed home and then the marriages suffered. I was frustrated. I am not an angel! I spent most of my life and my good years. I gave a lot but I also got a lot. I came to know different cultures and got different perspectives. Our economic situation was good. I didn't have to go to work but I learned many things and tried to do everything well.

I was miserable in Norway. It was too cold and dark.

I feel very Israeli. I feel more comfortable here than anywhere else with the language, the climate, the society. I like the landscape, the variety of people. Nowadays, I am kind of disappointed and apprehensive about the future. We have to reach a compromise with our neighbors and among ourselves — we have not yet succeeded in forming a fully democratic society. Israel is a miracle in history and became very successful in a relatively short time, but it turned into a society that is now too greedy and not so nice to one another. We have to make peace with our neighboring countries. We need to help each other more and get to know other parts of society. Maybe I am naïve, but optimistic and pessimistic at the same time about what is going to be here in Israel!

Ilan Elgar
Tel Aviv, 1947

Yes, Ilan is the friendly and hospitable husband of Ziva. He is now home from abroad, after being the Israeli ambassador to Switzerland. I have had the pleasure of being in his company at parties and in their beautiful home.

I think my career as a diplomat turned out to be such a good thing. This is a career of being a defender of your country abroad, especially a beleaguered country such as Israel. It means often working in difficult situations, representing the country that is not always seen in the best light. If you do it conscientiously, it is an uphill struggle. I never planned to become a diplomat — it just happened. Ziva saw an ad in the paper calling for candidates for the Foreign Ministry's cadets' course. We decided to give it a try, mostly out of curiosity, and six months later I started my training. I had a very interesting time, and I loved it, even if it was challenging.

It is more than a job; it is a way of life and the whole family is involved. Certainly Ziva paid a high price. You can't imagine this at the beginning. In my generation, it was expected that you reach eighteen and go to serve your country. This was before the age of individualism.

Now I am sort of in limbo, having returned from my last posting abroad about a year ago and awaiting retirement next January. I still work at the Foreign Ministry in my old department (International Organizations) but Ziva and I devote a lot of our time to getting our house ready. It has taken a long time and is more drawn out than we expected. The process of getting my bearings on how to spend my retirement time — it can be quite long and fulfilling. The thoughts are still whirling around and I am looking in different directions, but only to be self-employed, for which I am poorly trained by past experience and inclination. However, one has unfathomable reserves! You never know, I might strike gold!

Concurrent with our homecoming, our youngest son went to the army. This is central to an Israeli family. We had the rule that if we have a child in the army we would be in Israel, not abroad. We are living up to it.

My parents emigrated here from Czernowitz, in central eastern Europe that was part of the Austro-Hungarian Empire, so my grandmother spoke only German. Just before my parents were born it was annexed by Romania. Then it was invaded by the Soviets, and then the Germans, and now is part of the Ukraine. There was a thriving Jewish community there. Paul Celan, the famous German-language poet, was a childhood friend of my father. My parents came here separately. My father was eighteen and finished his studies and became independent and came here in 1938. His family stayed behind. My grandfather was lucky or unlucky. After the Soviet invasion he was deported to one of the gulags in Siberia and my grandmother and their daughter, my Aunt Ruth, accompanied him. My grandfather also spent some time in jail. His crime? Being a capitalist and a Zionist. In his house they had Zionist visitors for meetings. By the way, my grandfather was exonerated in 1992, long after his death. I found out from my only cousin here in Israel.

My mother arrived with her parents in 1940 with all their belongings, with the war already raging, on the last passenger ship to leave Romania. My grandfather was a dentist and they settled in Tel Aviv on Bialik Street, the doctors' street. In every apartment in their building was someone in the medical profession. In 1942 my parents married in Tel Aviv. They knew each other from before. I was born there in 1947, almost into the War of Independence. As a baby I saved my mother's life. She was hanging the washing on the tiny balcony when her baby, me, started to cry so she went inside to take care of me. When she came back there was a bullet hole in the wall where she stood a minute before. There were snipers firing from Jaffa. We never fixed the hole.

We also lived on Bialik Street, as my mother had to be close to her parents. Our apartment was tiny. The living room became my parents' bedroom at night and the kitchen could accommodate only one person at a time. My brother, Ronny, was born five years after me. Children get used to everything and we were happy in those cramped accommodations. We children lived mostly on the street anyway, as there weren't many cars and we could play on the road and in the back yards.

I didn't realize it at the time that I led a sort of pampered life. We were in the center of the city in a country that was taking in a huge influx of refugees who were living in *ma'abarot* (refugee camps.) In 1950 there was snow in Tel Aviv. I have a mental picture of me playing in the snow. For me it was a playground, but for those who lived in tents and tin huts it was a dreary time. My grandfather even had a telephone, as physicians had priority. He ordered it in 1940 and got it in 1953. I remember when it was installed and I still remember the number: 3567. Basically a very happy and carefree childhood, even if I was knocked down by cars on the road once or twice!

I still have a few friends from that time. Sometimes years pass and we still get together. My first language was German. My parents spoke Hebrew but said, "He will learn Hebrew, we might as well give him another language and he will have to speak German to his grandmother anyway." At the age of three I went to kindergarten with no Hebrew, felt completely out of my depth but picked it up quickly.

My parents shaped my life. I think that by the standards of the times they were very liberal. My mother was the intellectual of the family. She spoke Romanian, German, Hebrew, French, and English fluently.

In 1957, before we went to Italy, she studied Italian. I also heard her speak Yiddish to some people and she understood Spanish. I picked up the love of art from her. My love of music is from my father. In 1957, the Mann Auditorium opened and my family had a season ticket to the Philharmonic. When they gave it up, I used their ticket and attended a lot of concerts in my teens - not very common at the time! In the center of the city there was always a thriving cultural scene. Going abroad was a rare occurrence in those days, but I went with my mother in 1957 to Europe. She took me instead of my father. Being able to do these extravagant things was thanks to the support of my mother's rich uncle in Chile. They came to visit here regularly and even visited us in Oslo.

I was looking forward to doing something in aviation — I loved airplanes. As a child I was actually terrified by the Egyptian planes bombing Tel Aviv in 1948. Maybe because of that, paradoxically, I became interested. I never did learn to fly because of short-sightedness. Later, I had some notion of studying aeronautical engineering, but this turned out to be a dead end. I have some problems with certain aspects of my personality, like being lazy. However, we are burdened or blessed with a set of genes not of our choosing, so we might as well get used to it. Time travel is impossible so there is no going back. Our life is a series of crossroads, large and small, dramatic or mundane. We make our choices because of our background, upbringing, and experience. We take a particular road because we are what we are.

I am lucky to have had many nice, beautiful, interesting, experiences. Looking back I tell myself how lucky I am in more ways than one, including just being alive. I had quite a few close brushes with death during my military service in the Golani Brigade. I was almost killed by a fellow soldier who fired just over my head. Or when a Jordanian shell exploded just two meters from me. Or doing a patrol on a muddy path and seeing a mine come up out of the mud just after our vehicle passed over it. Or coming out unhurt from the Six-Day War despite enduring massive Syrian shelling.

I love living in Israel now! I think Israel is the greatest success story of the second half of the 20th century. I kept telling people abroad, but it was very sincere. If you compare it to other countries created after the Second World War, Israel stands out as a huge success story. I witnessed many of these changes, quite a few for the worse, but the broad picture is that it is a successful enterprise. Israel is the preferred posting for journalists and diplomats. Places that create news and excitement tend to be hardship posts, whereas high standards of living and comfort are associated with boredom. Israel is a rare exception in combining both comfort *and* excitement.

I am ending one stage and going on to the next one. I don't know where it will lead. The world is full of temptations. Both Ziva and I enjoy art and music. We devoted a lot of time to this and also money and will probably devote even more now. We travelled a lot, in the line of duty and on our own; we covered Europe extensively, made a few ventures into Asia, had a taste of Africa and the Americas. Ziva insists she must see Australia as she hasn't been there yet. Trying to cram a lot into life so far; we will go on doing it!

We have three children. They don't have to look after us yet.

Stella Isaharov, MBA

Uzbekistan, 1962

ONE OF THE FIRST THINGS TO DO WHEN YOU COME TO ISRAEL IS OPEN A BANK ACCOUNT. *Stella was in charge of the tellers and she helped me. Later, Stella started English lessons with me, but when the bank offered an English course, she switched to that. After a lapse of time, I went to a party at a kibbutz and Stella was there with a friend. She told me she was recently divorced. We arranged to meet for a coffee and have maintained our friendship since then, traveling to the north for a weekend, eating her delicious green rice, going to Middle Eastern music concerts, going to Paris together when she got her MBA. She has spirit!*

I'm a grandmother! I have a nice position in the bank as a department manager. I am a mother of three grown daughters. I am close to my three sisters and two brothers and my mother. My father died a few years ago. My youngest daughter just finished the army. She is working to save money for her trip after the army.

I want to help my children build their future in the very difficult situation here. And to promote myself in my work. I want to advance in my position. Now I am working on my well-being. I am in a detox workshop and feel better!

When I was eleven, my parents came to Israel after many years that they had not been allowed to leave the Soviet Union. Before we made aliya, my mother wanted to go to Israel but my father didn't. When we had to take a picture for the passport my father wouldn't come for the photo. Our passport photo is my mother and her four children. Eventually, my father had his taken separately. There was a superstition that if you have pictures including people not of the family it might cause trouble at the border, so my mother tore up all the pictures that were of us and our friends. People said things that were not rational and she believed.

And then we came to Israel. To Dimona! My mother saw the desert and said, "No, I can't do this. I can only be in Tel Aviv." The Jewish Agency, responsible for settling new immigrants, said, "Here in Dimona we give you a new apartment. In Tel Aviv you are on your own." We went by bus and stayed in a one-room apartment until my parents found work.

Some religious people came and said if they send us to religious school we don't have to pay. So they sent us to boarding school in Jerusalem. It was very difficult looking after my two sisters. My brother was sent to Bnei Brak (a religious town.) Our parents had to work very hard, but after nine months they bought a flat and brought us home. My father was a shoemaker and my mother worked in a chocolate factory. Because I had been in a religious school, I couldn't go to a regular high school, because in the boarding school I was only with girls so it was difficult for me to go to school with boys. So they took me to a religious school and I finished school there. I was so frightened and they threatened me with evil things — it was difficult.

My parents are from Uzbekistan — all the generations. My grandmother from my mother's side died a year before we left. As my grandfather was a hundred years old, and had another family, he didn't come. My grandmother was twenty-eight when she married my sixty-two-year-old grandfather. He had children and as a widower he was looking for a new wife. When he came to my grandmother's mother to ask her to marry him, he saw my grandmother and wanted to marry her instead. My grandmother was divorced because the children she bore had died at six months. She wanted to have children so she agreed to marry him because he had children already. Her mother agreed. His children were the same age as my grandmother. The first child was very talented at eighteen and very beautiful. She died on a trip when she fell off the mountain. Maybe someone pushed her. From that day my grandmother suffered and was never herself. My mother remembers her crying all day and night. I remember her as very beautiful, kind and so loving. She died when she was about sixty-two. She had lived with us for five years. My father was an orphan. His father died in World War II and his mother died young. He and his two brothers were in a boarding school for orphans. After some time, his uncle came and took two of them to his house and they grew up there. The other brother was not found.

When we came from Uzbekistan to Moscow to Vienna it was a very long journey with my parents and sisters and brother and we slept on the benches in the train station. We had a suitcase, which my mother watched over. I thought maybe it was full of money but it was our documents. We came through Austria, arranged by the Jewish Agency. Soldiers guarding us were very nice to us. In school I had learned German so I spoke to them. We children were playing with them. When I look at this now I remember the feeling of No Problems. We were just playing.

When we came to Israel the children were very mean to us. They said, Go back to Russia! And in Russia they had said, Jews go out!

There was nothing written in Russian here, unlike now. My mother took me to help her because I had learned Hebrew in that boarding school. And I translated everything for her in every government office.

My father died at sixty-six. I was with him in his last days in the hospital. One time he suddenly woke up and was looking straight ahead and welcoming his dead uncle. After a few days he died.

I grew up in Tel Aviv. I was working by age fourteen. I studied until ninth grade and then left to help my mother who had two more children. I studied in the evenings.

I had big luck that I met good friends along my way. My first was a friend who had her child in the same in kindergarten as mine. She was my first true friend. She is my friend until now — twenty-five years! She made me believe in myself. Two other friends I met in the bank taught me and guided me. And in my work I met you! I had another very good friend I met twelve years ago who encouraged me to go back to school. And now I have an MBA. You encouraged me and said if I get my MBA you will take me to Paris. And you did!

If I could, I would have kept studying and gone to the army. I was married at eighteen so I didn't do the army. But I am happy that I had my children at a young age. It was very hard to be alone after my divorce and to face everything, alone with your children, to handle everything alone.

I want to believe that I helped a lot of immigrants from Russia in '90-'91 because I spoke Russian. My bank was near the immigration office so they came to me and opened accounts. I was the address for all the questions and I was very happy to assist. One couple, the husband made dolls and we had a client who had a toy store. I tried to help. I taught Hebrew to new immigrants in the community center in our neighborhood for about a year.

It's difficult living in Israel now. But this is my country. I love to live here. But we need changes. We need stability in our government. We need a government that does things for the long term and not just three years before elections. We are not thinking ahead like other great countries. We don't do enough for the education for our children. I see that in other places in the world, the government invests more in teachers and motivates them to do more for children. I see that in the States the children know how to manage money in early years. Here, they don't teach anything to help them to learn to do something — to be someone. Here we are not preparing them for real life. Our government is held hostage in the hands of the religious parties. This is a disaster.

Doron Neev
Tel Aviv, 1951

As a cross-cultural consultant, I had approached Doron for work possibilities. In Israel, this is a hard sell and nothing came of my efforts — except to meet a very open, optimistic, energetic, charming, and friendly person!

I am married, father of two boys. One is thirty-two, married, a lawyer/economist. He has an MBA and works in one of Israel's largest companies in human resources. This is following my occupation! The younger, twenty-seven, is graduating now, in the social sciences. He works with me in our firm dealing with relocation, one of the best. We are here fifteen years, well connected to the larger world associations, customers, and partnerships, with a very long and nice list of companies that we represent. Israel is a hard place for consultants. We think we know it all! At my age, I am still working very hard, long hours, sometimes seven days a week. I am trying to have some time to sit on the roof in the flowers, read a book, even walk the dog! Time to have a telephone conversation with friends!

I am in Israel because I belong to a family that was really Zionist. My father came here early. Most of his family ran away from Soviet Union to America, but he and his sister chose Palestine and came in 1924 when there was nothing here. My mother was educated in Hebrew even before Polish. She came to Palestine on her own will. She had an aunt here, who had come the previous century, and she arranged for my mother's certificate to come. It was not because of the war. They were here during the War of Independence. My father was a member of the underground. They all served in the army. My two older brothers left the country, which upset my parents. They finally returned to Israel, when they were thirty-five and sisty-six.

The education was so strong in our family that we are all here. My sons wouldn't even consider going to the USA to live, even though both were born abroad. Whatever happens here, there is no chance we would go somewhere else. We did try to get European passports for the chance to study abroad or more easily to go to the EU, but as my mother gave up her Polish passport with no reversal there is no chance.

Up to a certain age, my parents shaped my life. My father was a contractor. When I was about six, they went bankrupt. I remember a lot of problems. We lived in a very nice house with an American refrigerator, a record player, and things not usual at that time in Israel. Suddenly they came to take these things. My father went to work in Eilat for two years. My mother went back to work. They worked very hard and paid back every penny. We lost the upper floor of the house, but somehow we managed. Slowly they were released from their debt and life returned. I don't think I missed anything in high school. When they went to America to visit to my older brothers I went, too. Their life returned to their higher level. I was impressed that they paid every penny. It's a value I appreciate today. I can't stand owing any money — either privately or professionally.

I always dreamed of trips abroad, even though half of Europe was closed to us at that time. And in other places we weren't welcome. I was just a global person. I wanted to go to strange places, wanted to be in the foreign ministry. My mother said she would give up a new sofa so she could go to America! I am the same. When I did go abroad for a few years, she came once/twice a year and wanted to see everything. The whole family has the tendency to travel. My two sons have already been all over the world in Asia, South America, Australia. We travel also within Israel — but sometimes it is easier to go abroad — and certainly cheaper!

I was accepted in the Foreign Ministry and started working but a "little war" came in October, '73. I was recruited, but the Ministry released me and called me back to Jerusalem. In January of 1974, I was in Ramat Hagolan in a stupid job so I was taken back to Jerusalem. I found myself going to Geneva as a very young guy, at that time with long hair in my diplomatic passport photo. I was an official member of the peace delegation. This period in Geneva was very special. I had the honor of working with Prof. Shabtai Rosen, who was a tough genius. He died recently at ninety-three, working on a committee about the last war in Gaza and the blockade.

When I returned, I wanted to go back to Geneva. I was only twenty-five when I went there again, this time for full mission of a few years. I was married in 1976. We were four couples at the same time. We couldn't have a honeymoon for everyone so we got one on the way to Geneva. It was winter and I wanted to go to Spain but we couldn't go on a diplomatic passport as there were no diplomatic relations with Spain at that time, so we went for one month in Italy.

My profession as a consultant is not easy as Israelis think that they don't need help, they don't need a consultant. Sometimes I am too careful, don't dare too much. Maybe I should be more courageous and spend more in the company for marketing. I am very, very, very conservative. I think it comes from childhood memories.

We are living in a culture, a country, a region where certain professions are not really understood. Sometimes we come to companies and they don't know what we are talking about. There is no word in Hebrew for 'relocation.' "Why do we need this?" they ask. In one case the husband didn't learn the French he needed for his work, but his wife did and she handled it all. He was never really there. Sometimes I feel like I am a foreigner here. There are things I do here that people are surprised. If you cancel, I say thank you for letting me know! Even though born here, I feel a little bit the foreigner — I still get surprises. Things have improved, but — We respond to people who approach our company looking for a job. A lot of the placement companies don't even answer.

Living in Israel now is a challenge — a country difficult for the quality of life. When you have to quarrel about everything — nothing is clear here. If you need some repair in the apartment: You call them, someone comes to look and then disappears. You have to chase after people. My son has twenty-four days of miluim. He will be out of the office. This is not a picnic. The current demonstrations are showing the difficulties for the young people. We paid for his education, as youngsters can't afford this. I have to pay a mortgage for them. Why to pay millions for an ordinary apartment? It's dirty and noisy and full of corruption everywhere. Relative to our size we have too much going on here. Recently, it is more and more severe. I am shocked by the religious corruption.

I would like to see a better quality of country here. More cooperation to help those who need help. We who can give must help them. We have become very cruel society — each one for himself only. Not very pleasant any more. It is a beautiful country, but the politics are terrible here. We should enjoy a country that is much better! I don't have regrets — I would not make major changes.

Jane Krivine

London, 1947

I MET JANE SOME YEARS AGO AT VIVIENNE SILVER'S HOUSE. THEY HAD BEEN IN THE WUJS program together years before. As a charming and vivacious person, Jane has many friends and I am happy to be one of them. She is the perfect guest for a dinner party: knows about all topics, has original ideas, is witty, relates to everyone, and is a good listener. We have done some rambles; one was to a gallery in Um el Fahem, another to a donkey reserve. We attend all the film festivals. She accepts me even though I can't abide her dogs.

For the first five years of living in Israel I used to say it was like being on a permanent holiday. Now that I work quite hard with the tennis charity and my activities with ESRA, I feel I am not on holiday anymore.

I would like to do something about the political situation in Israel. Israel is uniquely and extraordinarily fascinating, interesting, politically, economically, and socially. I am not frustrated by the politics. It is simply the huge effort of a society looking for the way through its challenges. It is like Britain during the Victorian age. Because of the Industrial Revolution, life became incredibly unfair, with huge gaps between the rich and poor. Parliament was going through massive changes because, at the time, only landowners could vote and the laws, inevitably, favored the rich. The country was always at war somewhere or other. The economy was building at a very fast rate. I think Israel is going through similar processes with a parliament that doesn't function very well, too much power in the hands of too few, too much control by minority parties, and worrying gaps between the rich and poor. But there is always the effort to improve ourselves and to be kinder and fairer to the disadvantaged and to achieve some kind of peace agreement. This is a painful effort, but you are always aware of it.

I have a perfect situation. I inherited a house from my parents in Caesarea that has three rentals so I am financially secure. I also run a program bringing tennis to Israeli Arab children from which I have a small salary. I am a very active volunteer with ESRA, which is Israel's largest English-speaking volunteer organization.

And I have two dogs and a cat, all found in the street.

Being in Israel is not the result of any Zionist dream. It is more pragmatic. My brother lives in Israel and has a young family. My father lived in Israel. I reached a point where I was ready to retire from my career in Britain. For many years I had worked under a lot of pressure and struggled financially. So my move to Israel was a huge relief—in the sense that I was no longer under stress and had greater economic freedom. In fact, I celebrated this new-found lifestyle with a series of exotic holidays with friends and relations to places such as Egypt, with a cruise down the Nile with my best friend Lucie; Jordan, where I took my daughter and niece for a fantastic five-day excursion which included Petra, and Turkey, with a magical week in Istanbul. Prior to that, for the previous twenty years, I had only come to Israel twice a year to visit my parents.

Since those geographically close trips, which I called "meeting the neighbors," I have been to India, South Africa, Uganda, and St. Petersburg. I have done more traveling in the last eight years than I had done all my life. This is the result of my good fortune.

I grew up in London. Both my parents were born in England. My mother was fifth generation English. However, my father's father was from Poland, and his mother from Russia.

When my father was two, my paternal grandfather took the family to Lille, in France. My grandfather was in the textile industry. They were there for nine years so my father and his siblings were all bilingual. He also spoke fluent Hebrew because he went to agricultural school in Pardess Hanna at the age of fifteen, returning to England at the age of eighteen in 1938. As the result of having a father who was fluent in three languages, it was perfectly normal for me to want to speak languages. I studied French and Russian at university, and subsequently lived in Italy for six months. Now I live in Israel and am certainly no linguist, but perfectly comfortable in four foreign languages. For this I thank my father. In St. Petersburg recently, I spoke Russian again. When I was a child in England there were few foreigners and no tourists. In 1954 there was still food rationing! No one in my class, except for one girl, spoke other languages, or went abroad, or thought it was important.

I remember once being worried that my life would be simply a series of routine events on the way to dying. I must have been about eleven. I never felt that ever again. I have a wonderful Aunt Dolly who says spend your money, do what you want to do. If anything, she has been quite an influence since my parents died.

I have been really fortunate. My parents lived to be an old age — I was well into my fifties when my parents passed away. I have a wonderful daughter. I am sure if I had three or four children I would never be so lucky as I am with Sophie. I have friends with children where the relationships are difficult and the children are not happy and some have turned to religion and split the family, and some don't even talk to their parents. I am very fortunate.

I don't think I have any *burning* issues, but there are several things I would still like to achieve. One is I would like to be more influential in improving Jewish-Arab relations in Israel. I would like to see my daughter in a happy relationship. And I would like to work more on my physical fitness. This list starts out with something I can't influence at all and ends with something I can, but probably won't.

I would like to include a bit about my career in England, because it was an example of fate, rather than planning.

This is what happened: At the age of thirty I married a classical music agent. And although I knew nothing about the world of classical music, I quite soon became a concert manager. And I was successful because I was a good organizer and it didn't matter that I couldn't tell my crotchets from my quavers.

After I divorced, I developed the PR side of the business and had a very interesting decade representing top international classical musicians. It could not have been more exciting. I employed five staff and was at last beginning to do well. However, when the CD was invented and the record labels started re-issuing their back catalogues, the record companies soon developed large international PR departments, a service they provided their artists for free. In a relatively short time, I lost most of my clients.

But I had another lucky break. I became the director of an annual classical music festival which took place at Windsor Castle and Eton College. For two weeks every September, I was given rooms at the Windsor Castle, at the top of a narrow winding stone staircase, above the Henry VIII Gate. I managed up to forty events, with a wonderful team of professionals and volunteers, every year for seven years. Festival management included everything from fundraising to selecting the artists. From the moment you finish one festival, you start the next.

It is a long way from booking an orchestra for the State Apartments in Windsor Castle to setting up tennis facilities in an Israeli Arab village, but I have been equally happy doing both.

Rachel Porat

Jerusalem, 1943

One of the first days that I was teaching at The Sadna, an architectural college, I was in the teachers' room eating a salad. Rachel came in and wanted to know, "Who is eating that salad?" As a graphic designer she was teaching CadCom. I have seen her develop into a yoga teacher, a traveler, and confident woman. She is full of fun. I am very grateful that she advised me to go to the US to apologize to my two stepsons for leaving their father, which has made it possible for me to have a deeply loving relationship with them and the grandchildren.

I am a happy woman. I am doing the thing I like. I have a boyfriend. I work as a yoga teacher. I do some spiritual work that brings me lots of happiness. I know I am on the right way, on the way of the light. I feel a lot of love for people that I meet in my life. What I like to do is to work with people and make them happy and healthy.

The most important is my spiritual way. I see people who are suffering because they have no knowledge about what is going on in the high level of the life. They don't want to hear about it. I want to show them something new, but they are still in their superstitions and beliefs. The time is now developing quickly and there is a lot of knowledge that people don't want. They want to live their lives for pleasure or for money. They have to make the development of themselves. That is the main reason they come to the world, as I see it.

Until I was twenty-five I was in Jerusalem and at Bezalel Art School. After, I went to Tel Aviv to find work. Then I moved from Tel Aviv after the '73 War and went to Kiriyat Shemona as a volunteer working with immigrants. After two years I moved to Beer Sheva to work as a teacher of art. I stayed in Beer Sheva for seventeen years as a pioneer. It was very undeveloped then and a graphic designer was necessary. I taught everywhere from Kiriyat Gat to the kibbutzim around. After my divorce, I moved back to Tel Aviv and shared a studio with a dear friend. My two daughters moved with me to Holon. My elder daughter died while serving the army. Now I live in Holon.

My father was born in Teheran, Iran. When he was very young, about thirteen, he started the trip to Israel, coming through Syria and Iraq, by horse, trucks. His parents had kicked him out. His father had died, and his mother married another man. He had heard about Jerusalem from the prayers so he wanted to come. He was seventeen by the time he got here. He decided to learn to be a tailor and he and his brother came to Israel.

At first, my father was working very hard all day. He didn't know to write and read. He wanted his daughter to be educated. He always sent me to the library to read. If I wanted to play he sent me to the library. Because I read many books I was more advanced than the other students.

My mother's family is seven generations in Jerusalem. I was born in Jerusalem; I feel every bone in my body is like the stones of Jerusalem. I am whole with the country. I am very patriotic. Even though my sister in Los Angeles wanted me to come to live with her, I never thought to leave, even though there are tough times here. This is where I was born and it seems I will die here.

When I was born, my mother ran away from my father. She couldn't stand his being jealous. I was a few years in an orphanage. When I was five he got married again and took me home. It was after the 1948 War.

I was raised by a step-mother from Bulgaria who didn't know Hebrew. My sister was like a mother to me. My father was very frightening. When he got angry he hit my sister. She didn't accept anything he wanted her to do, but I was the good one. I suffered because I wanted to please my father. My sister wanted her freedom. If she went to a birthday party against his wishes when she came home he hit her. For many years I didn't talk to him. When I was about eighteen my sister insisted that I go to a psychologist. Later on, I took many courses and read books and did the Landmark Education Forum for a few years and slowly repaired myself to bring me to who I am now.

I wanted to be a kindergarten teacher. But after my sister went to do this I decided to do something different. When I was in the army, I met a woman soldier who did the beautiful things in the army. In the army I took an advanced art course so that as soon as I finished the army I was accepted in Bezalel. Because my parents didn't support my decision to be a graphic designer, I felt all the time that I was not good enough, even though I was a very good teacher.

When my daughter died it was a big shock. She committed suicide while in the army. And I thought I was the best mother I could be. That made me think and ask many questions. The main question was how I continue my life, so I started looking for things that really interested me and made me happy. I found that yoga made a good feeling for me, to be closer to my body and my soul together, so I thought maybe I could do it for others.

I always liked to dance. My father didn't want me to. He thought it was a shame for a woman to dance — all those years I felt my body missed the chance to express itself. It was too late to start as a professional dancer so I used the yoga to make the connection to myself. Now as a good yoga teacher I found the way to the heart of the people and not only to their body. I bring to the lessons all my experience and wisdom of life. This makes me happy. When I was a graphic designer I worked with paper, printing machines and computers and now I am working with people.

I found that when you earn money and you are in good terms in your life, you have to volunteer and give to others. I volunteer and give my experience as a yoga teacher for a mentally wounded soldier, or people who are mentally sick. It's very important for me to do this. Today I am working with Holocaust survivors and people who have had a stroke.

It seems that these days each country has some problem and as a Zionist I see living here in Israel is the best life for me to live.

Abe Rosenfeld

Berlin, 1936

ABE WAS THE CHAIRMAN OF THE INTERNATIONAL GRAPHIC DESIGN ASSOCIATION AND hosted a conference in Israel. My friend Rachel, a graphic designer, (see Rachel Porat) was teaching computer-aided design at the architecture school where I was teaching English. She met Abe at a graphic design show, and I got to know how warm and welcoming he is through her. We have all had many good times together for lunches, parties, skiing, and in the desert.

I spoke with Abe in their light and airy apartment in Holon, across from the Cultural Center.

Being in Israel was the dream of my parents. My father was the chairman of the Zionist organization in Berlin and his ambition was to get to Palestine. My mother, with me in her arms, was arrested by the Gestapo. My father went to the police station to ask what happened. The policeman, a friend, told him that my mother and I were going to be deported to Poland. The first group that had been deported was not let in at night. The policeman then advised him, "Go home and get a suitcase and return in the morning. But whatever you do is your business." My father responded, "It's just before Christmas, can I wait for all the business?" "No. In a month when you're in another country you will hear about the plans I have here in my drawer." A month later was Kristallnacht.

When my father returned to the house, he took my brother and sister, gave the keys to our neighbor, and we escaped to the border. A guide brought us all to Italy, to Bari, where there was a ship that was supposed to go to Palestine. They were just about to leave when we screamed for their attention. A sailor heard us and dropped a ladder for us so we could get on the boat. My father had permission from the British Mandate with a certificate from the British Embassy in Berlin, for at that time no Jews could get in. We got to Palestine with nothing — all remained in Berlin. Our neighbor sent some stuff to us.

Later we found out that the clerk in the department of the embassy, Mr. Polly, was a spy who was later killed in Norway. Israel later granted him Righteous Among the Nations.

My mother got reparations every month after the war. My father had tried to open a business but it was not a success. He never returned to what he was in Germany. He never recovered from this. A year and half ago the city of Berlin invited me to visit the city. I saw my old house. They were very cordial and I was the guest of the *Bundestat*.

Mother was from a small town in Poland, Skiernewice, between Warsaw and Lodz. I visited. It is near where Chopin was born. And my father from Warsaw.

I really grew up on the beaches of Tel Aviv. We spoke German at home but as I was two when we came I learned Hebrew. I lived on the streets and on the beach, I ran away from school. No one cared. I grew up by myself. From time to time, my mother complained that I disappeared. It was a joke in the family. Actually, my brother and sister were in the underground at the time. My brother was arrested by the British and put in jail. My sister was on one of the posters that The Haganah put out.

I went to school — but most of the time I was on the run. I finished school, of course. Once I had to read an essay from my notebook, I just made it up. The teacher wanted to display it on the board but there was nothing to show. My art teacher and gymnastic teacher liked me. I lived as it came. No planning.

We lived at 117 Dizengoff where Café Kasit was. That was another place where I spent time. I met all the great people of Israel there, like Professor Chaim Weitzman who used to sit there. I learned to play chess from Abraham Shlonksy and Natan Alterman from time to time. One night I heard Danny Kaye singing — he was in the café. I ran out in my pajamas. He took me on his lap. I met many politicians and actors there. My family had started a custom shirt business - we made them at home, for Ben Gurion and Yitsak Sadeh. During the Independence Day parade I saw the tank commanders salute Yitzhak Sadeh. It was an emotional moment for me.

Ben Gurion was living nearby. The guard at his house called me over. "Paula (Ben Gurion's wife) wants to ask you something." She gave me some money to get him some butter on Ben Yehuda Street. At that time there was rationing. When I went to the Tnuva dairy store and told the shopkeeper the butter was for BG, he sent me away. I came back with Ben Gurion's ration book so he gave the butter to me.

One time when I was in the Scouts I had to go out collecting money for the orphans from Tehran. We debated whether to knock on Ben Gurion's door. As we waited outside, he opened the door. He invited us in and asked if we knew who those children were. Only then did he give us money and we put the *Paid* sticker on his door.

My biggest setback was when I went into the army. I wanted to be in the navy. At that time they didn't ask you — they just put me in a tank. Now my grandson is in the navy doing what I wanted.

I like what I do, I like what I did. After the army I got married and went to the Pratt Institute in New York to study design. And then I worked in the US for ten years, and even became a citizen. After I divorced, my ex-wife and two daughters returned to Israel, so I came back. I remarried, had another son, and now have seven grandchildren.

I remember when Israel became a state. The UN announcement was broadcast on a loudspeaker in Kikar David and we listened as each government voted in favor. That was a great day. I was standing near Dizengoff's house when Ben Gurion read the Declaration of Independence on November 29, 1947. Another memory was when I was Chairman of the International Design Congress; doing the opening ceremony was very exciting.

I like living in Israel, especially in Tel Aviv, where I have lived most of the time since 1938, but today Tel Aviv is so expensive that I moved to the city of Holon, which is pretty good to me.

I have lived for the past fifteen years with my girlfriend, Rachel. I am still working as a graphic designer. I also examine and write the computer design exams for high-school students. I volunteer. Right now I am a member of the selection committee for Israel's outstanding workers. Usually the ones I recommend get the prize. This is the sixth year of my candidates!

I'm alive and kicking! No hysterical goal. Just to live in peace.

Liora Loewenstein, MA
Buenos Aires, 1956

As we were both involved in cross-cultural training, a big need in those days for Israelis doing business abroad, we found many common interests. Liora, who also worked as a managing consultant for law firms, asked me to conduct a workshop for lawyers and I totally screwed up. She had to rescue me. I hope she forgave me.

I attended a super weekend birthday celebration she organized when she lived in the Galilee, in Hararit. On another visit she and I went for a ramble to the local Arab villages with not one shekel in our pocket and managed to have a fresh pita and a coffee. I accompanied her with a group of lawyers to visit lawyers in Gaza. With her organizational skills, she and Maya made a fantastic birthday celebration for me in the desert, with a busload of friends.

I was born in Buenos Aires and arrived to Israel as a student in Tel Aviv University almost four decades ago. My sister, Diana, and her husband, Yossi, live in Buenos Aires. She and her husband lived in Israel for three years but they left; and now two of their three children live here. Many of my sixteen cousins come to visit Israel from time to time and we are connected by Facebook.

I grew up in Buenos Aires. It was an upper middle class neighborhood, very central, near the subway — easy to get everywhere, near the botanical gardens that I visited very often. There was no Jewish community in the neighborhood. We lived in a big building with three elevators and a big parking area. We knew one Jewish family in the building. I attended the best secondary school in the country and I enjoyed good teachers and friends. I also attended the Jewish school and the youth movement. I made aliya, interrupting my studies at Buenos Aires University because of the hard times there during the military dictatorship.

Both my parents came from Poland — they came with their parents; they were very young. My grandfather told me they wanted to go the US, but as one of his best friends came to Argentina, he decided to join him. He came without his family and after getting a little established he brought the family. They didn't know a word of Spanish — they spoke Yiddish. They came from the shtetl. There was a big Jewish community in Buenos Aires. They came before the war, I think it was 1932. They were looking for another life away from anti-Semitism. The shtetl where my mother came from was near the border to Russia. During the war it became Russian.

After thirty years, my mother needed an Argentinean passport. They asked her for her birth certificate so she went to the Polish embassy but it was no longer Poland where she came from; it was in Russia, and the Russian embassy said it was Poland then. So she couldn't leave Argentina! My mother has a Yiddish name, Menicha. In Hebrew it is *menucha*, to rest. When she came by ship to Argentina she went to the Hotel de Immigrantes — someone who wrote her name couldn't understand so he wrote her name Mercedes — a very goy name! It was not easy for them to start a life in Argentina.

In Poland, my father's father was a tailor. In Argentina he opened a studio for men's clothing. At the time, many immigrants were coming and there was a flourishing of business people who needed suits. My father's brothers and he developed the business and were selling. Not Armani, but they were selling.

My father was one of six children — he came with two brothers and three sisters. And on the side of my mother they were four children. They told us stories about these times. My father died in 1978 and my mother made aliya in 1983. Now she is ninety years old

I got a Jewish education, a Zionist education in Argentina. I was active in the Zionist movement. But I arrived earlier than I planned because of the political situation there in 1975-76. I decided to come in the middle of my studies, and thought to return after one or two years. But I married and here we are! I was so sure I would marry and have a big family — I thought about four or five kids. I thought I will have an academic job — something connected to society and smart people! And to have an interesting life professionally.

I studied at Tel Aviv University for the first and second degree. I started a PhD but I didn't finish it. I studied organizational behavior and I am a member of the Israeli Organization of Organizational Development. My first career was in educational consulting. I taught also at TAU for a special program for people coming from South America.

I live now in Tel Aviv. Before, I lived in Herzeliya, Kfar Shmariyahu and in a lovely place in the Galilee, Hararit. I have two sons, Amichay, who is a lawyer and entrepreneur and Michael, a software engineer, and two lovely future daughters-in-law, Tamar and Danielle. I take care of my beloved mother. I have very good friends and — I have someone in my life called Isi who is a doctor.

I work as a managing consultant in KeyPeople. We specialize in business development for law firms in the private and public sectors and legal organizations, dealing with mergers, partnerships, and organizational consulting services for the legal profession. I developed a career and a profession and worked doing what I like to do. To write the book was very good. It has sold very well.

Liora wrote a book for lawyers about how to manage their practice.

We need to change something in this country so that it will be possible to live here for the next generation. We need to build a better place and a pluralistic country. For this purpose I am founder and active in a new group KANAL (KAN NIRTZE LIHIOT=WE WANT TO LIVE). The aim of this group is to stop the invasion of the *haredim* (ultra-religious) population to every city in Israel. The secular population has been excluded from many important decisions of our life. Unlike the religious, the secular are poorly organized, they have no religious teachers, and they do not receive instructions and guidance. However, when provoked, when forced to accept customs, institutions, traditions or neighbors against their will, they may wake up, organize.

I have developed intense and intimate friendships that during the years we feel more close and pass through our lives together, sharing good and bad moments. I think I also made a good decision to move to Tel Aviv after many years of hesitation. Living here there are many good and bad things. I feel totally part of this country. It is a very changing country, developing more and more. It is very difficult to make a living and I am very pessimistic about conflict with our neighbors. And there are many difficult people you have to cope with every day.

In the beginning, it was very hard to adapt myself to Israel. My divorce was also very hard. Fifteen years ago I was very ill and I thought I was going to die. The moment I recovered I promised myself to do every day something that will make me happy and I will celebrate every year my birthday as Life is a Gift.

Edna Mann, MA
Beer Sheva, 1958

EDNA WAS WELCOMING NEWCOMERS WHEN I MOVED INTO THE ABSORPTION CENTER IN *Beer Sheva. As it was Purim, she took me to a costume party. She was most hospitable and open-hearted. She still is! We went to the Arad all-night music festival, where I first heard Mati Caspi, and we watched a hot-air balloon rally just outside of Arad.*

Since that time, I have seen Edna progress in her profession to become a full-time psychologist, working for the municipality of Tel Aviv, attending to private patients, and dealing with children who suffer trauma from missile attacks. After I moved to a new apartment without a refrigerator, I came home from a weekend to find one she had installed! And when she moved from her small apartment in Basel to be with her new husband, I was first in line for this choice spot and got the family rate. She produced a son who has much of her charm. For many years she has studied meditation and the curing powers of Buddhism.

I hope we continue our adventures in the desert and commentary on life here.

Right now I feel like I was in a big storm that dumped me and now I must find my balance. I must do all that is necessary to clear up things from my divorce. I must also balance my son. And recently I thought that I would like to be a writer. I want to write a book interweaving the professional with the personal using my understandings of my studies about trauma to deal with my personal storms through my professional and philosophical understandings.

I just got divorced from my husband after ten years of suffering. I have a new love. I am working as a psychologist and developing my clinic, working with families, kids, and adolescents, but mainly with post-traumatic victims of terror attacks.

I was born here in Israel. But there was a time when I was married and lived in the United States. I chose to come back because I felt strongly attached to Israeli life and culture. There is a major significance to the songs of Israel. When I lived in the States, I took dozens of tapes with me. On one vacation from the States, I went to Israel and friends took me to Festival Arad. For the whole three days I heard Israeli music and felt how I am attached to the land and the history. I realized I had no other place where I belonged. That was when I confronted my husband, who was in the US, about our plan to come back to Israel. At first he had thought he would, but then he realized it was not a place for him. He insisted that we stay in the US as he had a teaching position at the university in Williamsburg, Virginia. He thought he would never be able to adjust to Israeli culture. And I thought I would never be able to give up my Israeli roots. I feel part of the culture and love the people and the way we interact.

I grew up in Beer Sheva and went to regular schools. I used to live on Freud Street and then became a psychologist — it was my destiny! My relationship to my grandmother was very precious to me. She was a very fine and intelligent person who shared her wisdom with me. She was very warm-hearted. I could feel loved by her. When I grew up I was the one who took care of her. The family gets together with good food and an atmosphere of caring for each other.

My father is from Fez, Morocco and my mother is from Tunisia. They speak French at home. They had been here about eight years before I was born so my first language was Hebrew. My father was a soldier in the War of Independence. As a Moroccan, he was not respected by other soldiers and had to prove that he was qualified. He saved the lives of his troop. He was honored by Chaim Weizman, the president at the time. The uncle of my father came by boat during the Mandate. He came from Morocco and was caught by the British and was sent to Cyprus. When he was released, he came back and joined the Palmach. In 1948, his kibbutz was attacked by Arabs and later he died. For sixty years no one knew where his grave was on Har Hertzl, until it was recently discovered and has been acknowledged that there were also Moroccans who came and were part of the history.

My parents used to tell me the history of the family. People who emigrated from North Africa felt deprived. They wanted me to succeed and do what they could not do for themselves. My parents, who are eighty, are still working because they need to help us.

When I was in eighth grade, one of my teachers told my parents that I was very successful in my psychometric exam, both verbal and manual. She wanted to send me to vocational school to get a profession faster than if I were on the academic track. I remember how my parents were offended. We had to convince the school that I could go on the academic track. At that time in Israel, kids who were not Ashkenazi were not sent to academia. I had to work hard to pave my way in spite of the prevalent norms. Being in the Scouts had an input for me. Walking the land — singing together. The whole class was sent to help to the kibbutz to help with the harvest.

I remember wishing that I would be successful with animals or with people, as a social worker or anthropologist. I knew I would work with the behavior of animals or people.

All my life was full of setbacks. I had to struggle. When I was in my studies of behavioral sciences I got 79.9 instead of 80. I was told I could not continue but I insisted that I can. I have had problems with my marriages! I invested in my studies in human relationships but in my personal life I was not so successful in choosing or in protecting myself.

I have been caring for and treating other people with their sufferings. I feel grateful that they give trust in me and in return I could help them live their life in a more joyful way. I think I have touched the lives of many people.

I need to survive! I feel that there is a continuous threat in the lives of people regarding the security situation. It seems like the government or the leaders don't care much for individual people whose basic needs must be supported. I work hard, but I will have to work harder in the future to support my child and my life. My new friend was fired from his work without the proper payments. People try to cheat each other. There is not enough justice, norms, or rules that can support regular people to live a normal life. Each one has to be on guard about the salary statement and conditions and to fight for what is due them.

We have a Zionist government but are held by the balls by the Religious. My son has to be in the army but the Religious don't think they have to share the load. Instead of helping, they are a heavy load with their dozens of children.

I feel I have a heavy load, even if I don't think of it every day. The nuclear threat from Iran, the Arab Spring — nobody knows what will happen. The government is in the hands of five or six rich families, while taking more and more tax from working people.

As I am getting to the age of fifty-five and the middle of my life, I wish for myself to be more at peace, instead of struggling and still paving my way. I try to live my life as if I had all that I wished for. I know at the back of my head it is somewhat naïve and I must be very alert and plan life and work in a way that I will be satisfied and stable.

Stanley Rubenstein
Staten Island, New York, 1942

I GOT TIRED OF BOUNCING AROUND ON A MOUNTAIN BIKE. A FRIEND AND I ORGANIZED A road bike trip to Riccioni, where we stayed in a bike hotel and rode every day up the mountains and to San Marino. Two days on a man's racing bike made me decide I must renovate my own road bike. I mailed my bike to Bob, the specialist at Elliot Bay Cycles in Seattle, for him to renovate it, flew there, rode for a few days with him and another friend and brought the renewed bike home.

In the meantime, I was looking around for someone to go touring with. Stanley was looking around, as his kids had given him a bike for his birthday. We had a coffee. This was a really good man! We met for a ride and have been riding together ever since.

The first time I came to Israel was because my father had been here on a business trip and was very excited about the country and wanted each of his three children to come. I spent a summer on a kibbutz and met a local young woman. After we married, we lived in New York for a few years. Then I came here in 1971. At that time in the US things were not so good; there was rampant racism in the South, Martin Luther King and Robert Kennedy had been assassinated, hundreds of people my age were being killed every week in Vietnam, students were mowed down on the campus at Kent State University, protestors faced brutal police violence at the Democratic Convention in Chicago, and Richard Nixon and Spiro Agnew were elected to lead the United States of America; Israel looked like a place with a bright future based on social justice and equality.

But it hasn't worked out that way. I was quite naïve. I wasn't a Zionist. I looked at this move as an adventure, and didn't think I would be here for the rest of my life. But I guess it is the rest of my life.

I grew up in Staten Island. I went to the public schools and had a regular 1950s childhood. I was probably like any other kid growing up in New York, like Paul Simon, or Art Garfunkel. It was the center of the world, undisputed! Even though I didn't pay too much attention to school, I got a good education. Each year I got more interested, especially when I went to college. I went to Hobart College, a small liberal arts college in upstate New York. It was an idyllic setting; we didn't have to worry about anything, except the weather. You could become immersed in classes and the academic life. I played tennis, travelled to nearby colleges as a member of the fencing team, and did a lot of skiing on the winter weekends.

My mother was born in Brooklyn, 1917. My father was born in Cleveland, 1913. My maternal grandfather was also born in America, on a farm in Massachusetts. They must have been from Germany with the name Holtz and never heard another language other than English. My paternal grandfather was from what is now Belarus and he came to America in 1905. He was a scribe, but I don't know how he made a living in America. After five years, he had enough money to bring his wife and the rest of his family to America and they moved to Cleveland. They spoke Yiddish. My parents lived through difficult times when they were young — the depression, World War II, and then they enjoyed the tremendous prosperity of America in 1950-80.

I never had a mentor or a guiding figure. I had to strike out on my own and figure for myself as I went along; some success and not a few setbacks. At Raquette Lake summer camp for fifteen summers, I learned about getting along with other people, following the rules, respecting the environment, about working hard and not quitting, especially on the camping trips. The training I had was just part of being in America. My parents didn't tell me to be a doctor or a lawyer. After graduating from Hobart I had to choose between going into the Reserve Officers Training program or to volunteer for the Peace Corps. I chose the Peace Corps. When I came back after three years in Malawi, I am sure my parents were not overjoyed when I told them I was going to Israel.

I had never really considered it. I was just growing up in America. People went to work. At that age I was impressed with sports people! Jackie Robinson, Mickey Mantle, Willie Mays. Eisenhower was President; he was like a relic from bygone days. Communications were not like they are today. Most of the reports in the newspaper were about politics, politicians, and sports people. I figured I'd finish high school, go to a good college, get a job and enjoy the upper middle class life that prevailed in America at the time. The turbulence of the 1960s changed all that.

I never was a great sportsman, even though I read the sports pages every day. So I had to settle for what Grantland Rice said, "It's not who wins the game but how the game is played." I had aspirations but nothing came of them, I didn't have any talent. I wasn't such a great student, either. I didn't get any awards in summer camp. I didn't get into the college of my choice and I never worked my way up the corporate ladder.

When I arrived in Israel, I was totally unprepared. I spoke no Hebrew; I didn't have pals from school or the army to help me get a job. I had to make my own way without help. For many years I lived on the Israeli overdraft, taking one loan after another to stay afloat. In the old days you could do this, as the banks were more lenient.

I don't know what would have happened if I had stayed in the US. I suppose Israel didn't pan out the way I expected. I didn't expect to be a colonialist, but that has been the situation for the last forty years.

I introduced skiing to a lot of kids in Israel who wouldn't have gotten into it. It played an important role in their lives, and gave them experiences at a different level than the usual life for young-sters here.

I tried to be good to my own three kids and tried to give them the tools so that they would able to manage in their lives, without me being too overbearing.

I'm concerned about the environment everywhere. It's the next big change that affects everyone. I'm considering going back to school to get a degree in this field so I can work and contribute.

I am not suffering, although I can't say my situation is typical, since I have chosen not to conform to the Israeli mode and mentality. I regret that the situation in Israel is so far from what I had originally anticipated. I hope it is OK to be hopeful about the future but it is far from certain.

The education system has achieved its aim of separating the differ-ent sectors of society — religious and secular, creating a fragmented so-ciety instead of one where everyone respects their fellow countrymen. I am not comfortable living in a place where the government tramples on the rights of our neighbors, treating them with scorn and humiliation. With all the posturing about being a Jewish Nation, we have forgotten that the essence of this would be to treat our neighbors as ourselves.

The greatest now is to go biking with Lori! And going off on great bike trips! One trip, riding through Umbria, we didn't know where we were going to spend the night but it worked out — we found a nice hotel at the top of the mountain.

I live in Caesarea; I'm sixty-eight years old. I don't work full time anymore. I am lucky to be living with Lori; she makes every day better for me.

Amos Yoran

Tel Aviv, 1946

A MUTUAL FRIEND INTRODUCED AMOS WHEN I WAS FIRST HERE. I ADMIRED HIS ANALYT-ical thinking, the books in his library, and his gentle manner. He helped me to get on the computer! And got my printer going so that I could submit a proposal. He was tech support for a long time. We both enjoyed the pleasures of Provence and drank to it. We swam in the sea from Tel Aviv past the breakwater from Bograshov beach to Gordon beach. When I had life-threatening pneumonia, Amos brought life-sustaining potato salad. We have celebrated many summer solstice festivities. As I type right now, my keyboard is set up with his board-in-a-drawer arrangement. We lived near each other in Tel Aviv and now are both a bit north. For the interview, we sat in the studio Amos built in his backyard.

How to make enough money to survive ! That's my burning issue.

Seriously: How to stop the crazy destruction of the planet, how to slow down, and hopefully reverse it. I have been asked to give a lecture to the WIZO college community entitled "Biosphere from the Perspective of Architecture." I actually named it "Biosphere 1, 2, 3." Biosphere 1 refers to that thin layer enveloping Earth, where life exists, that thin envelope, half a kilometer into the earth and 3-4 kilometers above. That little crust is all we have that has life in it. Biosphere 2 is a project in Arizona created in the late 80s. It is a huge, 15-acre enclosed structure modeled after the biosphere, to emulate our ability to create a mini working model of the real thing. Two years of testing it proved we still don't have enough knowledge to create a micro world. Biosphere 3 is where we are right now in affecting our world and where we're heading. These are my pressing issues; how to disseminate the knowledge to and for the general public and for professionals to keep our world sustainable for mankind. If I want to practice my profession I have to believe there is way to convince societies to change their ways and stop this crazy race.

I was born here in Israel. When I was five, my parents joined the Israeli foreign office and were sent to Europe representing the newborn State in the early '50s. We lived in Yugoslavia, and then we moved to Holland. My father was the Israeli ambassador to Holland in the mid-50s. We then returned to Israel, so I spent my early youth, high-school period, and military service here. Subsequently, I enrolled at the Technion to study architecture.

I spent more than a decade in the States while studying and doing research and had no plans to return. In the late '80s my mother became ill, and as an only child I returned to do what was necessary. I couldn't just leave her. My wife wasn't interested in coming back to Israel. So I stayed and this caused my family to break up. My wife stayed in the States with our daughter and I got involved in developing eco technologies in Israel. That's when I met Lori, in 1989.

My dad came from a family in Warsaw, Poland. As a child, he started his education in a typical Jewish *heder*, but was soon captivated by the Zionist movement, and left the religious environment of his family. He came to Palestine when he was eighteen or nineteen and worked in building construction, leaving his family in Poland. In his mid-twenties he decided to pursue an education and left for Europe to study law at the University of Brussels. He took a PhD in law and moved to Paris, and then to London. He wanted to have a profession. Eventually, he returned to Palestine in the late '30s to practice law and participate in the Jewish resistance, the Haganah. His true passion was not to be a lawyer but to have the opportunity to deal with law in a more theoretical way. So he left the attorney's office and he became a judge. The year the State of Israel was established he was asked by the Foreign Office to join Israel's first cadre of diplomats as he was something of a scholar with international experience and had a good command of several languages. After seven years in the foreign office, he returned to Israel to the judicial court and served as a judge for the rest of his life.

My mom was a lively young lady with a liberal education in Berlin of the early '30s. She got interested in photography and went to study with Lotte Yakobi, a leading photographer at the time, who later left for the States in time to escape the Nazi regime. My mother became quite an able photographer. In 1933 the Israeli Habima theater group came to Berlin. My mother met with them and was completely entranced by their bohemian character and Zionist spirit. They convinced her to join them and move to Palestine. She emigrated to Tel Aviv and joined the very colorful bohemian life of small Tel Aviv of the '30s. She took some marvelous photos of actors and artists.

My parents met in Tel Aviv; I think it was 1939 or 40.

I can't think of a single dominant personality who shaped my life. It was the exposure to different cultures as a child. I learned several languages, and met children from all over; children of other diplomats, Canadian, Norwegian, Pakistani, Indian, English, American, Dutch, and others. It shaped my life in knowing that we are all human beings, we are all friends. Race is an irrelevant issue. Other cultures are acknowledged and respected. That we live here with Arabs is made into a big problem. For me it was never an issue. I have friends in Furiedis, a neighboring Arab village. They invite me to join events. They don't regard me as a Jew from another town; they regard me as a friend. My early exposure to the variety of different human beings and different nationalities proved to me that relationships can work very well.

My father didn't insist on me following in his professional footsteps. I chose to be an architect because I felt I could do something worthy. I could easily have become a biologist – an area I had great interest in.

At that time I was very interested in biology. I created an impressive collection of dried plants and had all kinds of animals: rabbits, lizards, turtles, pigeons, roosters, and tropical fish. In the work I am doing now, there is a sort of marriage between the living world and the built world. My effort is to formulate a new balance between them.

I guess my most serious setback is a type of mental disorder, known as bi-polar mood disorder. It has disabled me from time to time. I'm on meds now.

The event that probably affected my life most was when I had to return from the States to take care of my mother and did not return to my family after a short while to save my marriage. Despite my efforts, my mother refused to move to the States. She said, "I came to live in Israel, I will not leave this country." When she couldn't handle things by herself, rather than leaving her with a caretaker or in a home, I felt I had to take care of her. Perhaps I should have done it differently.

To the cat: Arthur, can you say what good things I've done?

I don't see anything exceptional. Definitely not compared with what I would have liked to have achieved. Fostering community aware-ness, encouraging people to join and find value in contributing to a common goal; not in the sense of socialism but in the sense of finding satisfaction in sharing experiences.

My situation now is I'm an architect, specializing in sustainable architecture. I lecture at two colleges, live in Binyamina with a partner and we have a young son six years old. I am divorced, with a daughter from my first marriage who is now thirty-three and married with a baby living in Boston.

I am not very happy living in Israel. I am very critical of what Israeli society has become; the values, its socio-economic system. Although I am sure there are places that are much worse and I can't tell you there is another place where I would rather be. Professionally, I am not yet where I would like to be.

Some of this is because of Israel. It's a close-knit society; you have to know people to get ahead. In a larger environment one would probably have an opportunity to develop. Still, I have hopes and I am not resigned to my situation, I am pursuing other avenues. I am not young, and some people retire at my age, but I don't feel like retiring and feel that there are still worthwhile goals to pursue. There are still many promises to keep, to paraphrase Robert Frost.

Heeli Chaya Schechter
Santa Monica, 1981

HEELI IS THE COORDINATOR FOR THE ARCHEOLOGY LECTURE GROUP THAT I ATTEND *weekly at Tel Aviv University. She is responsible for the content, choosing and engaging the speakers, and all the administrative details. She does this with great knowledge, charm, and efficiency. What style!*

My Israeli mother married an American. They met on a kibbutz during the Yom Kippur War. And they went to California. He was a welder in the early '80s and my mother was an assistant to a gynecologist. Just before my sister was born, we came back to Israel to my mother's kibbutz, Kibbutz Tzor'a. This is home for me. So I grew up there, near Bet Shemesh. I am the oldest of three sisters and have memories of my sisters, rolling around and laughing with them. I now go every other weekend to visit my parents and my grandmother.

I lived in Marin County for three years after the army. A girl came to our kibbutz and we became friends and when she went back to California she invited me to her wedding. She lived in Marin so I went there and was a waitress — in the "dining business." I applied to Stanford, but I didn't have the SATs. I was in a relationship, engaged, and then I broke it off. But I don't regret it. I have been back here for six years.

I wanted to come back to study archeology. What better place to study archeology than in Israel, where every rock you pick up is ancient or if you throw it to the ground it hits something ancient?

My mother is from that kibbutz. Her mother is from Riga and her father was from Lithuania. My grandmother's parents were Hebrew teachers and built a school for the workers in Riga. They came to Israel in 1935 when she was six. My grandfather was from Lithuania. They were wood mill owners and in 1917 the mill was nationalized so they left and missed the Holocaust by going to the United States and South Africa. My grandfather was born in Israel, on Kibbutz Giv'at HaShlosha, in 1927. When he was a year and a half, his mother had a run-in with the other folks on the kibbutz so she took him and they went to South Africa. My father is an American from New Jersey. His parents died when he was very young. I didn't know them. I am named after his mother. She was very active in Jewish Women's Clubs. She helped refugees settle in the area. His father owned a clothing store.

My parents shaped my sisters' and my life. In the '80s all the gadgets began — only then did we have TV on the kibbutz. We were always outdoors, there was nothing to worry about as there were no strangers and no cars. I wanted to be alone just like the other kids. We were not brought up in the children's house. Even my mother slept at home in her childhood. There were lots of young people and other people around so we enjoyed them and learned how to deal with people not from our immediate group.

I had a sense of self-achievement. I was confident that I would do something great! Not now — feeling very comfortable with myself and being an achiever.

The setbacks I've faced were things that were my fault — not as if there was a war. I wanted to be a pilot. It was already OK at my age. However, I was injured during the tests. They gave me a chance to heal for a day and come back. But I didn't. I am still disappointed about this. My mother told me that for me things usually come easily, so if I need to make a lot of effort, I don't. I wanted to be a pilot for the prestige, to do something that mattered. I should have turned around and walked back to try for a different profile in the army.

Some things I did well. I volunteered after high school before the army, guiding hikes "to love the country with your feet." It's important. I taught in the local school and organized some of the activities. Some of the parents weren't there and the children felt neglected. No one was at home because the parents worked hard. So I did this after school, it was good for them.

Now I am not involved.

Now I am an MA student at Tel Aviv University. I must finish my thesis in the next month or so. I have been living with my partner for the last six years on his kibbutz, Kibbutz Hatzor, near Ashdod. We are quite happy there. My partner is a translator. He lived in Canada from the age of six to twelve, the best years to learn a language — but he is completely Israeli. He has a good job that pays reasonably in a law firm. They work together and have broad exposure to many disciplines, such as legal and medical. We don't have any children. We drive our beat-up car to the train station in Ashdod, go do our thing, and come back. I like living in the kibbutz, it's fine. We pay communal fees, but I don't participate much. I like that. We support things like having the gym open every Wednesday evening so that the kids can play.

It's hard to live here in Israel. We are underpaid, but it's hard other places, too. There is no money in archeology, but I chose it. I don't blame Israel for my financial situation.

I don't have many burning issues. This is out of choice, even though I live on a left-wing kibbutz. My parents are left-wing and I remember instructions for demonstrations if I got lost from when I was five or six: "Wait at the corner of Arlozorov and Ibn Gvriol!" I was in a left-wing youth movement. I was brought up to take a stand and make a difference. But now I just want to live peacefully and live a simple, comfortable life. I don't want to fight for anything. Not for me and not for everyone else. I try not to be involved. This probably means I am looked down on by other Israelis. My parents shaped me to be pro-active but also they shaped me not to take what they told me in stone. They have changed — their world has changed. The kibbutz has fallen apart. They are not fighting either.

Now I am studying — producing knowledge. I get an assembly of artifacts from excavations and I create a data sheet. After I have categories, I try to compare the data to create a picture. For instance, I studied an obsidian assemblage from the site of Ha'goshrim. There is no obsidian here in Israel; it had to come from somewhere. That means there was trade and international contact. They were hording, or trading — all the details lead to conclusions. Other people do research and we compare and describe.

I don't know if I want to stay in academia. It is a big struggle. It is always a battle for budget or time. The University considers us grunt workers.

One of the good things that I have done, I can say, is managing this group!

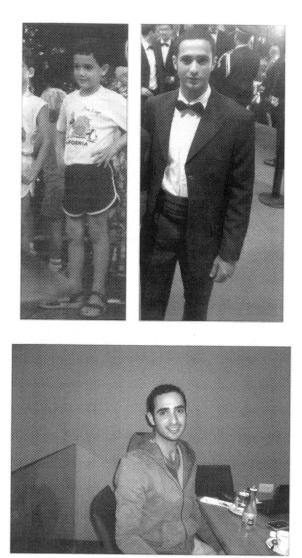

Daniel Matalon

Tel Aviv, 1982

I WAS HAVING LUNCH IN ZOZOBRA, A CASUAL ASIAN RESTAURANT WITH SHARED TABLES, when someone at our table forgot his cell phone on the table. Daniel was sitting across the table and tried to run after the guy to give it to him. When we started our conversation I realized I had found a treasure! We arranged for an interview some days later in Tel Aviv.

I recently came back to Israel after working out of the country in China and Hong Kong for three years. I wanted to study in the East. I was very curious about it. It was very challenging. It was an enigma for me. I didn't know anyone who had done this. My brother lives in Los Angeles. I also wanted to do something on my own. I was in Beijing. I just fell in love. My experience was amazing. Even though you communicate you can never be Chinese, even after thirty years, not like here, not in China. Once you learn the language you find out they are very nice and very warm. I wanted to learn from them and get into their life.

My family was very business-oriented. My family distributes films and owns cinemas. I wanted not to buy from China but to send something to China. After one year, I came back to finish my BA and then to Hong Kong to open a business. It is very welcoming to business in terms of taxes, and so on. But it is very expensive. I went with my girlfriend.

I worked in Macao selling cosmetics. Every morning it was two, three hours each way by boat. Then I decided to open something on my own. I found a guy who gave me a license for some enhancement products for men, among other things. I was fascinated how you sell. You need a call center and ads in the newspapers. And then there is the distribution. The most challenging part was selling — I had bikini girls for ads — but it was not possible to have this in the newspapers. So we used visuals of people kissing. The ads were about exercise and not sex.

When I published the first ad I sold about five hundred products in one day. It was the tops! I did this also in Taiwan. The Taiwanese are very open and warm — a very good experience. After two years I finished with my girlfriend. She was from Bosnia, and got tired of the weather at 91% humidity and wanted to go home. It's a crazy place but good for business as taxes are low. I had a lot of satisfaction living there for two years. I had a nice apartment. I wanted to do more, but after two years in the health industry with most of the products the same, most of the ingredients the same, this turned me off — I wanted to feel good about taking others' money.

I have been home almost a year. The *hevre* (long established group of friends) — the guys are something very important here. You are best friends and you spend all your time together. You have a lot of laughs and security. It's not like in other counties. This is more important than a wife! But you can't expand your point of view out of the group. Now I have found new books, interests, friends — after living abroad I don't need to be with my friends all the time. Staying home and reading a book is not something people do here — now it's different. I am more independent. I can allow myself not to see them all the time. When you grow up in such a group it's a different mentality.

In my group we used to be forty, now we are ten. If it is a birthday, we invite everyone but not on a daily basis. I am more focused. I think it is because I lived abroad. My buddies are not married, but one is engaged. One is unhappy and likes to complain. You can easily be drawn into bad relationships. I can say what I want now, but once I am with the group, it is totally different.

It looks boring to go with the crowd. From every bad experience I got stronger. I ask more questions about every new idea. I learned that not every great idea is good. Sometimes it doesn't fit your character or it won't make money. In business, I don't count on everybody. You have to write it down and see if people are serious. I used to be more enthusiastic and had big ideas. Now I see what is more suitable. It has to be genuine.

My older brother is an inspiration for me. He's a genius. He has a production company in LA. I knew if I wanted to do something I would have to be on my own. My parents took me back and it was nice for them because my two brothers were away.

I am now waiting for my next job with a clean tech company. In a small company you can do more, have more freedom. You are not tied to a job description. Two months ago, the company was in financial trouble and folded and they had to let me go. Now I am in clean tech — in solar. Waiting to get to work.

I have been studying meditation for seven years with a physics professor. I started in the army. I don't know how I got into this. Actually there is nothing to learn. Sometimes I think I know and sometimes I don't know. There is nothing more to it than to be aware. This is a kind of freedom, more than money and more than a woman. It's interesting because we try to find ourselves, to be more of ourselves. The most annoying thing about this study is that I don't like workshops. I don't like to share my personal life with everyone. All the mediations are the same. Buddhism is sort of a science of the soul, not a religion. Being practical and doing what you can do.

I was born here in Israel. My father's family is here for many generations, originally Spanish. My grandmother is from Germany. My father's mother is from Baghdad and my mother's mom is Greek and my mother's father is from Iraq.

I grew up in north Tel Aviv, not far from the sea. Very nice! We were probably the last generation to play outside. We were in the Scouts — super fun! We were outside, on trips, sleeping in tents. I went to a regular high school. It was special because it was very diverse. They brought people from south Tel Aviv. The integration worked somewhat, but many of them went to vocational schools. There were also people from the moshavim. We are still friends. To get to school I woke up at 8:00 but they woke up at 6:00. The time before school was busy until the last minute — talking! So much to do!

Many people shaped my life, but mostly my guide was my father. He is very humble. We are very warm tempered. He always shows me the other side. Even with Iran, he says to look at the other side. I am not the only guy in the story so I have to listen.

My mom also has influence. She knows how to push herself. She is like *pilpel* (hot pepper) I have those two elements: the humble and pushy together!!

My father is also the middle brother. My uncle went to Iran after the army. He was opening Columbia pictures in Iran and then in Europe, cinemas, video, TV, he did independent cinema. And also Puma business. I heard a lot of stories about business in my house.

My older brother is genius. He studied a week before and passed all the tests to become an accountant. If I have a business question he helps me how to look at it. It's good that he's far away because he could put a lot of pressure on me. We met in Dominican Republic, as my father is Counsel here for them. When we checked out of the hotel my brother wanted to know how come I don't know how much I paid a night!!!!

I had painful muscle spasms in Hong Kong and went to see a lot of doctors and spent a lot of money on this. After spending 100K on all kinds of meds I came back to Israel and found on the net that this is the result of repressed emotions. Stress! A breakthrough! That's why I am now in mediation. The book, MIND/BODY solved this problem in a few weeks. It was very helpful for me.

The day after I finished the army I flew to South America. The trip I did with my friends was liberating and fun all day long for eight months. We went from Argentina to Mexico to my brother in Los Angeles. We rented bikes, cars and we went places just because we saw it on the map. Every day was a new day — everyone was shining — genuine smiles.

I try to do good things on a daily basis: I listen to my friends, my family — that's what I do. I listen. I try to cater to their needs on a daily basis and help with decisions they are trying to make. They know the answer but I help them get to it. I try to pay attention to the people around me. I talk with my younger brother who just started a new semester.

I learned this from my father. He never said no. He listened and reasoned with me and I came to the conclusions. His father was very strict — if he did something wrong he had to stand straight for hours.

When I came back from Asia, Israel looked like a small town. Noisy, they miss consideration here. Good vibes on the street. In Hong Kong I went next door every day for a juice. It was the same salesman every day, but he never asked me how I am. Every time it was new. There was no communication.

Once I am here I have this warm feeling. It's amazing — I don't mind going abroad, but this is home. Networking for new ideas is amazing here. The atmosphere is great. And there are so many pools! I love to swim.

I have covered what my life is about.

Ephraim Zwanenberg
Den Bosh, Holland, 1927

Biking on a tour of the north of Israel, Ephraim was probably the oldest among us. But he was also one of the strongest! We toured the Golan on our mountain bikes, and we rode from Metula to Eilat, and around the Kinneret several times. He only feels whole on his bike, in spite of some difficulties.

I grew up in Den Bosh in Holland. I had a normal, middle-class childhood before the war. The mayor was living just around the corner. My father was a cattle dealer. He went to the surrounding villages to look for cows and brought the ones who were finished milking to the biggest cow market. I went to regular school and then college. I had mostly Jewish friends. Things were normal — we didn't feel anti-Semitism, maybe just children calling, "Dirty Jew."

In May, 1940 the Germans came. The first laws against the Jews began to appear, forbidding Jewish children to go to school. We had to wear the yellow star and couldn't go to restaurants, theaters, or parks. A Jewish school was started. Life was difficult for the Jews — radios, gold, and even bikes were confiscated. I studied during the hiding.

In the beginning of '48, I immigrated to Israel. I had my own passport, but a fake visa. I went by train to Paris and then to Marseille to sail to Eretz Israel. We intended to settle Ramot Naftali.

My Father was born in Holland, and his father was born in Holland. My mother was born in Germany. She was very beautiful. She was really the boss at home. She saved the whole family from going to the gas chambers. When the Germans came to Holland my mother said, "They won't catch us alive." My father was religiously observant. He was taken to prison, but my mother was able to free him. And then we went into hiding. We lived in a third-floor attic. Our former neighbor, an underground worker, brought us food once a week, and also news and books. The meat was from a non-kosher butcher who probably owed my father money. We knew nothing of what was happening outside. Isolating myself made it possible for me to concentrate on my studies.

Later, in September of 1944, things started really to move. The British were fighting the Germans, the house was hit by an English shell, and we had to leave. We stayed with some working class neighbors. I don't think they realized the risks they took. They had to behave as usual, and not do extra buying. They took care of food rations and falsified identification cards. For more than two years my family of six people, parents, brother, and two nephews, lived in the third floor attic with the housekeeper.

When we returned to our home the person living in the house left everything, including lots of things stolen from the Jews. Later more people returned, mostly ones who had been hidden. From the transported Jews, very few came back. Nearly all the family on my father's side disappeared.

Because they lost a big part of their possessions in the war they had difficulties paying for my studies. A good friend offered to pay for me. I think my parents had helped him during the war. I started to study medicine at Utrecht. At some point I started losing interest in my studies and got involved with Jewish youth clubs. One group was preparing to go on aliya. I decided to stop my studies and, influenced by their idealism and enthusiasm, joined them. When I left to study in Utrecht, I was in contact with the Zionist organization. This is the group that came to the moshav. I was mostly independent. My parents didn't like that I stopped my studies but they were OK with it. They sent packages. We lived on bread, onions, and tea. I learned to take care of cows, which I applied later.

I came in '48 as a halutz. I had started studying in '46 as part of a group. I was caught in the advertising aimed at youth and learned farming so I came to Israel before the War of Independence. We went to Kibbutz Na'an, then we went to the north to moshav shitufi Nahal Naftali. During the war, when everyone went to the army, because I had poor vision, I stayed and worked in the cow shed. I went to the army later when everyone was mobilized.

My wife also came from Holland; we were on the same track and met in the moshav. Life was hard; food was rationed, as was water. We tried to grow vegetables and raise our own sheep and chickens. We made lots of trips together, mostly on a horse, a mule, or even a donkey. My wife worked in the kitchen but she wanted to work with the animals. My first son was born in '50 and in '51 got polio. The place was breaking down, the situation was difficult. We went to a small village settled by Moroccans. I wanted to have a farm and perhaps enjoy life a little more. In those years we didn't even go to a movie.

Now I am in an assisted living residence — a parent's home. I have an apartment of about 55 meters and I am here all day. Not like when I had a house and big garden in Naharyia. We have catering so that my caretaker can take a serving for the two of us. I am busy with my physical activity. I ride about 15 kilometers around the compound. We have a pool here but I don't swim. I have been here four years. Every morning there is yoga, Pilates, or Feldenkrais. That keeps me on my feet. In the afternoon I nap for two hours. In the evening there is always some presentation: lectures, movies, always something. Once a month we have a trip. This time it's to Sfat. I only drive here in the surroundings. Sometimes I eat out.

In the '70s I stopped smoking. And then I started eating too much. I started walking and then running, even competitions. At the end of the '80s I had a total hip change and could not run so I started biking.

And I didn't stop! I joined the Carmel Mountain Bike Club and I still get their invitations for the Friday rides.

I had a job training people to be agriculturists. I built a good orchard of ten *dunams* (four dunams equals about one acre) and I was the agricultural supervisor for many villagers until I was eighty-two. Then I started to a build house in Nahariya and had an accident with my eye so I couldn't drive for a long time. I had to disconnect from my work and make a compromise to get payments. So I stopped working because of my eyes and couldn't read, so I did a lot of biking — tours in Cyprus, Turkey, France, Scotland, Slovenia, and Slovakia with the group. I rode twice from Metula to Eilat when I was seventy-two years old! The third trip was cancelled because of the Intifada.

I just want to be healthy and to be busy!

Ely Samoucha

Nes Ziona, 1953

ELY WAS ON ONE OF THE BIKERS WHEN WE MET EVERY SHABBAT MORNING AT THE Arlozorov train station in Tel Aviv. To do the annual ride around the Kinneret, I hitched rides with him. When my Jack Taylor bike was run over I took it to his bike shop for repairs. He was always very helpful and funny. There was a big conflict between a friend and him about the Bike Federation and I never knew who was right. Eli organized some nice parties under the trees on Shabbat afternoons, and he came to some of our parties.

These are the good things I have done:

Israel champion road race

Coaching cyclists

Deputy Mayor of Givatayim

Lawyer

In politics I helped a lot of people. I like to help people; it is my problem. I helped many who didn't pay me. So maybe it is good and it gives me a good feeling in my heart that I helped people.

I am happy that we start with the demonstrations now — people are saying what they think. With internet, Facebook, we start anew.

I divorced about ten years ago. It was a nice divorce without court. I have three children, two of them lawyers and one is an officer in the army. I have been working as a lawyer for the last six years. When I was seventeen, I started selling racing bikes to the racers and then imported bicycles. The main part of my nice life was racing and coaching. I was the big importer of Bertin racing bikes from France. I established four bicycle racing clubs. Now, once a year, I organize a meeting of all the racing cyclists in Israel. We hear the stories that we already forgot.

I am a little bit sorry that I stopped importing bicycles. But now the situation has changed. When I did it, we were about three crazy importers. Now it is mega-importing. My shop was 16m. and now the smallest in Tel Aviv is 100-200m. And now the market is controlled by people with a lot of money. When I worked about thirty years ago, we worked with the money we earned. Not money from outside. From about 1995 hi-tech people had money to invest and the situation changed and is too modern for me. I couldn't continue to work in such a situation.

I am one of four children, three were born in Iraq and I was born here. It's hard to recognize that my parents come from Iraq. Most try to hide it. I am proud of it. No one left for abroad. We are a "family" family. Since I finished the army we meet every Friday evening at my mother's home — good Iraqi food. You can only miss once a month. If you miss twice a month it means something is wrong with you.

My mother controls the family. She has to know everything. To involve her less you must tell her less. She is the chief — even when my father was alive. We had a nice house and garden and animals; sheep and a duck. We built things for the animals. My mother was the engineer, and my father was the worker. I helped him and from these days I have gold hands and can do nearly everything.

When I finished the army it was the fashion to go to the States. I didn't leave because I love Israel. It's a warm place, I feel safe here. I thought about it, but got into the bike business and stayed here.

The best period was when I was seventeen to twenty-two. I was the Israel champion of bike racing and coaching a racing club. I did it for thirty years. I was the first to bring Shimano to the market. I believed in it and sold it well. It was interesting when I was racing and coaching. I organized the racing around the Kinneret and around Kikar HaMedina and around the Hula Valley — and the first race to the Hermon. I organized almost all the racing 1978–1993. Now I am little bit tired of it. The bicycle union fights against me. I don't watch racing now as I spent too much time on this and now I must see that there is other life outside this. I ride a little bit, I swim.

When my parents came from Iraq in 1951, my original family name was Smocha or Smucha, and my mother's family name was Saltoun ben Zbeda. They lived in a tent. My father had been in the post office in Baghdad. He knew English, Hebrew, Arabic, and French; he was quite educated. When I was in high school he helped me with Arabic and French.

The immigration was quite hard for my parents. But my father was a leader like me so people tried not to fight with him and tried to help him. He worked for the army here as a civilian. The establishment didn't admire the education from the East. They were mostly Ashkenazi. If you were not, you were second level. Now we still smell it, but not so hard.

Father was my friend, my mother was my boss. Usually it is more difficult for the husband, but my mother was very strong and that didn't change. In Baghdad, my mother's family was very rich. They had purchased a *pardes* (orchard) from the local Ottoman governor. In the summer they slept on the roof. They fished from the river. Most of the water came from Turkey. They were able to sell some things before they left and bought a nice flat on Remez Street in north Tel Aviv.

The most influence was in the high school. It was a good school, with good teachers and I was an average student, but they gave me tools to think. These tools have followed me all my life and helped me. The teachers told us the first day, "You will learn here to think."

When one of the teachers retired, the education ministry organized a big event and he called me to speak there. The first thing he had told us was that everyone has something he loves to do and must do it in his life. Because of that, I went into cycling and racing and importing. He was gratified that I remembered.

When I was young, I thought there would not be many big changes. I was in a stable situation. I was healthy, had income, my friends were the same. I didn't see any revolution coming. I try to think forward all the time. I was born into a communist government — really communist with a communist economy. When I wanted to import 200 Michelin tires from France, the ministry of transportation got involved and limited me to import just twenty.

I needed a license for every shipment. They forced all importers to use the Standards Institute. This is one of the things that destroyed my business because they charged me a lot and the big importers pushed out the small importers. They still charge very high for bicycles. For airplanes, ships, cars you don't need the Standards Institute! The government is still involved here with a lot of rules like in Russia — the government is involved too much. In my economic view I am very liberal. It is a pity that Israel still has a communist point of view.

The first Israel championship in 1969 was my biggest event. Against me were a lot of cyclists who wanted to win. It was a rainy day from Ramla to Bet Shemesh with a *gesher angli* - British bridge (a ford) where the water was high and stones hidden in the water after riding uphill 20 kilometers. You could either ride through and win or stop and lose — I decided to ride and I won! Maybe a symbol of my life. If I have an aim, I do everything to achieve it. I don't turn back. I rode to Jerusalem and back once a week — alone for five hours on the bike. It is part of me to have an aim and achieve it. I rode in Germany for the Israeli national team, in a road race of 80 kilometers and I was in the second peleton. This was a very big event for me.

I started to be a lawyer when I was fifty-four. Learning at that age when your mind is not like the twenty-three–year-old other students! The exam was very hard; you have to remember so many things. This was my third aim: first was bicycling, second was politics, and third is being a lawyer. Now, there are so many lawyers, not like it was forty or fifty years ago.

At the time I was deputy mayor of Givatayim and had succeeded in this second goal of my life. No party was behind me; I was an independent with no outside resources. To become deputy mayor was very hard.

My biggest mistake was that I went to politics. The police are too involved in politics and they make dirty things in politics.

This Friday, I am organizing a demonstration against the mayor of Ramat Gan. Part of the demonstration will be in Arabic because I speak it and it's a good gimmick. I still want to go to politics even though it destroyed my business and then my wife ran away.

I can go again to politics — not too much to lose!

At my age of fifty-eight I must look I will get old. When I will be seventy-five, I would like to live on a farm with sheep, a camel, and a donkey. All my youth was with animals.

Eva Shaibe Rockman, PhD
Kansas City, Missouri, 1951

After arriving in Israel with my bike, I went on a three-day bike tour in the north, organized by Danny Be'eri. Eva was in the group. We were probably the only women in Israel who had biked in China, she in 1986 and me in 1980. That was the beginning of an enduring, devoted, fundamental friendship.

I came to Israel in my late twenties and wanted to get married. I didn't want to stay in the US and marry a non-Jew as I didn't want those problems. American Jewish men — oh my God — I wanted to have a family with the same tribal language I was used to; not far from a Polish/German background. I had to break off a relationship to do this and I still have lot of love for him, but I could see the problems about the children, and didn't want to deal with those problems. I came with the WJUS (World Jewish Union of Students) program. I learned Hebrew and it was lovely to live in the desert in Arad in the late '70s. My parents and four siblings were already here. They had hoped for me to come. It wasn't clear to me when they left the US that eight years later I would follow.

Living here is mostly good on a personal level with my work, family, being a grandmother of three, and immediate surroundings. I am very happy and have an involved and fulfilling life. Outside of that, it is

passionless and I wonder if I am contributing to the support of Israel —
do we still need Israel? A bit conflicted.

Until I was eleven, I grew up in Kansas City, the American Midwest
and a few years in Indianapolis. It was an area of mid-sized industrial
American cities, not like New York. Then we moved to Washington,
DC, not a big city then. I went to public school, and was not very involved with the organized Jewish community. Later, I did a big trip
around the States with the boyfriend with whom I was living. I went
to a small liberal-arts women's college, Goucher College. It had high
academic standards, and was intellectually challenging. I have never
had so much fun learning so much. I still have friends from there. I
stayed in the Washington area.

I saw myself in the US. My parents always talked about moving to
Israel but I was surprised when they did. I thought I would be married,
in a profession related to medicine, or biology. I thought I would be a
little more famous. Mr. Jones, my junior-high biology teacher, instilled
my love for biology. We had some really good teachers in the public
schools of the US. But I didn't want to be a doctor and deal with sick
people.

My parents are from Lodz, Poland. They are concentration camp
survivors. I am not going to use the word "Shoah" anymore. It's media
hype. They met before the War. They went to different schools, but like
here, everything was divided by politics. They were both first in their
class and a mutual friend said they should meet. But they were only
thirteen and not dating, just going out in groups. They got married in
Germany just after the end of the war after my mother found my Dad's
name on a Red Cross list. She conned her way with an ambulance driver
to transport her to the DP camp where my father was listed, found him
and they were married by the rabbi of the British occupying forces.

Their story is not a neutral story. We couldn't grow up and ignore
their experience in the ghetto, the War. Our parents talked about it.
Was that the best way to grow up, hearing about that? They did the
best they could. We had to live up to that. I have tried to validate my

children's lives rather than my own. My father's mother lived with us, even in Israel, and she helped raise my daughter Timna.

Now, my situation, in one word: Good. I am married, the mother of three, the grandmother of one and stepmother of one, and step-grandmother of four. Both parents are living, and I am working full-time as a scientific advisor for the Israel Science Foundation. I am living happily in Israel as long as I don't think about the situation. I would be as unhappy anywhere else. I am healthy, feeling fit, optimistic and pessimistic at the same time. In my personal bubble I am optimistic.

I wasn't as successful as a graduate student as I thought I would be. I did my Master's in Wisconsin but was not the top of my class. I then did my PhD at Hebrew University. I didn't do it fast or brilliantly but I didn't give up. I was brought up to believe I was smarter than other people, but it turned out that I was not smarter than everyone!

I would like to say I would not come here, given what I know now — but you only know what you know and would probably do the same. I wish I had volunteered for the army when I arrived. I think it would have really affected my absorption into society. Maybe I would have even learned to read Hebrew properly. If I had the chance, I would like to live as a grown-up in the US to see how it would be. My three sisters did that. They don't have as much fun as we do here, but they have comfortable lives in the US. They don't struggle about money as much as we do. The three Americans take Prozac, but the sibs here don't and we all have the same crazy mother. Makes you wonder.

Some good things I have done: a bike trip in China. I found work for a few people who wouldn't have without my help. I made a significant difference by keeping one girl in high school and contributed to her life.

I don't have a burning issue. I am very complacent, making do, easily satisfied. Everything is OK, but there is no passion in my life. Hard to get out of my comfort zone. I am not living up to my potential — this is life? Staying comfortable?

Leah Saporta

Jaffa, Christian Hospital, Israel, 1952

WHEN I PARTICIPATED IN A BOOK CLUB I NOTICED THE NICE HAIRSTYLES OF SOME MEMBERS *of the group — all from Leah, whose salon is in Basel Square, where I lived in Tel Aviv. I said, "Do me!" She made me blonde! I would never have imagined! Her salon is a haven of compassion and strength. She has the admirable patience to deal with all of us. And now she is continuing her mission to save lives by learning to be a driver for Magen David Adom, the ambulance service!*

I have many burning issues. The biggest is to change the world. If you look, only women should be prime minister or president and the secretaries should be men. We do most of the work at home. If we can do this part, we can save the world.

The second is to make some changes in my life with my husband. I am not going to change him.

I am married, bored, very occupied with the new life of my daughter, who is moving in with her boyfriend. I work full time, five days a week from morning to evening. It's like walking from the house to a social club. I am very lucky as I don't like working in an office with a computer. I sit with people and have a conversation.

And then there is a funny situation: I go home very satisfied, very tired and I have to stay in the living room to accompany my husband.

Part of me is very tired, so it's very nice that he doesn't talk. But the other part is not good because I am there and he doesn't talk. I am going to write a play about this situation. It gave me the idea of writing a comedy drama. The comedy is that he thinks he is still young and can do what he used to do! He has two separate personalities: one who thinks he is still twenty, the other one is over sixty and there is a big argument between them. Women have the same problem, but are more active than the men.

Every year, we eight friends, just women, go for a weekend to a *zimmer* (bed and breakfast). Two days of wine and talking — two days is not enough! forty-eight hours of talking about sex, politics, the situation in the world, playing cards, eating at a good restaurant, getting drunk a little, with a little bit of grass. We take a deep breath and then we go home. And we fix everything in 48 hours until the next year.

My parents were married in Budapest after the war, my mother, sixteen and my father, twenty-five. They came to Israel in 1948. They actually came in 1947 but the British captured them and put them in Cyprus for a year, then in '48 they came from Cyprus. My father was from Klus, in Hungary, but after the war it was Romania. They spoke Hungarian at home.

My father and mother went through the Holocaust. Since I was a child, I heard at home from my father that Israel is the only home we have. More than this, my father said that through the Holocaust he had a problem because he was a Jew. Now his children have a double problem: as a Jew and as Israeli, so Israel is now the only home.

When my brother got an offer to work in Silicon Valley he came home to tell my parents. I heard my father tell him about the two problems, so he didn't go.

I grew up in the Kibbutz Ma'agan in Emek HaYarden. I was born in Jaffa because when my parents came they didn't know where to go. The roof was full of holes with the rain coming in. One day my father met a friend, who asked, "Why are you here? Come to the kibbutz — all the Hungarians are in the kibbutz!" So until I was eight we lived in the kibbutz, and then my father decided to leave. It was hard for him to live on the kibbutz in the communist way, not like today. He was a *shiputznik* (interior renovations).

My father shaped my life. He is strong and independent. He would say, "Don't count on anybody. Don't ask anybody for anything. You must believe in yourself."

Like in the salon: One day I came home and said I rented a place. I shook hands on the deal without asking my husband.

When I was young, I wanted to go back to the kibbutz, but my father didn't want me to. I decided to become a hairdresser. I knew I loved it from playing with the hair of my mother's friends. They told me I had talent and encouraged me. I wanted to do something that helps people.

I got my adopted daughter after ten years of marriage. She was four days old when I got her. I stayed with her a year at home.

Then I went back to school to finish my bagrut, and then I went to learn to be a teacher. My father thought if I was a hairdresser it was a way of avoiding school. So at thirty-two I became a teacher.

I taught hairdressing in an Ort vocational high school for six years. And then I did the same in a prison for rehabilitating women. It was a very strict program for women who couldn't even read. I worked there for six years. And then another five years in a men's prison. It was easier to work with the men than woman to woman. The next teacher should be a man for the women, and for the men a woman because of the big difference in the ability to relate. One student didn't want to go from her cell to the classroom. I went to her cell to get her out, and said, "How do you look? Not washed, no make-up, you don't care about your hair? One day you will be out of here. You're still human." I came to her because it was the second time she didn't come to class and two misses and you're out. She came! Ten months later when the examiners came from outside to do the test she finished the course with high results. I taught twice a week and had to teach them chemistry and anatomy, and all about the hair. They had to learn to read and write. I helped them integrate their studies. For two or three years I went to visit to do a special day, usually on a Monday when the salon was closed. I gave them the tools — they had to use them! I knew I gave something to someone — sometimes when they got released I helped them. It was a big satisfaction. While I was teaching in the prison, I wasn't allowed to be in connection. But after, when I was a volunteer in a halfway house and I was working for Wella, I went every Friday to see how I could help them. I knew most of the hairdressers in Tel Aviv so I was able to help them find a job and give my guarantee. I could tell them, "She doesn't use drugs, she won't steal from you; she won't harm your business because she knows she would harm my reputation." One woman called me to tell me that she went back to drugs — she let me know she would be out of the program.

Most of my life I did exactly what I wanted. I wanted a business, but with two days free to do other things, I was afraid to open my own business because I would make too much money — so I kept my time to teach children. I think you feel much more effective when you do other things besides working. The hairdressing gave me a big space that doesn't connect only with women's hair — you hear many stories, know many people, and many troubles. You can get to the right person who can help. I also worked in between, cutting hair of wounded people: soldiers, people in accidents, or with a disease.

When I was sixteen, after the Six Day War, my big brother was wounded in the army and was one year in Poriya Hospital and then he went to Tel Hashomer Hospital. I used to go every day to visit him. That's how I started my volunteering.

I wouldn't change anything. I did everything by chance. I met some woman by chance who told me about the children in Yavne, so I was able to do something. She had a big place for weddings. She gave us a place one day a week to work with the children and came with all the material for the children bought with her own money.

My most precious memory is when I got my daughter. When she was in my hands, I wanted to run with her, so no one would take her away. I couldn't be pregnant because I had three out-of-womb conceptions. One year after the last one they wanted to start IVF. It was very expensive. The health department didn't have the budget, the religious didn't accept it, and doing the research on a chimp is too expensive. I took the name from the news article, and went to the University and said, "Tell the professor that the chimpanzee is here!" I was the first woman in Israel that they did the research on. And the first one where the research succeeded. The pregnancy didn't last, but it got published. I did this another seven times, but in between the whole process I got my daughter. She is wonderful — even if she were my own, I am sure she would not be so wonderful. She came to the salon with big flowers on her twentyith birthday. "For you, Mommy." She is a real gift!

Now I have to finish writing my play!

Ruth Strahovsky-Chalfon, PhD

Jerusalem, 1945

RUTHIE AND MICKEY LIVE ACROSS THE STREET IN A HOUSE THEY REMODELED. *RUTHIE IS a warm and welcoming neighbor! They taught me to be tolerant of the neighbor's noisy parties!*

They play golf at the club. Mickey walks to the beach to swim in the sea every morning. They tour China, Turkey, India and then invite friends to enjoy travel stories. We hear the laughter when the grandchildren visit.

When I was young, we didn't bother planning our "future life." I had no idea what I was going to do or be when I grew up. I enjoyed what I was doing at the time, concentrating on my responsibilities as a student, as a leader in the Scouts, and a member of other groups, as well as helping at home by taking care of my younger sister and fulfilling domestic duties, as both my parents worked very hard. We lived a modest life, our social lives centered in the activities of the Scout movement, going on hikes, camping, etc. In 1963, I joined the army and became an officer in charge of education in the northern area of the country. After saving some money for university studies, as an army officer I was accepted to Hebrew University in Jerusalem to study Hebrew and English Linguistics, where I graduated and was certified for teaching.

Later, I accomplished my MA as an educational psychologist in the US, and years later, my PhD.

Both sides of my ancestors originated in Spain. My grandparents on my father's side spoke Arabic between them, as well as French. I knew my father's grandparents, but only my mother's mother.

I am thirteen generations born in Jerusalem on my mother's side. They were expelled in 1492 and went to Greece. They immigrated to Jerusalem about three hundred years ago. The organization Yad Ben Zvi, which collects ethnographic histories, has the history of my family with all its branches. The name was Parnass. I am Sephardic, carrying the Sephardic tradition, spiritually, mentally, and culinarily. On my father's side I am fourth generation. In 1492, my father's ancestors fled Toledo to northern Morocco, to Tetouan. A hundred and fifty years ago they came to Haifa and Tiberius.

I grew up in Jerusalem during the first three years of my life. During the siege of Jerusalem in the War of Independence (1948), my mother and I left Jerusalem in an armored bus to Haifa, where my grandfather had built a house. He convinced my father, who was a soldier in a northern unit of the army, to move our family closer to where he was stationed.

My parents shaped my life. My father was an agronomist who studied in Toulouse. He was a pedagogue. He was very careful about educating my sister and me in moral behavior, tradition, and human relationships. These are the supports of building personality. And so did my mother. Our family was traditional, but not religious. All the holidays were strictly observed with ceremonies and holiday foods. I remember how our family gathered during my adolescence, a warm family always welcoming, supportive. As my parents were native speakers it was always in Hebrew and my father insisted in using correct Hebrew.

Later, my peer group helped shape my personality. I was always very active socializing in Scouts, at school, leading committees. I was also a good student!

At the age of sixteen in 1961, I was chosen by the school principal at the Leo Baeck School to represent the school as an exchange student in the Reform Movement in the United States. I spent six months living with a family in Buffalo, New York, studying in a public school and traveling during the weekends to Reform communities to tell the story of Israel. This experience had a formative influence on my life.

In many homes here at that time the economic situation was quite tight. We lived in a very small apartment. Both my parents worked hard. This taught us to manage according to our abilities. We had aspirations to be the best, to do the best. As I recall, I always succeeded in what I planned at the time. When I joined the army I knew I wouldn't be a simple soldier. At the university I knew a BA would not be my last stop. Hardships never stopped me from trying to achieve.

When I look back everything I, or we, my dear husband Mickey, a periodontist, did what was right for that time. I don't regret anything. After we had graduated from American universities, we didn't hesitate to return to Israel, rather than accepting positions in the US. It was clear that home is, and will always be, Israel!

Now I'm in an entirely new venue of my life. I am always a person who is caring for the other. I have done a lot of volunteer work for people. In the past, I was professor at the university, devoting my time and energy to both my family and my profession. I had very little time for hobbies, but did manage a lot of traveling. Today I am a lady of leisure! Free to plan my schedule and to try to combine intellectual, sportive, cultural, and family affairs. I am trying not to neglect any aspect and running my life as it flows. I focus one full day a week in a workshop, developing as a ceramist. I try to give as much attention to my children and grandchildren as my time allows, as well as devoting time to volunteer projects.

Living in Israel now, I don't know anything else, although we lived in the States for about three years as a young student family, with a child a year old at the time. Mickey went for periodontics studies in Philadelphia after graduating from Hadassah Dental School. I am rooted in this country, its beauty, the culture, the mentality, and the people. I have no problem getting along in another country, but I relate to everything that is happening here and now because it is my one and only home! I don't ignore the faults, the dangers, the bad behavior, and the hardships of the security situation. But home is home, especially as I am aware of the history of my family and my duty to my family and children, to carry on as one bead in a long, long chain of my family's rich heritage in Israel.

Israel today is not the Israel I've known throughout my life! The people, its values, its morals, political intrigues, and the priorities of life have changed. I do miss my old "growing" nation!

Eran Singer
Haifa, 1977

WHEN I WAS RIDING THE BUS TO JERUSALEM THERE WAS AN ACCIDENT ON THE ROAD. THE man sitting next to me jumped to look and then phoned to give full details. I asked if he was a reporter. "Yes, I work for Israel Radio." Because he speaks Arabic and English, aside from Hebrew, he is one of the editors of the feeds that come into the station and prepares the material for the announcer. I took him up on the invitation to visit the studio while he was working. It is a fast-paced, well-organized system that broadcasts to news-hungry Israelis. Today Eran is the Arab Affairs correspondent for Israel Public Radio. He is also a news editor in Jerusalem, and is considering TV journalism. For the last three or four years, he has been invited to the Arabic language satellite channels to tell about Israel.

He has joined us for parties. We enjoy visiting with him for his insights and his company!

I am preoccupied because of what's going on in the Arab world. I think I'm pretty lucky because I am now witnessing the beginning of a whole new era — not only the region, but in the world. I am one of a few to explain to my listeners what's really going on in our tough neighborhood.

If I have information about Israeli soldiers I won't say anything and not about Israel's national security. I will turn to the authorities to make sure that this info can be transferred.

In one line: I am not married. I think that my life is my job because my way of living is totally connected to the way I am working. I am sitting here with you and my phone is on my right and on my left is my laptop that I take everywhere I go, because if something would happen in Teheran or Damascus I would have to get on the air and let my listeners know. This situation has been like that for more than a year and half. I can't live a normal life — and I will never turn myself to Off as long as the Syrian president stays in his palace in Damascus. Everyone knows it's only a matter of weeks or months till something happens there and only after that will I be able to have a break.

I don't think I only have one burning issue. I think that my people here don't really understand what's going on in our region. And even more than that, they don't realize yet the tremendous changes this area is going through right now that will affect the lives of each and every one of us. Actually, it has already started to affect us. Israelis are very insular.

I don't like the weather here; it's too humid for me. I don't usually like all of my neighbors. And too many things that are connected with the Israeli way of living I don't like. Still, it's my country — I feel very connected to Israel and I still believe that many things can be changed.

I grew up in the Carmeliya neighborhood in Haifa, which is actually where I live today. I live about five meters from the house where I was born. It's a young neighborhood — I don't see many people my age here, and there are many people with children, which I don't have — I like it. It reminds me of my childhood, scenery that I am familiar with, the smells that I am familiar with. When I go out to my balcony I can see the sea.

In the army, I went to the Intelligence and I served with people familiar with Arab culture. Before going to the army, I went to a special course for six months and studied Arabic in a very intense way — this is why I speak and read Arabic today — there is no doubt that my knowledge of the Arab world is connected to my military background. I also had Arabic in high school. My initial connection to Arabic was my grandmother. She was born in Russia, and came to Israel as a young girl. For some reason, her parents sent her to Beirut to study nursing at the American University. She came back with fluent Arabic. I tell people and they are always amazed. A scene: my grandmother speaking Arabic to the gardener, Russian to the maid, and fluent English to her grandchildren. She tried to educate us.

This was my father's mother. My parents were born here in Haifa. Grandmother came between World War I and II. My father's father was born somewhere between Russia and Poland.

My mother's mother was born in Berlin. Originally, they came from Poland. As a young girl she had to escape when Hitler came to power. My mother's father was born in Lithuania. I didn't know my grandfathers — they were both gone, but I did know my grandmothers who lived in Haifa.

My father helped shape my life - my quality time with him, especially the feeling that I am secure and can trust. I think my late father was most influential in my life. We were good friends — and I think I can tell you that he was the only one who could really understand me and deal with my behavior.

He died ten years ago — I was twenty-five. He was a lawyer and he was killed in a car accident. He was riding his motorcycle. From that day my life really changed. We had a very, very good connection — in contact hourly! He would call me and ask what am I doing, where am I, etc. That day, when after a few hours of trying to locate him and he hadn't answered my calls, I started to worry. I was a reporter in Haifa and no one could tell me where he was. His secretary said she had tried to reach him at home and he didn't answer his cell phone. It was my initiative to call the Rambam Hospital spokesperson, who said, "Someone told me there had been a motorcycle accident but there was no name and they took him to Rambam. Why do you want to know?"

"I think it's my father."

His bag with his papers had been thrown by the crash so they didn't have a name. I took my mother to the hospital — she had been waiting at home. She had said, "He's riding his motorcycle today and I am not relaxed." I said, "We have to go to the hospital. You go in and I will find a place to park." When I got to the emergency room my mother already knew he was badly injured. He was critically wounded and passed away two days later. Up until that day, I was totally protected, even over-protected. Since then I have had to be on my own. I have a mother and a brother but it's not the same.

I can't tell you what I thought my life would be like. I do know that I always had something to do with mass media. As a child, I was amazed to see how sound speakers work at the supermarket. I saw the woman at the cash register, who was having a problem, push this mysterious button to call the manager by using the speakers. This started what I am going to do with my life!

In my personal life, I have faced many setbacks, but when it comes to my professional life, I don't let them interfere. I will always do the best I can to put things in proportion — but sometimes it's not worth it. I am a man of principles. And it's very hard for me to change these principles. Sometime I realize that no matter how professional I am, others aren't always and in these cases I try to change things but not for the long term.

His phone has been ringing every few minutes and Eran says, "This is a regular day."

I have met some people who really helped me and I did the best I could to help them in return. I am a good friend. And normally I would never hurt anyone. I don't like talking about it — I was raised and educated that it is improper to talk about your mitzvahs. I gave money in places where people really needed it. In addition, I give my support to others. Helping my mother after my father was killed is important.

Living in Israel is exhausting! Things are every rapid — hectic here — especially for me. Only two or three days ago, a friend asked me "When will we ever stop: I hear your name on the radio every day — morning, noon, and evening. When do you get the time to sleep?" Luckily, my job is totally connected — it's like a hobby: dealing with Arab language and culture and especially Arab diplomacy and at the same time having the privilege to explain to my listeners what is really going on.

I think we will survive — I am not pessimistic — this place as we know today, will change — the region — not just Israel — there are new mega-powers. I don't know where we will be inside this whole creation — I definitely don't think that we will be thrown out of here by our enemies — who are many. If there is a reason to be scared, it's because of what's happening inside Israeli society. People are becoming more religious, racist, intolerant and I think we are going backwards in many ways. I would even say that we're getting more and more like our neighbors — the way people treat the Other, xenophobia, the way men treat women, crime. We don't have a good reason to be proud.

Vivienne Silver-Brody

*Bulawayo, in the native language means the
place of killing Rhodesia, now Zimbabwe, 1942*

*I HAD READ AN ARTICLE IN ERETZ MAGAZINE BY VIVIENNE SILVER ABOUT A LOCAL PHO-
tographer. Strolling down King David Street in Jerusalem I saw the Silver Print
Gallery. I went in and introduced myself to Vivienne. I have been her fan ever
since. She has several books and numerous articles to her credit, a gallery in
Ein Hod, and is always busy with a new project. Because of her involvement
with Machsom Watch, I took a tour of the checkpoints along the wall that di-
vides Israel from the West Bank. We have had many good hikes, dinners, beach
parties, celebrations of the solstices, and desert rambles. When I was recovering
from pneumonia she offered to have me stay with them. She and husband Roy
are always good company.*

My life is full to overflowing. And I want to pack masses more stuff
into my life before I leave this earth. I have new projects that I want to
do: I am learning bee keeping, I want to print photographs on tiles, and
I have to have at least one container of olive oil from our own trees.

I'm happily married. I am a grandmother by marriage. I am a
passionate gardener. I worry about the sustainability of the earth. I
worry about my country; but it is still the most exciting place. That's
all about living. My intellectual pursuits revolve around my passion for

photography. I am a serious collector of local Israeli photography, which fascinates me because of its multiple facets of interpretation, together with its aesthetics.

I grew up in Bulawayo in a life of privilege in a colony of Great Britain — excellent educational system — lots of extra activities because my parents were culture conscious — art, dancing, elocution lessons. I was on the hockey team, played squash, tennis. I didn't really belong to the Jewish community. In junior school one day a classmate punched me on the nose. Why? Because I was Jewish! I had to ask my parents what Jewish means. I suppose experiences like that caused me to avoid having Jewish friends. During my school years and then as a young woman, most of my friends were rather *pukkah* (British upper class standards). One needs to be a psychologist to understand the complexity of this way of thinking. One thing I did share with my Jewish contemporaries is that few of us had grandparents, aunts, uncles, cousins. It was only when I was older that I realized why.

My father was in the RAF during the war. My sister was born in the new house that he had designed. He was good at many things — an artist who had not fulfilled his potential. He was a sought-after photo portraitist. People came from the capital Salisbury for sittings. My mother was a full partner in their photographic studio, Silvers' Studio. They worked together as a team — she played with the children when they came for sittings, arranged the groups tastefully, did a good deal of the retouching.

This reminds me of my own father's photo studio.

My parents were both from Poland. They met in my mother's brother's photo studio where she was working. They were very young, maybe twenty-one or twenty-two. They lived near the German border and were aware of unpleasant political changes concerning the Jews. The two of them left in 1937. My father cried when he got on the train in their home town, knowing that he was probably not coming back. My mother had a brother who was a violinist in Berlin, who was connected with Huberman, the founder of the Israel Philharmonic Orchestra, and went to Japan, where he taught at the university and thus survived the war.

Why Rhodesia? My father's father had worked in South Africa during the Boer War. But when they arrived, they didn't get permission to land, as the gates for Jewish immigrants were closed. The British consul got on the boat and suggested they go to Rhodesia. My mother didn't like Bulawayo at first. They counted up all their money hoping to get to New Zealand but they didn't have enough to get back if they had to, so they stayed and opened their photo studio.

My mother was well read and took care of my Latin and French homework and my reading list. My father shaped my artistic side, with art lessons, and the historical side and probably contributed to my workaholic nature as he was a hard taskmaster. I have a wonderful memory of my agriculture class. This has stayed with me and probably shaped my outlook on ecology. It's a great shame that this has disappeared from the school system here. In addition, there were the British mores which melded with my parents' European outlook.

I started to work in a local bank when I was sixteen and didn't want to go to university. Once a week I attended a forum, which dealt with current affairs. I was the only woman there and by this time, I was becoming politically aware. I also studied photography by correspondence. It was a vibrant community.

My parents had lost almost all of their families. They left Poland in '37 — I was born in '42 — My father thought maybe his daughters would marry gentiles and the problem of being Jewish would disappear. He had lived in Palestine as a boy and even remembered some Hebrew. I suppose he thought it was too hazardous to be Jewish! I do not know how, but out of fresh air my sister became a Zionist.

I came to Israel in 1971 with the intention of staying for a year to explore. I knew very little about my Jewish identity. In that first amazing year, I realized that I could really identify with this country and live here. My sister was here. I think it was an atavistic response, hard to define, a connection with a long history, and a fascination with a country building on that premise, outside the context of European destruction.

My father wanted me to have good professional experiences. They never went back to Poland, but they did visit Germany professionally; they did not boycott German products. I, too, took some professional training courses in Germany and later, in Israel I learned German for a while at the Goethe Institute.

I do not think I inherited my family's fears about Europe. These are emotions that have developed with age and knowledge. Now it is very difficult for me to even go to Yad Vashem (The Holocaust museum in Jerusalem). It sets off enormous sadness and brings on tears. I cannot be there for more than five minutes. My mother was an admirer of Polish culture. My father went to a Polish school because his father was a town councilor. He was a very assimilated person.

Just after 1967 I went to work in Switzerland in a very good photo studio in Zurich with a number of other young photographers, one of whom was a German. He said to me, in 1967, "Now the Arabs will finish off what we didn't finish." I went home and tried to work out what actually had happened that day. In Rhodesia, I functioned as a liberal — fighting for black rights, my sister and I would sit in the black part of the bus. I was willing to fight for blacks, but I couldn't answer this German arrogant young man? I worked in that photo studio for a year. It was never mentioned again.

Four years later when I came to Israel, it was the culmination of a process of exploring my identity.

First of all, Israel is not the same country I came to in 1971. When I was studying about the history, no one mentioned what had happened in 1948. I don't think the clock can be put back, but the political outcome of current Israeli policies cannot be sustained. So much short-sightedness in the effort to live in the historic heartland of the Jewish people, that in the end, I fear we will become one state rather than two states of one for the Arabs and one for the Jews. And then what will the Zionist dream look like? It will almost be like it was all in vain. It may not be gradual — it could turn into a nasty civil war. The people in the political center and the left are out-numbered. And there may be very unpleasant scenarios ahead of us. Even worse for me to watch is the growing inequality of society. I volunteer in a human-rights organization with a group of like-minded women. This is good for me; it's good for my conscience. But I must reiterate: I love living here. I have wonderful friends. I am constantly challenged and stimulated. I have a wide range of pleasures I can indulge in as I reach older age. I live in a privileged situation in a house rather than an apartment, in a village which is almost like a nature reserve and is not far from an urban center. The medical services still function as they should before the government tries to privatize them. Best of all, I have a wonderful husband, friend and companion — I have absolutely no reason to complain. But I am aware that around the corner, the edges are far from perfect.

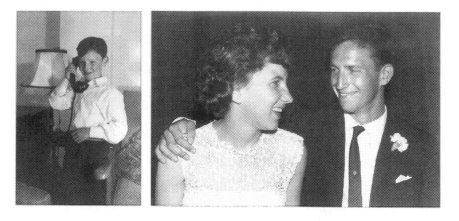

Robbie Sabel, PhD

Knebworth, Hertfordshire England, 1941
My parents lived in London, but because
of the German blitz, my mother had
moved out into the country.

I MET ROBBIE ON A NATURE ORGANIZATION HIKE IN THE GALILEE. WE SPENT THE WHOLE *day talking and on into the night. This was the first of many hikes with Robbie, in a group or on our own. With friends from Paris we did a hike with elaborate dinner arrangements. We once found some abandoned graves in the Jerusalem hills, and we saw the Roman mile markers on the trail from Jerusalem to Caesarea. He introduced me to another hiker who has become a good friend. He was always very gracious and charming and modest about his many professional accomplishments in international law. I have enjoyed reading his articles about the legality of border issues here. And he makes a wicked lemoncelo!*

I am retired from the Foreign Ministry and am now a professor of international law at the Hebrew University Law Faculty. I also teach at Tel Aviv University.

Both of my parents were born in England. My grandparents came from Russia. I grew up in a suburb of London. I come from a prosperous, non-Zionist, Anglo-Jewish family. During the Second World War, my father was an officer in the British Army, stationed in Intelligence in Cairo. He came on vacation to Palestine out of curiosity. He fell in love with the *Yishuv* (the pre-state Israel). On demobilization, he returned to England, to his clothing business (known to Anglo Jews as the *shmatte business)* and became active in his local British Zionist Movement. When war broke out in 1948, the *Yishuv* was looking for experienced army personnel and he volunteered to serve in the newly created Israel army. He was appointed officer in charge of counter-Intelligence in Jerusalem, under Moshe Dayan who was overall commander of the Jerusalem district. One incident he told me of his experience was that his agents reported that they had seen a suspicious looking Englishman. He instructed them to trail this person and my father discovered, to his amusement, that he was receiving daily reports of his own movements; security being so strict in those days that the field security agents were not aware of the identity of their own commander. When the War of Independence was over, he left the army and spent the rest of his career as a director of the Jewish National Fund, the organization engaged in reforesting the barren hills of Jerusalem and the Galilee.

When the fighting died down, at the end of 1948, my father brought my mother, my sister, aged twelve, and me, aged seven, to Jerusalem. Mother didn't like it; she had lived through austerity in the war in London and she now had to face it in Israel as well. Using her experience from war-time Britain, my mother volunteered to teach the new immigrants from Arab countries how to use milk, eggs, and potatoes in their powdered form, which was the only form available. Mother never learned fluent Hebrew and made herself understood in a combination of English, broken Hebrew, Yiddish and snatches of Russian that she had learned from her parents. It was very difficult here for her with rationing. Israel had no foreign currency to purchase meat from abroad and there was no indigenous beef farming at the time. The main source of protein was frozen cod from Norway cooked in endless varieties. We had a ration of one chicken a month. My job was to take the chicken from the store (the chicken was alive) to the *shochet* (slaughterer) and then nearby to some old ladies (or they seemed old to me at the time) who plucked it, leaving enormous piles of feathers. I carried the now naked chicken home and Mother had to eviscerate it. We had little fruit; we did have lots of aubergine that she made into "chopped liver." In 1950, on a vacation to Europe I saw fresh apples and peaches for the first time.

When I came at seven, I had no Hebrew, and knew nothing about Israel. There was no special instruction in Hebrew for new immigrants, as was introduced later, so I went to a regular Israeli school. I found it hell. My clothes and manners were English and here everything was informal *Palmach* (independence fighters) style. My sister and I went to the same school and we were used to discipline. I didn't know what hit me with the casual Israeli style. I discovered to my surprise, that for the average Israeli the English were the enemy because of Bevin's policy of not allowing Jews to immigrate to Palestine. In the winter of 1949, there was heavy snow in Jerusalem. I assumed that kids had snowball fights and when I threw a snowball at a passerby I was accused of throwing stones, something they associated with Arab gangs.

However, there were compensations. Walking in Jerusalem, I was overwhelmed with the bright sunshine, compared to the dreary atmosphere in London. I went to a kiosk for fresh orange juice that I had never seen!

At that time Jerusalem was the end of the world — you could only go west. The life however, was very cosmopolitan, more than it is now. It had been the center of the British Mandate, with Arab Christians, foreign journalists, UN personnel, and German Jews. In Zion Square, Café Vienna served coffee and apple strudel and one could *kibitz* on endless games of chess.

In the religious quarter of Mea Shearim, Yiddish, of course, was the language. We lived in the Rehavia suburb of Jerusalem, where all the public notices were in German, and people had signs on the door "Don't ring between 2:00 and 4:00." The German-Jewish residents had come in the '30s and were mostly educated professionals and lived the sedate German way of life, eating sponge cake washed down with egg brandy. They refused to speak English, "the language of the enemy." As the British had imposed curfews, we children moved through the gardens, through holes in the fences. One favorite pastime was collecting empty rifle shells left over from the war. When we went to Mt. Zion and had a glimpse of the Old City we often saw the red *kafiahs* of the Arab Legion guards on the walls of the Old City.

To get to Tel Aviv took two hours and there was only one narrow road. In one place near Motza, the road, built by the Ottomans, had a sharp turn and was so narrow there was only room for one car to pass at a time and traffic from Jerusalem had to give way to traffic coming up the hill. There were few hotels in Tel Aviv and one stayed with relatives or friends, usually on a sofa in their living room. Air-conditioning was unknown. The sea was polluted as, in the 1950s, there was no other way of disposing of Tel Aviv's sewage. Swimming in the sea was therefore strictly prohibited. However, I used to sneak in to swim, without my parents' knowledge, and seem to have survived it.

Some years later, I returned to England and went to an English boarding school, with its strict discipline. There, one learns not to show emotion, a trait I think retained for life.

I returned to Israel, served in the army, artillery corps, studied law and became a private lawyer. As a student in 1964, I needed income so I took a night job working for the military censor, reading through the Jerusalem Post and other publications looking for key military words. I learned to read very quickly and can still scan a document for a word, though I now find, of course, that computers beat me to it.

I had always been interested in politics and international affairs and in 1972 the Foreign Office was looking for young lawyers so I applied. My wife thought the job posting was probably "cooked" and that in reality they had someone, but they were really looking and I got the job.

In the Foreign Service at first I did only legal work. I was later sent to Washington, DC in 1981-85 and again in 1993–94. I found Washington delightful. I had fascinating work and we lived the comfortable life of suburbia in leafy Bethesda. I was appointed ambassador to Canada by Shimon Peres but because of a family health problem did not take the post.

Although I have lived in Israel for over sixty years I still feel more at home in English culture than in Hebrew, the litmus test is that I count in English and if I have a choice of an English book or one written in Hebrew, I choose to read in English.

Lina Slutzkin
Tbilisi, 1964

SOME YEARS AGO (I COULD CALCULATE BY THE AGES OF THEIR CHILDREN.) VLAD FOUND *Lina and so she became a friend, too. They each sold their Jerusalem apartment and bought an old farm in Kfar Uriah. They had big plans that have now been realized: building their own beautiful house that faces the long valley all the way to Ashdod, bringing up their adorable, active, brilliant, and charming children, and now developing the winery. Lina has brought the organizational talents that she used working for Intel to her own project of the winery. www.kadma.com– a lovely place to visit and taste the significant wine!*

We are sitting in the much-used kitchen of the house, sipping soup made from the pumpkins in the garden.

Living in Israel is very good for me. I don't think we need to be anywhere else. There is no other place for Jews to be! I am very glad that we have the chance to build this house and develop the area where we live — us and our children — to have the connection to the land — not just the idea of Israel. I have a family that I love very much, a nice home, and nice things that I do every day — so it's all good!

I'm in a new adventure that I started three years ago. I like what I'm doing with the winery — building a new thing from scratch — we created something. I lead this, but the whole family is doing it. It turned out to be a family project. Vlad said this is my thing, but he takes part in all the decisions. I would never do this alone. The fact is that I am executing the things that need to be done, but he is really supporting me so much.

Not all of the kids work with us now — the little ones, Ruth and David, are really with us in this. Joel is interested but is not able to spend enough time and Assaf is in the army and also doesn't have enough time, but it is more because of the family dynamics — he went away from us — it happened before — before he went to the army he wanted to be distant from us.

David and Ruth work every weekend unless they have something else planned. Sometimes they come later, so as not to have to wake up so early on Shabbat.

When I worked for Intel, I had just one direction. Now, in these three years I use other parts of myself, designing the winery, also singing in a choir. It's more like looking at the harmony of things in life. It is much better for me now for two reasons: The first is because of my father, who was a mathematician. When he taught us math he was giving us the *spirit* of math — how to intuitively understand math and algebra — what is a straight line. I loved this. When I went to university I wanted to learn math. But for the army, I learned computers. In reality, I could earn money with computers but not with math! I never got back to the university for a second degree in math like I had hoped. I got married and had Assaf.

The other factor is my dyslexia. In the first grade in Russia you had to come to the front of the class to read. I just learned everything by heart. Some of my children also have this. But I am very stubborn to beat this. What depended on reading I was always behind. My first husband went to law school and I was interested, but I didn't have a diagnosis — I couldn't go to law school! I am getting better. I have learned to use other logic. I guess this had a big influence on the choices I made in my life. I gave up some things.

The two things I do are the winery and the children. Right now the winery is taking everything. The children are already launched. Now, a lot of what the children need they can do for themselves.

I came with my parents when I was a little girl in '72. They were very Zionistic. We left Russia when it was pretty dangerous. Actually, my grandparents came before us. My great grandfather was in *Hovevei Zion* (a Zionist organization). My grandmother spoke fluent Hebrew.

My aunt came in 1971 to join the eighteen families from Georgia. It was easier to get permission to leave Georgia than from Moscow. In '69 they asked and got permission in '71. The whole *hamula* (extended family) went. My great-grandfather from Lithuania had been sent to Georgia to be the rabbi. He founded the Jewish education system in Georgia. He was the rabbi in the town of Zkhenvali. He was a great rabbi and established a *yeshiva* of a very high quality. My aunt came to Israel with his family. My father was the grandson of the big rabbi.

I remember when I was really little my grandfather doing the Seder and telling us the story of Pesach in Russian. He told us the whole story.

They went to Israel to give us the proper place to live, a proper life. They thought Israel was wonderful. They came to build and to participate in the building. They never thought to get something from the State. They admired the local people. My father was always talking about the good people — the willingness to help. They never felt that they had left anything, not only the socialist regime that they hated — they had no doubts about going to Israel. The fact that it was not so easy here was not considered a problem.

I grew up first in Tbilisi until I was eight. We spoke Russian at home. We came and lived in Meir Shfeya near Zichron and I went to school in Kerem Maharal. We had learned a little Hebrew at home in Tbilisi, but it was secret at that time. When I went to school here I learned Hebrew in six months. I used being an olah hadashah to cover my dyslexia. By high school I admitted to myself I was not telling the truth.

My mother is an important figure in my life, but my father was much more significant. My sister was my father's daughter! My mother was not so dominant, but she had a lot of influence on us and taught us different things. She is a very strong character, but she was also influenced by my father. He was the center of the larger family — he took care of everyone. Everyone came to him for advice. Now that I have lost him I always think of what he would say. My father put the *mezuzah* (prayer case) on the winery — and three days later he died.

I thought my life would be similar to my parents'. What they had I imagined having — a family like my family. My mother was very dependent on my father: she didn't drive, or do finances. I knew I would be more independent. I definitely thought I would not be dependent on anyone.

My divorce was a big setback. This was the most difficult thing I experienced in my life, except for the death of my father. It was surprising to me that I was divorcing — I never thought it would happen. Because I saw my parents so together I couldn't imagine the idea of divorce. They were always together, for sixty years! No doubts about being together. When my (first) husband came to me to divorce, my mother said, "Tell him to go!" I couldn't believe it.

I don't do enough good things. Like a *mitzvah*. One thing we have done is take a soldier into our house. We took the chance to help someone who really needed our help. We didn't do enough — a friend got divorced who we hosted when she needed.

Maybe it doesn't come out — how much I like taking care of the children. This is the real challenge — it is also fulfilling. You get back so much — I feel great satisfaction when I see my children doing something.

Vlad Slutzkin

Leningrad, 1961

VLAD LIVED WITH HIS THEN WIFE IN THE APARTMENT DOWNSTAIRS FROM MY FRIEND Maya. When they divorced, I stayed friendly with Vlad. I knew he would be all right. Later, he married Lina. When they moved to their farm I helped clear the land! I don't think there is any topic you can mention that Vlad doesn't know all about it. He knows everything!

He and Lina visit us in the summer with her son from her first marriage, his son from his first marriage, and their children together. They are eager participants in my frivolous summer and winter solstice celebrations.

Now they are busy with their winery, Kadma, and have less time for socializing.

I am busy! I'm fine. Not enough time for anything. Juggling too many balls in the air: work, house, children, winery, start-ups, volunteering activities. Every hour it's something new! Right this moment, and not relevant in two hours, is that son Joel called me and he is having a party in our winery for fifty people! There is a lot of work: reorganizing at work, new ideas for how to promote the winery, one start-up needs investment, and we have to decide what to do with the vineyard — a lot of things! Last weekend we had no children at home: one in the army, the second had to stay for a weekend in army preparation camp for leadership skills, the third child was in a seminar of the youth movement, and the fourth went with his hiking club.

I do not refer to living in Israel as a commandment or a need. It's a choice. But in my perception, it's a clearly privileged choice. We cannot, in our day-to-day life, live with a feeling that basically we are returning the nation to its historic homeland after two thousand years. Once a month sounds sufficient. There is a very good saying of Jabotinsky that to be a Zionist you don't have to be insane, but it helps.

I came here when the Soviet Union gates were opened. The choice of coming either to Israel or another place was not fully obvious. But I never regretted that for a second. I am trying to be fully objective. Perhaps if I made different choices I wouldn't regret it either.

My idea of Israel at the time was extremely limited. I had met some people from Israel and knew a lot about general facts but knew nothing about living a normal life. A couple of days before I was leaving, in those days of endless drinking, a friend told me, "They have no potatoes." So I said, "OK, we'll have oranges." Perhaps he knew something! You can know the history but you don't really know day-by-day life.

Perhaps we all look for something to identify ourselves with. The country I was born in and grew up, and served in the army, and went to university, clearly didn't fit this. It was a matter of self-identification. Moving to Israel wasn't a popular trend, but I knew some guys who came. Most of the people I grew up with were not Jewish. I grew up in Leningrad — in an apartment — my parents worked. My father was an engineer and my mother was an economist, basically an engineer, as well.

I applied for leaving in 1989 and received permission by the end of 1989 and I came in 1990. My Soviet citizenship was revoked.

My parents never opposed it — I think they supported my choice. Naturally they worried; they didn't like the idea of separation. Moving to something unknown. It wasn't clear that I would be able ever to come back. Russia is a country with an unpredictable past — and also future — I hoped they would come. When you change your place of living, and especially a country, our choices are never 100% for the sake of something or because of something. It's always a combination of both. I was twenty-eight when I came.

In Lina's case they knew they would never come back for sure — since it took place much earlier.

My mother was born in Leningrad — originally Belarus. Her parents moved to Leningrad after the Revolution in the beginning of the '30s. My father was originally from Belarus as well.

They escaped during the War. They were not far from the border and knew the Germans were coming. My grandfather had been conscripted so they just started walking. The two boys were nine and ten, one was my father. Along with my pregnant grandmother and two little children of five and three, they walked to the East carrying a sheet bundle on a pole. Eventually, they met somebody with a carriage. They found a train and went east and finished somewhere in the steppes. My grandfather's brother, who was not married and was a pilot, had special permission. They found themselves in the Ural Mountains, just staying at the railway station. Everyone was sent to another house in the village. They lived in the room of another woman with her children, looking for wheat seeds for the next year. My grandmother succeeded in hiding some seeds in her boots for the next planting. The two brothers did the work that could be done. When they came back after the war, everybody had been killed, by the Germans or the local ones. Somehow my grandfather survived. And somehow he found them. It was such a mess. It is hard to understand the meaning of WWII for Russia: I am almost sure that I was among the very few children in my class who had two alive grandfathers.

Books helped shape my life.

I remember specifically for a lot of years, 'till I was twenty-five or twenty-eight, I had a feeling that I hadn't started yet. It was preparation for something. One day it would start. I don't have this feeling any more — whether it is because of age or coming to Israel.

Living in Israel is promising. I sincerely believe that it is perhaps the best place to live. I am very impressed with the progress that was made in the last twenty years. And I am quite optimistic about the general direction. There are some things that could be improved — like the general attitude — the self-perception — the strange approach of disregarding real things and constant concentration on invented issues.

Marrying Lina is one of the good things I have done.

Netanel (Nati) Monty

Tiberius, 1985

*S*OME TIME AGO THERE WAS AN ARTICLE IN *H*A'ARETZ ABOUT *"*LONE SOLDIERS*"* NEEDING *a place to celebrate Pesach. I responded by contacting the army. To our delight, Nati came to enjoy the holiday with us. We went for a bike ride in the valley. We were totally charmed by his good nature, his thoughtfulness, his openness and warmth. He has continued to be in our lives and we are happy to follow his adventures in life.*

I live better than any other place in the world. But I would be happy maybe to live somewhere else. It is very difficult here. You need to pay a lot for an apartment, food is expensive, gas is very expensive. And it is not quiet here — always there is going to be war and all the people are in stress. So it's difficult. But after all this — it's my country.

I am working. Single. I will be moving to a new apartment in Ramat Gan with a woman roommate who has a dog. I have to survive, to manage my life in a good way. I am working for a company that sells cell phones but I am looking for something better.

I grew up in Tiberius, in Kibbutz Ma'anit, in Sfat, in Tel Aviv, and now Ramat Gan. My mother is from Gibraltar, and my father from Morocco.

My mother put me in boarding school when I was seven years old. From that day I stopped seeing her. When I grew up I changed boarding schools. And I had people who took me for Shabbat and holidays. If I could change one thing, I would change my mother and my father! I would be born again! I found my father after I had not seen him all my life, when I was living in Canada and I connected with him. I talked with him about all this time that we had not seen each other.

God gave me a spark here, a spark there! Maybe from the people around me.

When I was a youngster, I thought I would do the army, and I would go to travel in the world, and hope to marry, and stuff like that!

Every day I have some setback; the life itself — every day. When you're alone, you have to think about what will happen next.

My good memories are everything that I was successful at.

I try to help people. I give money to people who ask. I try to live as a good person.

Nurit (Nukie) Yaffe

Petach Tikva, 1951

ON THE BUS ON THE WAY TO ONE OF THE HIKES I DID WITH ARCHEOLOGIST ZVIKA TZUK, *were Nurit and Hezzie. What a beautiful woman with such a warm smile! So we chatted all day and thus started a friendship. I don't remember how many years ago. She invited me to her place in Herzliya and we exchanged our stories. We go to events like the holiday celebration in Wadi Nis Nas and to the beach for a quiet walk, and to have a lovely breakfast, and to enjoy parties. Nurit used to make beautiful jewelry but then she got involved in Jahara water therapy and became a teacher of the Alexander technique.*

I am after a big trip to New Zealand and Australia and dreaming about another one with the motor home — I don't know where. We want to feel our home here after being away for half a year. We organize the garden; I want to make curtains. My boyfriend Hezzie and I live together. I love to say "boyfriend"! It makes me feel young! We have been together twenty-two years!

Now I want to be a good grandmother for my own four grandchildren and with the others from Hezzie; fourteen, and two great grandchildren.

I was born here; it's my country. My parents got married here and I was born here. It would be nice to live somewhere else, but I don't have the courage and not the partner. I thought about going to another country for one year, two years. Greece, maybe.

I grew up in Bat Yam. I went to regular school. I am the oldest of four children. When I was sixteen my father died but it didn't change my life. At this time I was on a kibbutz and I wasn't in such a good relationship with my father. I wanted to go to the kibbutz. I organized this for myself, chose the kibbutz, and then let my parents know they had to pay for it. It was Kfar Szold. I came home on the weekends. The kibbutz wanted me to be a nurse so they made a deal with the army and sent me to school instead of doing the army. I didn't like it, but I didn't say no. After one year I got married at nineteen. So I didn't do the army.

I don't think it's so different that I didn't do the army. The time I spent in the kibbutz I grew up. What changed my life is that I got married so young, but it was usual at that time.

My parents are both from Germany. They came before the war. My mother was nine years old and my father nineteen. My mother came with her mother and my father with his family.

My mother's mother was a lawyer in Germany and couldn't work anymore and some of the family were killed already. In my father's family were six children. His oldest sister had two children and they were killed in the Holocaust, maybe after he came. I never asked about it.

My grandmother shaped my life. We had a very good relationship. She was very warm to me and I felt she could accept me as I am. Not like my parents. My father was never happy with me. My mother was not dominant. My grandmother died when I was about twenty-five. She met my daughters Tal and Galit, but not Haggit, my third child. I saw her a lot. I went by myself to visit her and take care of her. Here, she worked in a factory that made soap, and then as an insurance agent. A very strong and very elegant woman. She was very generous with her time and money and everything. It was special for me, unlike with my sisters. I was the one she loved the most. With my mother I wanted to be the opposite so this was an influence also. She didn't tell me stories about her life — no one talked in those days.

I wanted children. I thought I would take care of babies for work. Not like being a nurse.

When I was at school I wanted to live outside the house. When my first husband loved me I was so happy and felt so lucky I didn't pay attention to other things and ran to his arms. He shaped me from the other side. Now I know about good behavior, quiet, good relationships. I didn't have this when I was married. All the time I thought I was guilty. No matter what happened I thought it is was my fault. I didn't know how strong I am and how much power I have. I felt at the time either I was wrong or I have to go out from this marriage. I understood that I have to do something. I tried to get divorced — he died during that time. I felt sad, but not guilty. I didn't want him to die, I just wanted to divorce, but I didn't feel guilty.

I wouldn't get married so young. And if I hadn't, I would have gone to the university to learn something. I was forty when I tried to divorce and had three children.

I have many precious memories. *She laughs.* When the MOD (Ministry of Defense) told me that I am an IDF (Israel Defense Forces) widow. So now I felt I had a father for all my life — someone to take care of me.

The good things are that I have children and that I still want to learn and to listen and to change. When I am sick and my body doesn't behave as it should, I am afraid my life is going to change.

Living in Israel is nothing to think about — my family is here. That's it. I don't think about. I am sad about the situation with the Arabs — not happy, I don't think we behave nicely to the Arabs and things have to change — not only with Arabs. I don't like when people fight. And when my people make bad things to other people I am really ashamed about it.

I want to say that I find myself healthy in my soul — mentally healthy. If I really, really want something I do it. For example, I wanted to divorce and I did it even though it was very, very, very hard. I wanted to leave the town and live out of the town, and I did it. And I wanted to travel for a long time and I did it.

Yosef Abromovitz
Brooklyn, New York, 1964

WHEN I MET WITH GERSHON BASKIN AT THE WORKPLACE THAT HE SHARES WITH *Energiya Global Capital,* "An innovative, multi-national renewable energy company focused on the development and management of utility-scale solar fields in emerging markets," according to the company overview, he suggested I also interview Yosef.

The very day I met with Yosef, "a well-known figure in the Israeli solar power industry," according to Ha'aretz newspaper, he was in the middle of negotiating to buy a Better Place, the company established to provide service for electric cars.

I was grateful for the time he managed to squeeze for our interview.

My burning issues is how do I provide for my family when I am trying to do different things for Israel and the world? We want to stop global warming, kill the use the diesel fuel. We are trying to save the dream of electric cars in Israel — but this could die! Global energy is where I spend my professional time. Our family is also very involved with Women of the World.

I am married to Rabbi Susan Silverman. I have five kids from ten to twenty years old. We live in Jerusalem. And I am completely overwhelmed with the opportunities to do good things for Israel. And I feel I live a charmed life.

I did the Young Judaea year course program at Kibbutz Ketura. Gershon was there, too. This was in February, 1983. Now he is working on establishing solar power in Palestinian schools.

I fell in love with the life in Israel: the community, the nature, the whole package. I had a scholarship to Boston University. I told my then partner and she said go and come back. But on the third or fourth visit I brought girlfriend Susan with me.

Susan and I decided in 2006 — a fateful day! to take time out of our busy life in Massachusetts and move to Jerusalem. I had just run for the Knesset for *Atid Ahad* (one future) the Ethiopian party, and got 14,007 votes. Susan said, "You live in Boston and you are going back and forth!" so we moved here as a family in 2006 to have a quiet life. We lived in Ketura for three years. It is a mixed community with Israelis and non-Israelis and has an American sensibility of entrepreneurship. We still consider ourselves part of that community. They decided to abandon some of their agriculture and come up with new enterprises. When we showed up they were ripe for us.

Growing up, I moved a lot as a kid. It probably served me well. I was in Brooklyn until I was three and lived in Israel from ages five to eight and at eight we went back when my dad did a PhD at Brandeis. Later, my parents divorced. I bounced around in high school; urban communes, and then went to Young Judaea. My girlfriend was in it and I was a social-action coordinator. I had basic Hebrew and was an activist! It was a fun and good thing to do! I am not sure I was thoughtful about it. Thank God!

Both parents are from Brooklyn, they met on a handball court. My grandparents are also American. On my mom's side from the USSR. Great-grandmother Sophie and great-grandma Molly from USSR. Sophie escaped with a circus troupe by hanging on under a train for three days. My dad's dad was from Romania.

Who helped shape my life? Who didn't? Moving around a lot, living in communes, traveling, conferences, being in the right place at the right time during major Jewish and other social movements. It's like a jigsaw puzzle — millions of DNAs from other people. My dad was at the I HAVE A DREAM speech and my mother was involved in social action. I got the benefit of a lot of great people at a very young age — also as a young journalist I was on the White House lawn at Oslo. I met the change-makers and leaders. I am not a traditional learner — I learn from interacting with people. That was one the great things about Ketura. You eat in the dining room and talk to everyone.

I thought I was going to be an astronaut when I was a kid. Not original! I had played with little science kits, blowing things up, all that. Science was then all fun and no math. But I have average to minimal math skills and I discovered the astronauts have to be engineers!

One of my kids went deaf the first year of our aliya. He has cochlear implants — it is a miracle. We've been lucky.

Being in the non-profit world has meant certain financial constraints. I have started more Jewish websites than anyone on the planet and closed more. Maybe they have natural life cycles. I work hard to do meaningful work. It's about juggling. I just needed to travel for the last four or five weeks and that's a setback. I have never done that.

Luckily, we landed in the kibbutz at a time when we could cover our basic needs. Maybe it was a blessing because that's where I got into the solar energy business. That's a good one. I didn't script the incredible journey I am on!

On the work front, we suffered a big setback with a major deal of five million with a major international company and then they reneged on it. It was a big hardship. But we were able to recover.

On multiple occasions, I have had the double privilege and opportunity to take the impossible and make it possible. That's all I really do. Then real professionals take the possible and make it happen. It manifested in so many unpredictable ways. The way I helped Hebrew teachers out of the gulag in Siberia, the Ethiopians — I know how to do the first part — I don't know how to do anything myself.

Living in Israel now is very exciting. It feels like the fulfillment of a dream connected to my early life coming full circle. Ended up in the center of some storms, but good storms — as a family we are able to connect with the pluralism of Judaism. Just now the government has recognized Reform rabbis. My wife is a Reform rabbi. This was unthinkable a year ago. And now there is solar power industry.

It's nice to have a little country as a platform to express our values to resonate around the world. I love the rhythm of life here and the holidays and access to kosher food! We will end up being more than a footnote in Jewish history by doing what we're doing. I hope my children, by being part of the family, by observing their kooky parents, will conquer their fears and take reasonable risks and feel the thrill of their innate ability to change the world by being Jewish.

Afterword

We are many from different places. Why do we feel so at home in Israel? What is that feeling of home? What are the political implications? Does it make us understand other people's feelings of home? Most of the participants feel strongly positive about life here, in spite of social issues and political issues that are yet to be solved, like ending the occupation, peace with the Palestinians, the separation of religion from government, equal rights for all citizens, and affordable housing. With a system of desalinization and grey water for agriculture, lack of water is no longer a problem. The country flourishes, in spite of trends that threaten the original design.

Yes, each one of us is part of the complicated story of this little strip of land, in the middle of Mediterranean trade for more than seven thousand years (per Heeli Schechter) that has developed and hosted major ideas, that was defined for politically determined reasons without regard to reality. This mosaic of about eight million people combines an indigenous population with a wild assortment of old settlers and new, in a land that shares the biological diversity of three continents.

Lori Mendel
Israel
2014

Participants in Alphabetical Order

Yosef Abromowitz
Adi Amorai
Shai Ariel
Connie Azulay
Doreen Mirvish Bahiri
Doron Bar Chen, DMD
Gershon Baskin, PhD
Sara Beery
Florence Benhamou
Ofra Ben-Zion
Tali Benzvi
Ashkar Sandrine Canella
Zvi Crohn
Yair Dalal
Ilan Elgar
Ziva Elgar
Munther Fahmi
Rachel Ann Gambash, MMS
Yael Gavish
Vered Giladi
Abu Hamad Hader, MA
Moni Haramati

Stella Isaharov, MBA

Yair Kenner

Jane Krivine

Liora Loewenstein, MA

Edna Mann, MA

Husam Massalha, PhD, MPA

Daniel Matalon

Tal Medvezky

Bat-ami Melnik

Oded Melnik

Oz Mesilati

Erika Miron

Netanel Monty

Maya Mendel Morag

Noa Suzanna Morag

Bishara Naddaf

Doron Neev

Milton Novak

Rachel Porat

Shirley Raphaeli

Eva Shaibe Rockman, PhD

Abe Rosenfeld

Natalie Rubenstein

Stanley Rubenstein

Robbie Sabel, PhD

Ely Samoucha

Annette Samuels, MM, OTR

Lea Saporta

Heeli Schechter

Vivienne Silver-Brody

Eran Singer

Lina Slutzkin

Vlad Slutzkin

Ruth Strahovsky, PhD

Chava Vester
Zev Wanderer, PhD
Nurit Yaffe
Amos Yoran
Maha Zahalqa-Massalha, MA
Ephraim Zwanenberg

Acknowledgements

Thank you to all the participants for being their usual charming selves.

Title suggested by Stanley Rubenstein from a ten minute film, *The House I live In,* starring Frank Sinatra, made in 1945 to oppose anti-Semitism and racial prejudice.

Thank you to the following for your time, suggestions, critical assessments, and strong support.

Ruth Almog, proofing and editing

Linda Coleman, suggestions

Teri Damisch, encouragement

Lenora Genovese, photo preparation

Judy Goldman, reader

Shelley Goldman, professional advice

Sally Kaufmann MD, reader

Anne Kleinberg, publishing consultant

Jane Krivine, copywriter, reader, editorial consultant

Howie Lascy, reader

David Laskin, suggestions

Lori McKenzie, reader

Jennifer Posen, facilitator

Abe Rosenfeld, suggestions

Ameed Saabneh, facilitator

Stanley Rubenstein, constant support and good ideas

Andrea Talmud, reader, editorial consultant

Patrick Tyler, suggestions

Joanna Yechiel, encouragement

Photo Credits

Doreen Mervish Bahiri
    Edi Sands, St. James, South Africa
Ofra Ben-Zion
    Photo of the family by Gerda Mathan
Vivienne Silver-Brody
    Roy Brody, Ein Hod
    Leo and Dorothy Silver, Silvers' Studio, Bulawayo, Rhodesia
Bat-ami Melnik
    Dan Keinan
Amos Yaron
    Dvora Goldman Yaron

About the Author

LORI WAS BORN IN NEW YORK CITY, THE ONLY CHILD OF RUSSIAN-JEWISH immigrants. The family moved to California when Lori was four and she grew up in Marin County. Lori completed her studies at UC Berkeley, taught school in Long Beach, San Francisco, and Paris. In 1963, she travelled by train and boat to Israel, spending the summer picking apples on Kibbutz Neot Mordechai in the north. Returning to California, she taught school in Los Angeles, managed her publishing company, Mara Books, did PR for the city of Beverly Hills, fundraising for USC Medical School and Daniel Freeman Hospital.

She settled in Israel in 1986, taught Business English in Tel Aviv, did cross cultural training for the Ministry of Defense, taught English for the Israeli Air Force, and taught at Shenkar College for ten years.

Lori lives with her partner, coaches students applying to university abroad, and enjoys friends, bike touring, the desert, and the Mediterranean life.

Her four grandchildren live in the United States.